Reimagining Democracy

Reimagining Democracy

Communication Activism, Social Justice, and Prefiguration in Participatory Budgeting

Vincent Russell

LEXINGTON BOOKS
Lanham • Boulder • New York • London

Published by Lexington Books
An imprint of The Rowman & Littlefield Publishing Group, Inc.
4501 Forbes Boulevard, Suite 200, Lanham, Maryland 20706
www.rowman.com

86-90 Paul Street, London EC2A 4NE, United Kingdom

British Library Cataloguing in Publication Information Available

Library of Congress Cataloging-in-Publication Data

Names: Russell, Vincent, 1989– author.
Title: Reimagining democracy : communication activism, social justice, and prefiguration in participatory budgeting / Vincent Russell.
Description: Lanham : Lexington Books, [2025] | Includes bibliographical references and index. | Summary: "This book presents findings from a community-based critical ethnography of two participatory budgeting processes in Denver, Colorado. Providing detailed descriptions of activists' communication, the book offers lessons about the state of democratic culture in the United States and illuminates alternative pathways for public decision making that can realize social justice"— Provided by publisher.
Identifiers: LCCN 2024037482 (print) | LCCN 2024037483 (ebook) | ISBN 9781666942538 (cloth ; alk. paper) | ISBN 9781666942545 (epub)
Subjects: LCSH: Local budgets—United States—Citizen participation. | Local budgets—Colorado—Denver—Citizen participation. | Social justice—United States. | Local government—United States—Citizen participation. | Democracy—United States.
Classification: LCC HJ9147 .R867 2025 (print) | LCC HJ9147 (ebook) | DDC 352.4/82140973—dc23/eng/20240920
LC record available at https://lccn.loc.gov/2024037482
LC ebook record available at https://lccn.loc.gov/202403

™ The paper used in this publication meets the minimum requirements of American National Standard for Information Sciences—Permanence of Paper for Printed Library Materials, ANSI/NISO Z39.48-1992.

To all those in the struggle for justice

Contents

Preface

This book is about people reimagining democracy as they worked to realize a more participatory and just governance system through the implementation of participatory budgeting (PB). For readers who are unfamiliar with PB, I want to offer a brief explanation of the process and its attendant vocabulary. I offer a more thorough explanation of PB later in the book, but for now, it may help to understand the basics. First, PB is "a form of participatory democracy in which citizens and civil society organizations have the right to participate directly in determining fiscal policy" (Marquetti, Schonerwald da Silva, and Campbell 2012, 63). PB is a directly democratic public deliberation process that structures communication values and practices such that residents control the allocation of a portion of a public budget in their geographic locale (e.g., housing authority, neighborhood, city, or school). PB was initially created for the purposes of advancing social justice by encouraging participation from people marginalized by or excluded from typical decision-making processes and by directing material resources to historically underserved communities. For example, every year, young people (12–22 years old) in Boston, Massachusetts, decide how to spend $1 million from that city's capital budget on community improvement projects.

THE PHASES OF PARTICIPATORY BUDGETING

The standard PB process implemented globally, including in the United States, occurs in five phases/stages, with the entire process lasting, on average, eight to nine months.

Phase 1: Forming the Steering Committee

In this phase, process organizers recruit residents of a geographic area to form a *steering committee* that typically comprises 15–45 members, depending on the population size of the city. Once appointed, steering committee members write a rulebook that includes rules for people's inclusion and participation, eligibility criteria for funded project ideas that PB participants submit (e.g., projects' cost limits, feasibility, and effects on social equity), a process timeline, the number of events to be held (e.g., steering committee meetings, budget delegate meetings, idea collection events, and PB voting locations and dates), and goals for the process.

Phase 2: Idea Collection

In the second phase, organizers and steering committee members recruit residents living in the geographical area where the process takes place and who meet the participation criteria (such as age limit) to identify their community's needs and submit ideas for projects to improve their community. This phase often includes hours-long *neighborhood assemblies* where residents of the geographical area gather in person to discuss problems experienced in their community and brainstorm potential solutions to those problems.

Phase 3: Project Proposal Development

In the third phase, residents volunteer to serve as *budget delegates* who vet the submitted project ideas using the steering committee's project eligibility criteria. The budget delegates work with community stakeholders and city officials to develop eligible project ideas into full-fledged project proposals that include estimated cost, project design, and completion timeline.

Phase 4: Voting

In the fourth phase, project proposals that meet the eligibility criteria are placed on a ballot, and residents vote for projects to fund, with those receiving the most votes being funded, within the constraints of the PB budget. Projects are funded until the pot of money is exhausted. For instance, imagine that a community has $100,000 to allocate through PB. Let's say the top five projects (ranked in order of the number of votes they received) were new bus stop shelters (at a cost of $50,000), playground renovations ($20,000), new computers for a library ($30,000), a scholarship fund ($10,000), and new bike lanes ($100,000). The bus stop shelters, playground renovations, and library computers would be funded because those three projects cost $100,000.

However, if the bike lanes project had received the most votes, then it would have been the only project funded in that cycle of PB because that single project would have exhausted the available funds.

Phase 5: Project Implementation and Process Revision

In the final phase, the local government implements the PB-funded projects, the steering committee revises the rulebook (e.g., to increase participation rates; refine project eligibility criteria; and/or improve collaboration among steering committee members, budget delegates, and city officials), and the process is repeated the next year.

There is no simple solution to the myriad injustices people face today, and PB is but one policy option that has the potential to restructure democracy and advance social justice. Nevertheless, I hope this book will inspire its readers to pursue their own experiments in participatory democracy as they work to improve their schools, neighborhoods, and cities. The flame of social justice burns brightly in the hearts of the PB participants I profile in these chapters. May their example fuel the fires of liberation struggles already happening in communities across the United States and around the world.

Acknowledgments

A manuscript such as this is not possible without help from numerous colleagues, comrades, co-conspirators, and loved ones. Most importantly, this community-based project would not have been possible without the participation and support of the numerous community members who collaborated with me. I want to especially thank Roshan Bliss, Candi Cdebaca, Candace Johnson, Brande Micheau, Tash Mitchell, Jenette Preciado, and Evan Weissman. Their devotion to building community was awe-inspiring and taught me, by example, the meaning of solidarity and the necessity of grounding the fight for social justice in love and joy.

I owe them an enormous debt of gratitude for taking a chance on me, a recently arrived North Carolina transplant who knew almost nothing about Denver, to serve as their research partner. I could not have been luckier to join this incredible team of organizers, and I am grateful for their contributions to this study, including their collaboration on the data collection instruments we used and their feedback about the preliminary findings of the study that I shared with them throughout the process, as well as their help in recruiting study participants.

Furthermore, the PB processes I studied occurred because hundreds of community members on the Auraria Campus and in the Cole neighborhood participated, and I thank them for the time and energy they put into PB to improve their campus and neighborhood. I am deeply grateful to the community members who agreed to participate in this research project. I also want to express appreciation to Nathan Schneider at the University of Colorado Boulder for introducing me to Evan Weissman, which effectively was the catalyst that launched this multiyear research project.

This project was made possible with the help of three undergraduate students at the University of Colorado Boulder (all of whom have since graduated). Helen Citrin provided valuable research about the sites of study that helped me become familiar with the Auraria Campus, the Cole neighborhood, and the City of Denver. Gracie Hanson transcribed most of the interviews conducted for this study, and she provided essential copyediting, formatting, and graphic design assistance on numerous documents related to this study, such as the evaluation report about the Cole Has a Soul PB process. Most importantly, Therese Gardner was an irreplaceable collaborator who was involved in nearly every step of the research process, including co-designing the data collection instruments, administering and entering the data collected from questionnaires, recording fieldnotes at PB events, helping to interview PB participants and transcribing the recorded interviews, offering insightful advice that benefitted the preliminary analyses of the qualitative data collected, and co-authoring with me several reports and essays about these Denver PB processes. Therese was an invaluable comrade, and I am immensely grateful for her work on this project, our countless conversations about how best to conduct this research, and for her friendship.

I want to thank Dr. Larry Frey for his unwavering support of me and this research project. I am grateful for his confidence in my abilities, his willingness to explore unconventional approaches to doctoral studies, his mentorship, and his thorough copyediting of prior versions of this manuscript. Larry never shied away from asking me challenging, necessary questions that forced me to maintain focus, think deeply, and develop my perspective. It was at his suggestion that I conducted the second round of interviews with PB participants that comprise the findings presented in chapter 4. His feedback on earlier iterations of this manuscript left the final artifact much improved, and I take full responsibility for any errors, oversights, opacity, and other flaws that readers may find. I also want to thank other colleagues for their sage guidance throughout this research project, including Dr. David Boromisza-Habashi, Dr. Stephen J. Hartnett (whose feedback inspired my focus on prefiguration in this book), and Dr. Ben Kirshner. Lastly, I want to extend a scholarly thank you to Dr. Spoma Jovanovic. Although she was not involved directly in this research project, she was my first model for scholar-activism, and her work exemplifies community partnerships for social justice. It was under Spoma's tutelage that I first began studying PB and communication activism more than a decade ago, and it is her life example that continues to inspire my communication activism. This book would not have been possible without her ongoing mentorship, our numerous collaborations, and her irreplaceable camaraderie. In sum, all of these scholars' contributions provided incalculable benefits for this research project.

I also want to thank three organizations for providing funding support for this project. First, CU Engage at the University of Colorado Boulder provided a fellowship that included a stipend to conduct this research, as well as some additional funds to support my community partners and to pay for Therese's work. That fellowship connected me with a cohort of community-based scholars, including Dr. Kirshner, who helped to develop my expertise in community-based research methods. Second, the Department of Communication at the University of Colorado Boulder provided numerous research grants that funded the valuable work that Therese and Gracie contributed to this research, as well as awarded me a summer research fellowship that provided essential material support during the time that I was interviewing PB participants and starting the process of drafting this manuscript. Third, the Department of Communication at Western Carolina University granted a course release that provided time for me to revise this manuscript. I thank all of these organizations for their generosity.

Finally, and most importantly, I simply could not have completed this project (and many other things in my life) without the help, support, and love of my wife Carly Bachman. My adoration for her, and my gratitude for her presence in my life, is vaster than the night sky.

Introduction

Democracy in Crisis

On a cold afternoon in December 2018, I drove from the University of Colorado Boulder to Denver's Auraria Campus[1] and met up with two of that campus's students who, for the past two hours, had been recruiting fellow students to vote in a PB process that was occurring there. These votes were the culmination of an intense, student-led, four-month PB initiative that involved more than a thousand students deciding how to spend $30,000 to fund campus improvement projects that addressed the material needs of students who, predominantly, were members of nondominant, oppressed, and underresourced populations and communities (e.g., people of color), and whose typical exclusion from campus decision-making added to their many experiences of marginalization.

Jeremiah,[2] an African American graduate student who was quick to share his opinions about how to improve the Auraria Campus, and Kyle, a white graduate student with a calm and casual manner, stood at the table they had set up outdoors in the campus's well-trafficked square located between the Tivoli Student Union and the Auraria Library. Despite the long, ongoing stretch of cold weather prior to that afternoon when I joined them, Jeremiah, Kyle, and other Auraria students had been tabling outdoors for a week and a half, encouraging their peers to vote in what was Colorado's first PB process, along with another being conducted at that same time in Denver's Cole neighborhood.

During the time I spent with them that afternoon, Jeremiah and Kyle unrelentingly encouraged students passing by to stop at their table—piled with candy, stickers, PB ballots, and voter guides—to complete a PB ballot. The students could vote for up to four projects they wanted to fund from a list of 12 projects created by students. That list of potential projects included a retreat for Indigenous students, a textbook rental program for students who struggled to afford books, and a food pantry for students experiencing food insecurity, among others. When Jeremiah asked one group of students if they wanted to vote, they laughed, explaining that they had voted already, and adding that Jeremiah had approached them "like six times" encouraging them to vote.

After about 30 minutes of nonstop recruitment, during a lull in foot traffic, Jeremiah and I were able to have a conversation. He talked about the difficulty involved in getting permission from campus administrators to recruit PB participants, and how bureaucratic red tape had been an obstacle throughout this PB process. As he explained with visible frustration:

> I tried to get permission to set up a table in front of one of the buildings on campus, and I was appalled at how difficult they made it! The administrators wanted two weeks' notice and to set up a walkthrough of the building, just for us to sit in front of the doors and ask people to vote in PB! I wanted to tell them that's why students don't engage on campus.

After months of organizing and implementing the PB process, and with its end in sight, Jeremiah was fed up with campus administrators' obstruction of this student-led effort.

Despite the bureaucratic barriers that had to be navigated and the inclement weather, for two weeks, Jeremiah, Kyle, and about ten other student volunteers spent hours outside inviting their peers to engage in direct democracy by voting for projects that emerged from the PB process. The students participating in PB were persistent, deliberate, and fueled by their passion for civic engagement, desire to improve their campus, and commitment to using the PB process to fund campus improvement projects that addressed the material needs of students who were underresourced. These student volunteers were kept warm during that frosty December in Colorado by an internal flame generated from sparks of hope that this PB process would result in widespread participation by Auraria students in public, collective decision-making to create a more just campus. They hoped the participation engendered by PB would be a far cry from typical, opaque, and oppressive governance processes in the United States—a first step toward reimagining democracy to foster people's liberation.

*****

The United States faces a public political participation crisis (hereafter, public participation). In 2018, the Science and Security Board of the *Bulletin of the Atomic Scientists*, an independent, nonprofit organization that tracks and offers information to reduce human-made threats to life on Earth (i.e., nuclear risks, climate change, and dangerous technologies), moved its "Doomsday Clock" to two minutes before midnight (which signals the end of the world), the closest that it had been to midnight since 1953 ("2018 Doomsday Clock Statement" 2018). That change in the clock was made, in part, because the organization believed that people around the world had experienced a "loss of trust in political institutions" and needed to mobilize to demand action from political leaders and "seize the opportunity to make a safer and saner world" ("2018 Doomsday Clock Statement" 2018, 5). That loss of trust may be one reason why voter participation rates in the 2014 U.S. midterm elections were the lowest that they had been since World War II, when much of the voting-age population was abroad (DelReal 2014), representing the culmination of a decade-long trend of declining public participation in civic affairs (Abramowitz 2010). Although voter turnout increased for the 2018 U.S. midterm election (Stewart 2018) and a record number of people voted in the 2020 U.S. presidential election (Schaul, Rabinowitz, and Mellnik 2020), the United States continues to trail most of the other more economically developed countries (MEDCs) in voter participation rates (DeSilver 2018).

The problem of voter participation rates is but one sign of a lack of U.S. Americans' involvement in civic affairs. From the 1990s to the 2010s in the United States, public approval of authoritarian governance systems and political apathy increased, whereas approval of democratic governing systems decreased (Foa and Mounk 2016). Research suggests that democracies in MEDCs may be deconsolidating (i.e., marked by increasing periods of instability and potential regime change; Foa and Mounk 2016). From 2012 to 2022, the United States and 41 other countries (the largest number in 50 years) underwent autocratization—defined as a substantial decline of liberal democratic traits (Varieties of Democracy Institute 2023). This decline erased the last 35 years of democratic advances worldwide, with "the level of democracy enjoyed by the average global citizen in 2022 . . . down to 1986 levels" (Varieties of Democracy Institute 2023, 6). Furthermore, in 2018, nearly half of U.S. Americans (45%) reported that they were not engaged at all civically or politically, with regard to, for instance, signing petitions, participating in boycotts, attending community meetings, following political campaigns online, encouraging others to be active politically on social media, joining activist groups, or contacting elected officials (Jones et al. 2018).

One cause of the U.S. public participation problem is increasing income inequality, which creates significant resource barriers to involvement in civic affairs for those with low income, such as the inability to take time off work and the lack of reliable transportation to travel to political events. Income inequality is at the highest level in U.S. history (Lindert and Williamson 2017), with the richest, compared to the poorest, 20% of U.S. Americans being responsible for 1.8 times the number of votes, more than 2.6 times the number of hours working for political campaigns and causes, and 76 times the number of dollars spent on those campaigns and causes (Schlozman, Verba, and Brady 2012). Since at least 1981, economic elites predominantly have shaped U.S. federal public policies, causing researchers to conclude that the United States should not be considered a democracy, but rather an oligarchy (Gilens and Page 2014).

U.S. residents increasingly are aware of the fact that existing governance systems are neither designed nor intended to benefit the common good, resulting in declining trust in their government. In 1964, approximately 80% of U.S. Americans reported that they trusted the federal government most of the time, but by 2010, that figure was only 22% (Pew Research Center 2010). Elite capture of democratic institutions and processes has created a negative feedback loop, with members of other economic classes lowering their public participation because they distrust the government, which leads government officials to be less responsive to those societal members' needs and views, which further decreases those members' trust in the government and their public participation in civic affairs.

Lower public participation has significant consequences for U.S. democracy and for particular U.S. populations. For instance, when voter turnout decreases, young people, people of color, and people with less income are underrepresented disproportionately (Lowndes et al. 1998). This state of affairs leads to marginalized populations being "doubly disempowered" (Lerner 2014b, 9)—possessing less influence than privileged populations at the voting polls and in between elections because politicians tend to listen to people who voted for them in their last election and to people they believe will vote in their next election. Growing income inequality, increased distrust of political institutions, and decreasing public participation rates have led scholars, at least as far back as the early 2000s, sounding the alarm that the United States is in the twilight of democracy (Hartnett and Stengrim 2006), with authoritarianism on the rise (Zakaria 2007).

In many ways, the contemporary democratic system of the United States was designed to engender a lack of participation from everyday people. Antidemocratic, vestigial aspects of the U.S. Constitution remain in effect today, including the Electoral College, which was designed to prevent the people from directly electing the president; the U.S. Supreme Court, an unelected tribunal of justices, appointed for life, who determine the fate of legislation, regulation, and civil rights for the entire country; and the flawed Thirteenth Amendment to the Constitution, which legalizes slavery for people convicted of felonies, effectively disenfranchising 5.2 million U.S. Americans in 2020—citizens who, disproportionately, are people of color, disabled, and/or low income (Chung 2021). Beyond the Constitution, election days are not national holidays, and citizens are not automatically registered to vote, two policies that differ significantly from other democracies around the world, and easy policy changes that could significantly increase voter participation.

In addition to these historic forms of disenfranchisement, the 2010s experienced an escalated offense against voting rights in the United States that continues to this day. In 2010, the U.S. Supreme Court ruled in *Citizens United v. FEC* that spending on political campaigns was protected by free speech, effectively gutting many campaign finance regulations and opening the floodgates to unlimited political spending, which systemically privileges the wealthy (Moskowitz 2019). Three years later, in 2013, the U.S. Supreme Court dealt another blow to voting rights when it invalidated key sections of the Voting Rights Act, clearing the path for states to implement extreme gerrymandering and voter ID laws designed to disenfranchise people of color and the poor.

As a result of these discriminatory policies, one political scientist concluded that the state of North Carolina no longer constituted a democracy (Reynolds 2016). In another example, in 2018, Democrats in Wisconsin won 53% of statewide votes for the state assembly, but due to racist gerrymandering, won just one-third of the seats in the state assembly (The Gravel Institute 2022). To have won even a slim majority in the state assembly, Democrats needed to clinch 65% of the vote, a nearly impossible feat (The Gravel Institute 2022). More than a decade since this latest assault on voting rights began, elected representatives have failed to take meaningful actions to address such rampant, ongoing disenfranchisement.

Of course, voting is just one means of public participation, and as liberal, capitalist democracies have failed to adequately respond to twenty-first-century polycrises, people's discontent grows, raising questions about whether liberal democracies are capable of serving their citizens in this new century. The climate crisis, rampant income and wealth inequality, unending war and imperialist foreign policies, the risk of nuclear annihilation, and entrenched white supremacist ideologies are just some of the global problems facing, and often exacerbated by, capitalist democratic countries. As a result, a large majority of U.S. Americans desire substantive change to the political system (Wike et al. 2021), think most politicians are corrupt (Brenan 2021), and say U.S. democracy is at risk of failing (Newall, Jackson, and Diamond 2022).

In 2020, many of these crises came to a head in the United States. As the COVID-19 pandemic spread like wildfire through the country, people watched as millions of their neighbors fell ill or died—disproportionately people of color, people with low incomes, and/or people with disabilities or pre-existing conditions—witnessing the utter failure of the state to implement adequate protective measures. In the summer of 2020, after the murder of George Floyd by police, historic uprisings occurred around the world in defense of Black lives. The prospect of revolution was in the air, and, in the United States, people began to advocate for some of the most radical social justice policy proposals in decades. Residents began to reimagine their country and took to the streets to demand change: abolish police and prisons, abolish debt, housing as a human right, eviction moratoriums, healthcare for all, and more. In the wake of those uprisings, support for labor unions reached its highest level since 1965 (McCarthy 2022), and young people increasingly support socialism more than capitalism (Saad 2019).

As discontent with democratic institutions grows on the left and is channeled into social justice protests and campaigns, discontent with democratic institutions grows on the right and is channeled into authoritarian movements. In 2016 and 2020, nearly half of the United States voted for an authoritarian in the form of Donald Trump, believing that a strong-man ruler was the only way to reclaim the (white) nation's waning prestige and (white) people's diminishing quality of life. Reactionary police forces in the United States brutalized, oppressed, and killed Black Lives Matter protestors in 2020 and then were rewarded with increased budgets in the years since (Adams 2021), further entrenching the police state. Then, in January 2021, the country witnessed an attempted coup by right-wing forces in an effort to install Donald Trump as president.

These upheavals suggest U.S. democracy is on the brink of something transformational. Will the people of the nation reimagine democracy for the twenty-first century so that it promotes social justice, or will the country slide further into an authoritarian, fascistic state of repression? One glimmer of hope is that, even as U.S. Americans lose faith in the institutions of liberal democracy, they seem to retain faith in each other. A majority of U.S. Americans support reforms to promote participatory and deliberative forms of democracy, such as citizen assemblies, national referenda, and deciding directly how to spend portions of a public budget (Schleifer and Diep 2019).

Public budgeting, in particular, is a significant but obscure element of government operation that both affects people's material conditions and can sow (dis)trust among a populace. For example, the U.S. Department of Defense (the largest recipient of discretionary funds in the federal government) has never successfully passed an audit of its spending, with experts documenting widespread fraud, waste, and corruption at the agency (Lindorff 2018). In 2020, at the beginning of the COVID-19 pandemic, the U.S. government implemented the Paycheck Protection Program (PPP), which provided $800 billion in forgivable loans to businesses and business owners, ostensibly so those businesses could continue to pay their employees. However, investigative reporting has found that more than 15% of those PPP loans (approximately $120 billion) were acquired fraudulently, that most of that money is unrecoverable, and that the program was structured in such a way as to facilitate this plundering by the capitalist class (Dilanian and Strickler 2022; DiNardi 2022). The current opacity of public budgeting, thus, tends to benefit wealthy elites while preventing oversight and participation by everyday people, providing plenty of evidence for citizens' perception that government officials are corrupt.

Rather than simply technocratic, actuarial accounts of fund distribution, public budgets are moral documents that lay out taxpayers' priorities (Lerner 2011; 2014a). However, public budgeting's opaque and exclusive nature prevents most people from understanding how governments spend tax dollars, let alone providing input on governments' budgetary decision-making. Therefore, participation processes ought to be implemented that demystify public budgeting. Doing so, especially at a local level, could increase citizens' trust in governing institutions (Clark and Teachout 2012), as well as generate changes in public budgetary priorities that would improve the unjust material effects of income and wealth inequality, and thereby address two of the underlying causes of the ongoing U.S. public participation problem.

One such policy that encourages people's engagement in local politics with regard to budgeting, especially by people who, historically, have been marginalized, oppressed, and/or excluded (hereafter, oppressed communities) is PB: "a form of participatory democracy in which citizens and civil society organizations have the right to participate directly in determining fiscal policy" (Marquetti, Schonerwald da Silva, and Campbell 2012, 63). PB is a directly democratic, public deliberation process that structures communication values and practices such that residents control the allocation of a portion of a public budget in their geographic locale (e.g., housing authority, neighborhood, city, or school).

Although PB encourages all residents of a geographic locale to participate in making decisions about public funding for their community, from its inception, PB was intended to promote participation by oppressed communities in redirecting capital funds to meet their collective needs (de Souza Santos 1998; Fung and Wright 2003). Since its creation in Brazil in 1989, PB has been implemented in more than 3,000 locations worldwide, with research finding that PB increases governments' transparency (Goldfrank 2011; Shah 2007; Wampler 2000) and accountability (Alves and Allegretti 2012; Goldfrank 2011; Shah 2007), as well as promotes social equity (Gonçalves 2014; Touchton and Wampler 2014). These and other findings led the World Bank, the International Monetary Fund, and the Movement for Black Lives, among others, to endorse PB as a best practice for democracies (Lerner 2011; Phelps 2016). PB, therefore, is an important type of public communication process, with the potential to revitalize embattled U.S. democracy.

PB, despite its prevalence worldwide, is still nascent in the United States, with the first PB process not occurring until 2009 in Chicago (Lerner 2011; 2014a), and, as of 2019, only approximately 20 citywide processes having been conducted (Participatory Budgeting Project, n.d.-a). In 2018, a coalition of nonprofit organizations implemented two PB processes in Denver,

Colorado, the first use of PB in that state. One PB process (called Cole Has a Soul) was implemented in the Cole neighborhood, which is located in the northeast of the city in an area called "East Denver," where residents decided how to spend $30,000 of a privately funded grant to improve their community. The other PB process (called Auraria PB), as described in the narrative that opened this chapter, was implemented on the Auraria Campus in downtown Denver—approximately 3 miles southwest of the Cole neighborhood—with college students allocating $30,000 from the same grant to fund projects to benefit that campus. Both the residents of the Cole neighborhood and members of the Auraria Campus are comprised disproportionately of people from oppressed communities, including people of color, those with low incomes, and people who do not speak English as their first language (more will be said about these communities in the following chapter).

Given the limited number of PB cases conducted in the United States, PB is a relatively understudied process in that country, with many questions about it left unanswered, including its ability to advance *social justice*, "in which people have their human rights and freedoms respected, receive equitable treatment with regard to opportunities and resources, and are not discriminated against because of their class, gender, race, sexual orientation, and similar identity markers" (Frey and Blinne 2017, 12). For instance, a lack of empirical data caused some scholars to conclude that it was "too soon to tell" whether PB reduced inequality in the United States (Leighninger and Rinehart 2016, 12). In general, much is known about who participates in PB and the outcomes of PB processes (e.g., effects on PB participants, communities, and governing systems). However, with some exceptions (Jovanovic and Russell 2019; Russell and Jovanovic 2020; Russell 2023), almost nothing is known about communication that occurs during PB, including what discourse participants value, whether and how participants communicate explicitly about social justice concerns, and participants' perceptions of their and other participants' communication (e.g., with regard to it being socially just).

In this book, I offer insights related to those topics from a study of the first two PB processes in Colorado's history. Given the ongoing polycrises of U.S. democracy mentioned earlier, and the potential of PB to address those crises, my purpose in this book is threefold. First, I aim to document these historically significant events. The two PB processes I studied in Denver were the first in the state of Colorado, and some of the first grassroots PB processes in the United States.[3] Second, I sought to understand the cultural themes that emerged as PB participants deliberated to promote social justice and policy change. What communication values did PB participants draw upon to achieve their goals, and what could others learn from these activists as they worked to reimagine democracy? Based on those findings, my final purpose is to argue that the deliberative activism performed by these PB participants functioned as prefiguration: that the PB processes were spaces where participants simultaneously imagined and created through their communication a vision for a just society, robust communities, and new models of citizenship. The radical reimagining of democracy engendered through PB offers lessons for the transformation of society that is necessary to respond to the numerous crises of the twenty-first century.

The analysis I present in this book is drawn from a multiyear (May 2018–October 2020), community-based, applied, critical ethnographic research project. *Community-based research* (CBR) is "a partnership of students, faculty, and community members who collaboratively engage in research with the purpose of solving a pressing community problem or effecting social change" (Strand et al. 2003, 3). Importantly, community partners with whom academic researchers conduct CBR must be "people who are oppressed, powerless, economically deprived, or disenfranchised" (Strand et al. 2003, 3). For this study, my community partner was the nonprofit coalition that implemented the two PB processes in Denver (described in more detail in the next chapter). This study was also informed by *social justice communication activism scholarship*, which, as Frey and Blinne (2017) explained, can be categorized into two types:

> The first type analyzes communication engaged in by activist individuals, groups, and organizations to promote social justice. The second type involves researcher-activists and teacher-activists employing their communication knowledge and skills, in collaboration with oppressed and marginalized community members, and with social justice groups and organizations, to intervene into and reconstruct unjust discourses in more just ways, with scholars documenting their purposes, practices, processes, and effects. (13)

My research project straddles the two types of social justice communication activism scholarship. In line with the first type, this research project describes and interprets the communication of PB organizers and participants as they embarked on a deliberative process (PB) to include and benefit people from historically oppressed communities. With regard to the second type, this research project involved some aspects of partnering with oppressed community members to intervene in and reconstruct unjust discourses, through my partnership with the PB organizers, my efforts to make a positive difference in their social justice campaign to make PB permanent in Denver, and my publication of evaluation reports with findings and recommendations that, potentially, could aid their campaign.

The final methodological approach that informed this study is *critical ethnography*, a type of ethnography that addresses social injustice and inequality through the research process by incorporating critique of the methodological choices and practices of the researcher (Norander 2017). Critical ethnography shares with other ethnographic approaches the methodological foundations of fieldwork and qualitative data analysis, but it differs from other forms of ethnography by engaging in an explicitly political project of "deconstructing taken-for-granted assumptions to uncover the workings of power and control and advocating for social change" (Norander 2017, 297), with this ethical responsibility to address injustice making critical ethnography distinct from other forms of ethnography (Madison 2020). Critical ethnographers move from describing "what is" to describing "what could be," for they recognize that current circumstances prevent some interlocutors from realizing their full potential. To this end, critical ethnographers concern themselves with the applied aspects of their work, consistently asking what they can do with what they have learned so as to advance social justice (Norander 2017).

The findings I offer in this book are drawn from extensive fieldwork, including participant observation and two rounds of participant interviews. During this project, I attended as many PB events as possible; in total, I observed 34 events: 17 steering committee meetings, 14 budget delegate meetings, and 3 idea collection and PB voting events. These participant observations generated 411 pages of typed, single-spaced field notes (217 pages from steering committee meetings, 184 pages from budget delegate meetings, and 10 pages from idea collection and PB voting events). I also met monthly (sometimes more frequently) with PB organizers to discuss the project and preliminary findings. These regular meetings provided invaluable iterative feedback on my process and the lessons learned.

I also conducted two rounds of interviews with PB participants throughout this research project. The first round of interviews was conducted shortly after people's participation in their PB process ended (September 2018–January 2019). For example, the Auraria PB process concluded its idea collection phase in mid-September 2018, and, on September 29, 2018, I interviewed someone who had submitted a project idea for consideration. In total, for this first round, I interviewed 18 PB participants: 6 steering committee members, 4 PB organizers/facilitators, 4 budget delegates, 2 Auraria Campus staff members, and 2 idea submitters. Interviewees' ages ranged from 18–70; 53% were women and 47% were men; and 40% self-identified as White, 33% as Black, 20% as Asian, and 7% as Latine.

A second round of interviews was conducted during September–October 2020, which was 19–20 months after the two PB processes concluded in December 2018. The purpose of these interviews was to learn how participants perceived their PB process after some time had passed since it concluded, and whether it had long-term effects on them. In total, for this second round, I interviewed 16 former PB participants: 7 budget delegates, 5 steering committee members, and 4 PB organizers/facilitators. Interviewees' ages ranged from 20–62, with 77% being women and 23% being men, and 40% self-identifying as Black, 33% as White, 20% as Asian, and 7% as Latine.

I'll have more to say about my research partnership with the organizers of these PB processes and my fieldwork in the next chapter. However, before proceeding further, I want to offer a brief overview of PB in general, including the unique vocabulary of the process, its history, and some of the findings from prior research on the process, because these terms are used throughout the book, and the broader context of PB in the United States informs the conclusions I present in the final chapter.

PARTICIPATORY BUDGETING: AN OVERVIEW

PB began in 1989 in Porto Alegre, Brazil, the capital of that country's southernmost state, which has more than one million residents and is a relatively affluent municipality (Wampler 2007). In 1985, Brazil's government transitioned from a military dictatorship to a fledgling democracy, and in 1988, Luiza Erundina, of the leftist Workers' Party, who campaigned on reversing a decades-long trend of investing public resources in middle- and upper-class neighborhoods, won the mayor's office in Porto Alegre and implemented PB by making public participation accessible to members of oppressed communities and prioritizing an equitable distribution of resources. Thus, from the outset, PB "was intended to help poorer citizens and neighborhoods receive larger shares of public spending" (Wampler 2007, 23).

The results of that program were impressive. For example, before PB was implemented, approximately one-third of Porto Alegre's one million residents lived in slums on the city's outskirts and lacked access to basic infrastructure, such as clean water, sanitation, medical facilities, and schools. However, after nine years of employing PB, 98% of the city's households were connected to sewer and water infrastructure, and the city increased spending on public housing, schools, and health services (Bhatnagar et al. 2003). During the first two years of employing PB in Porto Alegre, less than 1,000 citizens participated in the process, but by 1992, more than 20,000 people participated each year (Wampler 2007). Approximately 20% of Porto Alegre's population participated in PB over a span of 20 years (The World Bank 2008), and as of 2016, as much as 10% of the city's population had participated in a single cycle of PB (Leighninger and Rinehart 2016). These levels of PB participation, compared to U.S. public deliberation processes, which rarely involve more than a few thousand people in a single process (Nabatchi and Leighninger 2015), are impressive, especially given the time-intensive nature of PB, with a typical PB process lasting between eight and nine months, and requiring many volunteer hours from local participants.

The material results promoting social equity were due, in part, to the fact that people from oppressed populations participated in the process. Residents with low income and less education participated in Porto Alegre PB processes at rates equal to and, sometimes, higher than residents who were richer and more educated (Pateman 2012). Additionally, approximately 30% of people who submitted a project idea, 20% of people who developed those ideas into project proposals, and 15% of people who chaired the process came from households in the lowest 20% of the population by socioeconomic status (The Center for Urban Development Studies 2005). Indigenous Brazilians and Afro-Brazilians were also overrepresented among Porto Alegre PB participants, compared to local census demographics (The World Bank 2008).

The PB process continued to gain popular support, the Workers' Party continued to win reelection, and by 1999, Porto Alegre residents used PB to allocate 21% of the city's budget (Bhatnagar et al. 2003). With PB, elected officials in Porto Alegre achieved "something that had eluded leftists up to that point: the combination of good governance, redistribution, and political good fortunes" (Baiocchi and Ganuza 2017, 55).

The early years of PB in Porto Alegre required innovations in governing through direct, participatory, and deliberative democracy. In implementing PB, Porto Alegre officials closed nearly all other formal communication channels for citizens to make demands of their elected representatives (Baiocchi and Ganuza 2017), such as public hearings about infrastructure projects. Consequently, if citizens wanted to see something (de)funded in their community, they had to participate in the PB process rather than lobby elected officials. The adoption of PB effectively stifled other privileged communication channels for those who were wealthy and/or politically well-connected (e.g., bribing officials; Baiocchi and Ganuza 2017). However, this radical formal implementation of direct, participatory, and deliberative democracy had nuanced effects on people's political communication channels. For instance, although PB effectively "circumvented politicians and cronyism, . . . it also cut out urban social movements and protest tactics as a way to make demands" (Baiocchi and Ganuza 2017, 60).

Over time, PB spread throughout Brazil, then Latin America, and, eventually, across the world. First, during the 1990s, the process spread through Brazil and Latin America, with Brazil's Workers' Party adopting a standardized model of PB into its policy platform and encouraging political leaders in municipalities across the country to use that model (Baiocchi and Ganuza 2017). By the late 1990s, nongovernmental organizations (NGOs) partnered with the Workers' Party to disseminate PB across Brazil. That version of PB relied on "a mix of good governance (such as transparency), social justice, and civic goals (such as cooperation)" (Baiocchi and Ganuza 2017, 65). As PB expanded across Brazil, it began to lose its affiliation with the Workers'

Party; by 2001, center and right political parties implemented 40% of the country's PB processes, with by 2003, more than 140 of the 5,571 municipalities in Brazil (2.5%) having implemented PB (Bhatnagar et al. 2003). PB was "attractive on the left and the right because the Workers' Party had separated PB from local social movement influence *and* associated it with a transparent and efficient administration" (Baiocchi and Ganuza 2017, 69). However, the widespread use of PB by center and right political parties focused more on technocratic rules for participation than on the material outcomes of the process, resulting in PB's goal of achieving social equity being deemphasized (Wampler and Avritzer 2005).

Nevertheless, Brazilian PB processes—regardless of the political party that implemented them—have reduced material inequalities across the country. Municipalities that implemented PB processes, compared to those that did not, increased spending on healthcare and sanitation by 6%, increased the number of civil society organizations operating in a municipality by 8%, and decreased infant mortality by 11% (Touchton and Wampler 2014). The implementation of PB in Brazil reduced the number of people living in poverty and increased their access to basic social services (Baiocchi et al. 2006). Furthermore, cities that have implemented PB not only allocated more money to the health and sanitation sectors but, even in cities that allocated similar amounts to these sectors, the money was spent more effectively in cities that implemented PB (Gonçalves 2014), leading to greater reductions in infant and child mortality compared to cities that did not implement PB.

The implementation of PB in Brazil also had positive effects on government efficiency and transparency. Government-funded projects developed through PB were more likely to be completed and less likely to run over budget compared to projects developed through standard government processes (Schneider and Goldfrank 2002). Cities that implemented PB, compared to those that did not, also had less corruption (Touchton and Wampler 2014). Perhaps due to the increased efficiency and reduced corruption in cities that implemented PB, those cities' residents reported greater levels of trust in their local governments, which increased those governments' democratic legitimacy (Wampler 2012). Overall, the effects of PB on Brazil have been drastic:

> The big picture behind these numbers is that Brazil, one of the world's most inequitable countries when the period of military rule ended in 1989, has become steadily more equitable since PB and other participatory reforms were introduced. . . . It is worth noting that over the same time period, income inequality in the United States and Canada started out much lower and has steadily increased. (Leighninger and Rinehart 2016, 8)

By the early 2000s, PB was being implemented across Latin America, including national laws that promoted or mandated its use at a municipal level in Bolivia, Guatemala, Nicaragua, and Peru (Goldfrank 2012). As PB moved beyond Brazil, it attracted a global audience, with the World Bank and the International Monetary Fund becoming leading promoters of the process because these institutions believed that PB could reduce the amount of corruption occurring in many countries' governments. In line with that belief, the World Bank, for instance, provided millions of dollars in loans to Peru to support the mandatory use of PB by all 2,040 subnational governments (Goldfrank 2012).

During the 2000s, support of PB by those and other global development institutions and networks (Goldfrank 2012; Lerner 2011), in part, led to the process becoming popular in Europe, Africa, and Asia. South Africa's constitution, for example, requires municipalities to develop cultures of participatory government that complement representative government, with several cities adopting PB to meet those requirements (Shall 2007). In 2004, the World Bank, UN-Habitat, and several local NGOs signed a letter of intent to promote PB across Africa (Baiocchi and Ganuza, 2017). International development agencies also aided the implementation of PB in numerous other countries, including Albania, Bangladesh, Bosnia, the Dominican Republic, Ecuador, El Salvador, Gambia, Honduras, Indonesia, Kyrgyzstan, Madagascar, Mozambique, the Philippines, Uganda, and Uruguay (Goldfrank 2012).

Europe was the first continent beyond Latin America to adopt PB, and by 2010, more than 200 processes had been implemented across Europe (Baiocchi and Ganuza, 2017). In 2014, Paris launched the largest PB process in the world in terms of money allocated—pledging €500 million between 2014 and 2020 (Carlson 2017). In 2015, the United Kingdom planned 200 PB processes, Germany expected to engage in more than 100 processes, and Portugal was planning a national PB process (Baiocchi and Ganuza 2017). The global spread of PB has been breathtaking:

> By 2005 there were roughly 200 PB projects outside of Brazil; by 2008 there were at least 500; and by 2010, the sum total of PB experiments was at least 1,500. The estimates for 2015 were that there were at least 2,000 ongoing PB processes. (Baiocchi and Ganuza 2017, 75)

Moreover, this growth in PB's movement from the Global South to the Global North defies the conventional flow of development and governing processes from the "developed world" to the "developing world."

However, as mentioned previously, as PB spread across the world, its radical leftist political roots were severed, becoming, instead, a tool of "good governance" detached from a social justice political project (Baiocchi and

Ganuza 2017, 75). For example, a review of the World Bank's promotion of PB raised concerns that PB processes would be watered down and lose their transformative potential (Goldfrank 2012). The study found that some actors within the World Bank promoted PB as part of the institution's standard pro-market agenda because PB could co-opt the ideas of civil society opponents and neutralize them, and, simultaneously, legitimize capitalist hegemony through a democratic process, a departure from the leftist origins of PB intended to create a people's budget that advances social justice (Goldfrank 2012). Eventually, the World Bank's globalized model of PB arrived in the United States, and its unique phases and vocabulary (used throughout this book) warrant explanation before discussing the state of PB implementation in the United States.

Phases of Participatory Budgeting

The standard PB process used globally, including in the United States, occurs in five phases/stages. During the first phase, process organizers recruit residents of a geographic area to form a steering committee that, typically, is comprised of between 15 and 45 members, depending on the population size of the city. The process used to recruit steering committee members varies. In Europe and North America, members are often appointed by city councilmembers; whereas in Latin America, typically, members are nominated by and serve as representatives of civil society organizations and their constituents (Leighninger and Rinehart 2016). Once appointed, steering committee members write a rulebook that includes rules for people's inclusion and participation, eligibility criteria for funded project ideas that PB participants submit (e.g., projects' cost limits, feasibility, and effects on social equity), process timeline, number of events to be held (e.g., steering committee meetings, budget delegate meetings, idea collection events, and PB voting locations and dates), and goals for the process (Hagelskamp, Rinehart, et al. 2016b).

After steering committee members create the rulebook, PB moves into the second phase of "idea collection," with organizers and steering committee members recruiting residents living in the geographical area where the process takes place who meet the participation criteria, such as age limit (for North American PB processes, most commonly, the minimum voting age is 14–16 years old; Hagelskamp, Rinehart, et al. 2016b), to identify their community's needs and submit ideas for funding projects to improve their community. This phase often includes hours-long "neighborhood assemblies" where residents of the geographical area discuss common problems experienced in their community and brainstorm potential solutions. In the 2014–2015 cycle, the average North American PB process held six neighborhood assemblies (range = 1–19), with 38 people attending a typical neighborhood assembly (range = 3–200; Hagelskamp, Rinehart, et al. 2016b).

In the third phase of PB, residents volunteer to serve as "budget delegates" who vet the submitted project ideas using the steering committee's project eligibility criteria. Those budget delegates work with city officials[4] to develop eligible project ideas into full-fledged project proposals that include estimated cost, project design, and completion timeline. In the 2014–2015 cycle, the average North American PB process included 30 budget delegates (range = 8–75; Hagelskamp, Rinehart, et al. 2016b).

In the fourth phase, project proposals that met the eligibility criteria are placed on a ballot, and residents vote for projects to fund, with those receiving the most votes being funded within the constraints of the PB budget. The average North American PB process in the 2014–2015 cycle allocated $1,015,756 ($9.85 per resident) and ranged from $61,000 to $3,365,644 ($1.18 to $69.85 per resident; Hagelskamp, Rinehart, et al. 2016b).

Finally, in the fifth phase, local government implements the PB-funded projects, the steering committee revises the rulebook (e.g., to increase participation rates; refine project eligibility criteria; and/or improve collaboration among steering committee members, budget delegates, and city officials), and the process is repeated the next year. Although, typically, U.S. government officials (and elsewhere) approve PB to be repeated indefinitely, the two PB processes in Denver I profile in this book were one-time occurrences because they were funded by a nonrenewing grant and implemented by nongovernment actors (i.e., nonprofit organizations).

The State of Participatory Budgeting in the United States

The uptake of PB in the United States has not been as rapid as in other parts of the world, and where the process has been adopted in U.S. cities, its scope often is limited to funding only capital projects (built environment infrastructure projects, such as bus benches, sidewalks, repairing streets, and so forth), rather than both capital and programmatic projects (social programs, such as summer camps, Meals on Wheels, scholarships for postsecondary education, job training, and so forth). After two decades of cities across the globe implementing PB, the first use of PB in the United States was in 2009, when Alderman Joe Moore in Chicago, IL, decided to use PB to allocate $1.3 million in municipal discretionary funds, with 1,652 residents participating in that inaugural process (Lerner 2011). Gradually, other Chicago alderpersons adopted PB in their communities, and by 2020, nine wards were conducting PB on an annual basis (PB Chicago, n.d.), although those wards account for only 18% of Chicago's 50 districts, and each process is run independently. Hence, Chicago has nine separate PB processes instead of a single PB process that occurs across all nine wards. In the more than ten years since the process first was used in Chicago, PB has failed to be adopted citywide, and the amount of money allocated, as well as the number of participants, therefore, has been circumscribed.

In 2011, inspired by Chicago's implementation of PB, four New York City (NYC) councilmembers used PB to allocate a portion of their discretionary budgets. NYC proved to be fertile ground for PB, with, by 2016, 28 of the city's 51 districts (55%) having implemented the process (Hagelskamp, Rinehart, et al. 2016a). In 2018, NYC voters approved a ballot proposal to create a Civic Engagement Commission charged with establishing a citywide PB process, which was expected to more than double the size of dollars allocated and the number of PB participants in the United States (Lerner 2018). However, the mayor did not apportion any funds for a citywide PB process in the fiscal year 2020–2021, mostly because of decreased public revenue caused by the coronavirus pandemic, and the prospects of a citywide PB process in NYC remained uncertain (Khurshid 2020).

By 2016, 61 PB processes were occurring across the United States and Canada, but only seven U.S. municipalities had implemented PB citywide: Boston, MA; Cambridge, MA; Clarkston, GA; Greensboro, NC; Hartford, CT; Seattle, WA; and Vallejo, CA (Hagelskamp, Rinehart, et al. 2016a). Eighty-eight percent of PB processes funded only capital projects; the remaining 12% also allowed spending on social programs. That overemphasis on capital spending in U.S. PB processes may be a barrier to PB promoting social justice because social services (e.g., policing, education, and healthcare) are more effective in addressing social inequalities in MEDCs (Leighninger and Rinehart 2016).

In addition to the number of PB sites and their funding criteria, another important metric for assessing the success of PB processes is who participates. A typical PB process requires participation from numerous residents across its five phases. However, researchers often measure the reach of a PB process by the number of people who voted in the process because the voting phase involves the single largest number of participants at one time, and it provides a useful statistic that is easily comparable across sites. In the 2014–2015 cycle, 1,595 people cast ballots in the average PB process in North America (range = 85–6,299; Hagelskamp, Rinehart, et al. 2016b). From 2014–2015, in total, 73,381 PB ballots were cast in North America, which translated to an average voter turnout of 2.6% (range = 1%–14%) of the census-estimated population eligible to vote in places where PB had been implemented (Hagelskamp, Rinehart, et al. 2016b).

Participants from that cycle of North American PB processes, in general, were diverse, too. In comparing demographics of jurisdictions that implemented PB, residents under 18 years old and older adults were overrepresented; additionally, "in nearly all communities, black residents were overrepresented or represented proportionally to the local census among voter survey respondents" (Hagelskamp, Rinehart, et al. 2016b, 6), although Latine residents were underrepresented in most PB sites. Residents from lower income households (less than $50,000) and, in most communities, women were also overrepresented or represented proportionally to local census figures, but people with less formal education were underrepresented. Overall, young people, older adults, African Americans, women, and people from lower income households, but not Latine residents and residents with less formal education, participated in those PB processes.

In some cases, a group's participation in PB was higher than participation in local elections. For instance, in one cycle of the NYC PB process, Latine residents constituted 39% of voters in the most recent municipal elections at that time, but they comprised 48% of PB voters, and although only 4% of municipal voters had household incomes of less than $10,000, they comprised 22% of PB voters (Su 2012). These results may be because participation requirements in PB are less restrictive than U.S. elections. In many PB processes, one does not have to be a citizen, possess a permanent address, or be at least 18 years old to vote[5] (Hagelskamp, Schleifer, et al. 2016).

A final significant characteristic of U.S. PB processes is how and why PB is adopted, because those factors can have a significant influence on the design of the PB process, the number and demographic representativeness of those who participate, and the types of projects that are funded (Lerner and Secondo 2012). Overwhelmingly, the decision-making process in the United States to adopt PB has been top-down, with, most often, a city government official learning about PB (e.g., at a conference they attended) and deciding to implement the process in their city, which was the case in, among other cities, Boston, Chicago, NYC, and Vallejo. Rarely does the desire to implement PB bubble up from grassroots community organizing and advocacy.

A survey study conducted by Public Agenda (a nonpartisan research and public engagement organization promoting democracy) about why elected government officials adopted PB found that most did so because they perceived the process as an opportunity to increase their constituents' excitement about local politics, educate residents about how government works, and increase those officials' popularity among citizens (Hagelskamp, Schleifer, et al. 2016). Government officials, in line with the values attached to the global standardized model explained previously, therefore, did not adopt PB because they wanted "to make budgeting decisions more responsive to community needs or to transform the political system" (Hagelskamp, Schleifer, et al. 2016, 4). PB, thus, is adopted in the United States not because city residents organize and advocate for it in an effort to transform local politics or because government officials see it as a way to advance social justice, but because those in positions of political power believe that they will benefit (Hagelskamp, Schleifer, et al. 2016). Hence, many PB processes in the United States face an uphill battle in fulfilling the promise of social transformation seen in the Global South.

Some U.S. PB processes, however, have been adopted because of *deliberative activism* engaged in by local residents (e.g., attending political protests, signing petitions, and staging sit-ins) to institutionalize public deliberation processes (Fung 2005) that can promote social justice. For instance, in the NYC example I described earlier, local residents organized and advocated to place on the 2018 municipal ballot a measure to implement PB citywide, and they then engaged in a coordinated get-out-the-vote campaign in support of that ballot measure that, ultimately, secured a people's victory when it was approved by a majority of NYC voters.

The earliest successful example of deliberative activism driving PB implementation in the United States occurred in 2014, in Greensboro, NC, which became the first U.S. city to implement the process because of a grassroots social justice effort, with local activists organizing a three-year campaign to convince government officials to adopt PB citywide (Jovanovic and Russell 2014; Russell and Jovanovic 2020). Activists' desire to foment political change was integral to that campaign; as a participating community organizer explained, "We saw PB as an excellent opportunity to bring about much needed positive change by tapping into the energy and creativity of people talking about and making public decisions to address community needs" (as cited in Hagelskamp, Schleifer, et al. 2016, 34). Specifically, the PB process engaged local residents, many of whom were members of oppressed communities, in critical reflection about who held political power in the city and shifted public discourses about public spending priorities from a focus on austerity and self-interest to a focus on collective well-being and the common good (Russell and Jovanovic 2020). In their performance of deliberative activism, "organizers relied on the tripartite power of rhetoric, collaboration, and participatory democracy with the goal of empowering historically underrepresented communities to contribute to budget decision making" (Jovanovic and Russell 2014, 19). The Greensboro PB process, thus, was driven by a grassroots social justice effort that sought to transform the City of Greensboro's power dynamics and decision-making processes to a motivation more aligned with PB's origins in Porto Alegre, compared to the globalized, standard version that has been adopted across the United States (and elsewhere). Of course, PB is just one example of a public deliberation process, and the field of public deliberation has struggled sometimes in its efforts to promote social justice.

DELIBERATIVE ACTIVISM, SOCIAL JUSTICE, AND PREFIGURATION

Public deliberation is a process rooted in particular normative principles that have adapted as scholars and practitioners have refined their ideas about the subject. Jürgen Habermas (1991) advanced theories about the value of the public sphere, which was characterized by "the people's public use of their reason" in "rational-critical debate," such that "the public process of critical debate lay claim to being in accord with reason" (26, 54). Other normative values advanced by Habermas (1982; 1984; 1991) in public deliberation included consensus, the relative equality of participants in discussion, and an absence of power among deliberating parties. However, some scholars have critiqued Habermas's emphasis on homogeneity of communication practices, use of rational argumentation, and rosy view of power equalities among deliberators (Dryzek 2010; Gutmann and Thompson 2004; Young 1996; 1997).

Rather than abandon the project of public deliberation, several scholars have sought to redeem the idea. Iris Marion Young (1996) imagined a form of public communication, called the "theory of communicative democracy," that pushed past Habermas's (1982; 1984; 1991) ideas of deliberation to open up public participation to people who are oppressed. Young (2002) placed justice at the center of public communication, which must respect others' being and voices. Such respect must value heterogeneity; that is, deliberative communication requires participants to recognize and incorporate differences in values, cultures, ways of life, and histories. Therefore, despite their differences, communication among diverse people—with care and trouble—still is possible (Frazer 2006). Young (1996), however, argued that to accomplish that goal, "reason giving" for supporting an individual's stance in public deliberation should add forms of discourse that include "greeting" (explicit mutual recognition and conciliatory caring), "rhetoric" (forms of speaking that attend reflexively to audiences), and "storytelling" (which people who are marginalized often use more than rational debate to communicate their values, goals, etc.).

Expanding the communication practices relevant to public deliberation is one way to promote social justice, and public deliberation can advance social justice in other ways, too. First, socially just communication is promoted when all people have the maximum freedom to talk about who they are, what they do, and how to envision their future (Swartz 2006). Public deliberation can generate educative effects on participants, and including members of marginalized communities in deliberative processes can address social inequities by providing opportunities for them to further develop their democratic skills (e.g., contacting elected officials, knowing where to find information about civic life, and giving speeches). Including historically marginalized populations in deliberation also potentially counteracts hegemonic discourses by encouraging other participants to consider nondominant worldviews and cultural norms. Furthermore, deliberation processes require that they end with participants making decisions about the issue/topic they discussed—decisions that can have both material and symbolic effects for oppressed communities.

For example, residents of a town might engage in a deliberation process to decide how to reform their local police department. After days of deliberating and considering diverse perspectives, participants decide that the police department's funding should be reduced drastically because of systemic issues that disproportionately negatively affect people of color and those with low incomes. Even if that decision is not formally binding, it can send a powerful symbolic message to communities of color and the larger locality that affirms many minority members' views about the police department as an oppressive institution.

Lastly, deliberation can engender participants' dialogic encounters with the Other that increase neighbors' empathy for, mutual understanding of, and trust in one another. Deliberation processes that create such dialogic encounters within larger racist, colonial, and capitalist cultural systems that emphasize competition, dehumanization, and self-interest, thus advance social justice by "promoting values of inclusion, care, and equity" (Russell and Jovanovic 2020, 4).

One way to assess the extent to which public deliberation promotes social justice is by evaluating its impact on the political self-efficacy of people from oppressed populations. *Political self-efficacy* is the extent to which people believe they can participate competently in political conversations. For instance, a study of one large public deliberation event found that, prior to the deliberative event, people of color and women had lower political self-confidence than did white people and men (Nabatchi and Stanisevski 2008), but after the event concluded, the political self-efficacy of people of color and women increased. That finding was supported in a review of scholarly literature related to issues of inequality, exclusion, and marginalization in public deliberation processes, with the authors concluding that "deliberative engagement can positively affect minority perceptions of their own internal political efficacy and . . . that although deliberative civic engagement exists in a world of inequitable conditions, the process can indeed help ameliorate some inequalities" (Siu and Stanisevski 2012, 89). That review also found that public deliberation processes are most effective when they encourage participants to raise questions about and make space to address participants' identity differences (Siu and Stanisevski 2012).

To accomplish those goals, organizers must address *external exclusion* (when people from oppressed populations are not present to deliberate) and *internal exclusion* (when people from oppressed populations are present, but they are not able to contribute meaningfully to the deliberation; Young 2002). Scholars and practitioners have identified several strategies that facilitators and deliberators can and have employed to effectively address problems associated with inequality, exclusion, and marginalization in public deliberation processes (e.g., Esterling, Fung, and Lee 2015; Gutmann and Thompson 2002; McBride 2005; Ryfe and Stalsburg 2012; Siu and Stanševski 2012; Leighninger 2006).

First, external exclusion of members of marginalized communities can be prevented by making their inclusion mandatory for public deliberation processes. For mandatory inclusion to succeed, public deliberation organizers must set a goal of making those processes as representative as possible, with representation drawn from the geographic community or communities that will be affected by decisions made in those processes (e.g., if a geographic community is 20% Black, then 20% of deliberation participants should be Black). Meeting that goal requires organizers to recognize structural barriers (e.g., racism, lack of transportation to attend events, and inability to take time off work) that might prevent or discourage members of oppressed communities from engaging in public participation processes (Siu and Stanševski, 2012). The most frequent practice that organizers employ to address some of those structural barriers and achieve mandatory inclusion is proactive, targeted, network-based recruitment (Leighninger 2006; Ryfe and Stalsburg 2012), which is effective for recruiting members of most underrepresented demographic populations, except for Latine people, perhaps because of the high numbers of immigrants in that population (Esterling, Fung, and Lee 2015; Fung and Lee 2008).

Second, public participation processes need to incorporate and promote an *ethos of deliberative reciprocity* by establishing the expectation that participants' interactions demonstrate mutual respect, with, for instance, those who disagree stating their recognition of the value of how each other justifies their claims (e.g., giving reasons, telling stories, trying to bargain, and/or seeking compromise). In addition to deliberative reciprocity, to address issues of inequality, those engaged in public participation should demonstrate their appreciation of one another's cultural practices and values (McBride 2005; Young 2002). These suggested practices emphasize the importance of public participation organizers proactively recruiting culturally diverse participants who appreciate, encourage, listen openly to, and respond positively to diverse viewpoints and the many ways they are communicated (Habermas 1994).

Deliberative reciprocity, of course, is an ideal that can never be achieved fully, leading Archon Fung (2005) to argue that the concept ought to be understood as being interdependently relational with deliberative activism. Although those engaged in such activism are committed to deliberative ideals, "due to unfavorable circumstances, they may be forced to adopt nondeliberative means" (Jennstål and Öberg 2019, 648) to achieve their goal of institutionalizing public deliberation. With regard to such circumstances, Fung (2005) argued that an ethic of deliberation recognizes the value of engaging in civil disobedience when those in power refuse to abide by deliberative reciprocity principles.

For example, for 21 days, Harvard University students and employees occupied administrative buildings and demanded that the university pay a living wage, engaging in that deliberative activism because the university's administration had failed to adhere to an ethic of deliberative reciprocity (Fung 2005). Although the direct action of the sit-in did not force the university to pay a living wage, it did cause the university to create a deliberative committee charged with offering recommendations about Harvard's wage policies, which ultimately endorsed activists' demands for a living wage floor for university employees and contractors (Fung 2005).

Deliberative activism is distinguished from other forms of activism because, although some situations may require using nondeliberative tactics (such as the sit-in described above), those tactics are intended to get other parties back to engaging in deliberation. Deliberative activists must maintain fidelity to deliberative methods whenever possible and assume and act as though their would-be interlocutors are willing to engage in good-faith deliberation until those interlocutors prove themselves unwilling to adhere to the norm of deliberative reciprocity (Fung 2005). That situation often necessitates activists engaging in nondeliberative, even coercive, forms of public participation, especially to challenge injustice and inequalities, because "sometimes forces more compelling than the better argument are necessary to establish fair and inclusive deliberation, or the conditions that support such deliberation" (Fung 2005, 401–2).

However, to constitute deliberative activism, activists must remain steadfast in their ethical commitment "to engage in dialogue characterized by responsiveness and reflexivity" (Jennstål and Öberg 2019, 653). That ethical commitment emphasizes dialogic encounters both among allies and between allies and adversaries, such that people are willing to listen to one another and their adversaries, consider multiple viewpoints, and be open and ready to transform their beliefs (Jennstål and Öberg 2019). According to these criteria, activists who presume to know with certainty what is just, and who are unwilling to put their arguments to the test of public criticism, do not engage in deliberative activism, whereas deliberative activists offer justifications for their views and actions and engage in dialogue with those with whom they disagree (Talisse 2005).

The implicit role of activism has been central to deliberative theory, with many scholars and practitioners assuming that the development of the field is the result of a grassroots movement that promotes public deliberation (Lee 2011). That assumption contends that deliberative democracy is a "progressive, bottom-up movement to reform politics" that draws from "participatory democratic movements of the 1960s" (Lee 2011, 11). However, a study of deliberation practitioners found that they do not use the language of social justice movements to describe their work implementing and facilitating public deliberation processes, and that much of the development of public deliberation theory and practice has been driven by elite experts (e.g., scholars, certified deliberation professionals, and government employees; Lee 2011). "It is fair to say," therefore, "that the deliberative movement around the globe is spearheaded by a relatively small cadre of experts" (Button and Ryfe 2005, 21). Deliberative practitioners regularly downplay perceived associations with progressive activism to avoid criticisms of possessing a "leftist bias," and they often avoid explicitly discussing social justice because doing so is perceived as divisive (Lee 2011, 12). Such a concern reflects a dialectical tension between the values of *equality* (ensuring that all deliberators have equal opportunities to contribute to discussion) and *equity* (from each according to their ability, to each according to their need).

Friction between the principles of equality and equity occur at all stages of public deliberation, from the design of public deliberation institutions and projects, to naming and framing issues within deliberative forums, to recruiting community members' participation, to creating rules for participating and making decisions, to implementing outcomes of deliberations (Abdullah, Karpowitz, and Raphael 2016). For example, during PB's design phase, questions about equity and equality occur as steering committees consider rules about, for instance, which community stakeholders will be allowed to participate, whether participants must be adults who are at least 18 years old (vs. including children) and legal citizens (vs. immigrants), as well as whether project proposals will be evaluated according to whom they will benefit, as opposed to considering only their cost efficiency (e.g., budget delegates score highly a project proposed in an underserved community because of the history of divestment in that locale). With regard to soliciting community members' participation, questions include whether steering committee members will hold the same number of idea collection events in all areas of the city (valuing equality) or hold more events in oppressed communities to better solicit their participation (valuing equity).

Participants' communicative practices during the process also may produce conflict between equity and equality principles, such as when participants' differing cultural backgrounds lead them to privilege (e.g., respond to positively) only some of the many communicative practices used in deliberative forums, such as rational discourse, storytelling, greetings, rhetoric, humor, and testimonies (see, e.g., Curato et al. 2017). For example, white and male deliberators tend to prefer engaging in rational discourse, whereas African Americans and women tend to prefer telling stories and offering testimonies (Polletta 2006).

Cultural differences also exist within the same communicative practice, such as storytelling. For example, storytelling by middle-class white, U.S. Americans commonly employs a temporal structure, with story details told in the order they occurred chronologically, whereas Black and working-class U.S. Americans tend to tell stories using a topical structure that emphasizes relationships between actors and their surroundings, with less emphasis placed on the chronological order of events (Miller, Cho, and Bracey 2005; Tracy and Robles 2013). Values of equality and equity can come into conflict in a deliberative forum, for instance, if there is a rule that all participants can tell stories (valuing equality) but no consideration is given to whether Black storytelling styles are granted the same legitimacy as white storytelling styles, and the implications of that lack of consideration on decisions reached in the forum (valuing equity).

The normative principles of equality and equity within deliberation processes, such as PB, also affect the outcomes of those processes. For instance, typically, scholars and practitioners are concerned about the effects of deliberation processes on participants and their communities, such as whether and how those processes reinforce participants' social statuses, and, in PB, whether projects are implemented across all areas of a city (again, valuing equality) or are concentrated in neighborhoods that have been neglected (valuing equity). These concerns about the equality versus equity of deliberative outcomes also affect who participates; for example, those who have been "historically marginalized are often drawn to politics more by a hunger for more equitable policies than for opportunities to deliberate" (Abdullah, Karpowitz, and Raphael 2016, 2). Participants from historically marginalized communities—people who, oftentimes, are overworked, underpaid, and struggle with the material impacts of racist, classist, and sexist social structures—may be less interested in taking time to deliberate with fellow community members if there is not a definitive opportunity to improve their material conditions.

Tensions between principles of equality and equity also involve concerns about who has power and how it is exercised in a public deliberation process. Deliberative democrats' nuanced view of power "recognizes that coercive power pervades social relations, but understand[s] that certain kinds of power are needed to maintain order in a deliberative process, to address inequalities, and to implement decisions" (Curato et al. 2017, 31). In other words, dominant, hegemonic discourses are coercive forces that infuse all social relations, including deliberative spaces; to counteract those forces, deliberation practitioners employ rules and structures that, among other things, seek to temper elites' power (Druckman and Nelson 2003; Niemeyer 2011) and that provide opportunities for members of marginalized communities to develop further their civic capacities and political self-efficacy (Pogrebinschi and Samuels 2014; Rao and Sanyal 2010).

However, issues related to equality and equity remain relatively underexplored in deliberation scholarship (Lee 2011; Abdullah, Karpowitz, and Raphael 2016). Empirical issues of equality and equity have received little attention in public deliberation scholarship.

> Full and fair inclusion of all perspectives is a foundational element of deliberative democracy, but we still have much to learn about how such inclusion is achieved in practice, given connections, tensions, and trade-offs between competing values at all stages of deliberative processes. When it comes to issues of equality and equity, not enough space has been given to the insights and lessons that practitioners learn on the ground and to the benefits of conversations between scholars and practitioners about the hard choices that arise in different parts of the deliberative system. (Abdullah, Karpowitz, and Raphael 2016, 8)

If scholars are to address concerns raised about deliberation with regard to promoting inclusion, equality, equity, and social justice, broader engagement with these tensions is warranted. Hence, the focus of this book is on deliberative activism for social justice, as it manifested in the two PB processes I examined.

Prefigurative Politics

A final concept important to explain before delving into the Denver PB processes described in this book is "prefigurative politics." *Prefigurative politics* are "typically understood as experiments in living, laboring or provisioning that are alternatives to 'what is' and prefigure 'what could be'" (Lin et al. 2016, 302), and a preponderance of scholarship has focused on their economic and political structures (Wright, 2010). However, prefigurative politics also can reimagine social and power relationships as activists organize to resist oppression, for they include "a sense of relationality borne of desire, bids for self-determination derived from lived experience, and intersectional engagement in coalitions" (Lin et al. 2016, 303).

Prefigurative politics is similar to, but distinct from civic imagination, which is "the capacity to imagine alternatives to current social, political or economic institutions or problems" (Jenkins 2016, 29). Civic imagination and prefigurative politics may have aspects of utopianism (e.g., some ideas will be impossible to achieve); however, if activists are to create a just society, then there is value in articulating future goals to provide a means of measuring the shortcomings of the present society and identifying structural impediments to the realization of those dreams. After all, "changing how the American public imagines democracy may be a key first step toward altering how Americans perceive and treat each other" (Jenkins 2016, 36).

An important distinction between prefigurative politics and civic imagination, however, is that, while civic imagination is simply the *capacity* to imagine new democratic relations, prefigurative politics captures the simultaneous nature of imagining, practicing, and creating those relations, often through discourse. In other words, prefigurative politics is an alchemical, iterative process of imagining, practicing, reimagining, re-practicing, and on and on, as people strive to affect social justice.

The first component of prefigurative politics, relationality, emphasizes that the relational dimensions of collective action (e.g., friendships, disagreements, and trust-building) are necessary components for imagining/realizing political possibilities (Lin et al. 2016). The dialogic encounters that occur through relationships for political struggle open spaces for transformation (Bakhtin 1993; Levinas 1982; Lipari 2004), where interlocutors are capable of practicing the communication values, narratives, and discourses required for liberation. Indeed, the relationships and deliberative spaces comrades create through activism can imagine and practice the identities, relationships, and societal rules necessary to realize social justice (Lin et al. 2016).

Second, the component of self-determination calls for restructuring power relations both in society and in social movements so that demands for change come from those most impacted by the issue. Collective self-determination involves groups of people or communities engaging in intellectual work, deliberation, and political struggle to prioritize and take action on issues that emerge from their shared experiences and interests (Lin et al. 2016), just as the participants of the two Denver PB processes I describe later strove to accomplish.

Finally, the third component of prefigurative politics is intersectional engagement in political coalitions. To prevent "siloing and divide-and-conquer dynamics of single-issue politics," intersectionality "requires everyone to bring their full selves into struggle so that movements don't leave anyone behind" (Lin et al. 2016, 305). In other words, prefigurative politics necessitates the realization that my liberation is bound up with your liberation, and that no one is truly free until everyone is free.

The organizers and participants of the two PB processes I studied demonstrated the prefigurative nature of deliberative activism because of their emphasis on developing intersectional public relationships and self-determination rooted in the experiences of PB participants. The deliberative activism of these PB processes, as a form of prefiguration, sought to imagine "what could be" for local governance systems and the relationships among residents. Just as a new prefigurative politics exists within the context of people's struggle for liberation (Lin et al. 2016), the prefiguration of deliberative activism occurred within the PB participants' communication as they created relationships and collectively determined a common interest. These transformations may be at a smaller scale than the policy changes that other deliberative scholars have imagined as they theorized deliberative activism, but, as will be made clear in the following pages, such transformations are still impactful for the individuals who experience them, especially those from oppressed populations who struggle for liberation, dignity, and justice.

The effort to implement PB in Denver, CO, began in early 2017, when a group of community organizers strategized how to convince local government to adopt a budgeting process that promoted social justice by offering oppressed community members an opportunity to exercise collective power over public budgets. Those Denver activists, however, did not perform deliberative activism to *get* PB approved by a reluctant city council (as done in the Greensboro case described earlier). Instead, the Denver group decided to implement PB *as* deliberative activism, engaging in the process independent of any government institution, and believing that their successful implementation would convince city officials to adopt a permanent, citywide PB process. The organizers wanted to reimagine local democracy from how it operated to how it could be more just, participatory, and life-affirming, and they wanted to put that vision into practice. Those community organizers sought to inject humanity, creativity, fun, spirit, and soul into a public budgeting process that stood in stark contrast to the traditional, exclusionary, technocratic, top-down process used by Denver's government. To signal their resistance to the traditional city budgeting process—which they perceived to be dehumanizing—those organizers christened their effort "This Machine Has a Soul."

NOTES

1. The 150-acre Auraria Campus, located in downtown Denver, is shared by three institutions of postsecondary education: Community College of Denver, Metropolitan State University, and the University of Colorado Denver. Additional details about the campus are provided in the next chapter.
2. All study participants' names are pseudonyms, including the names of individuals who organized the two PB processes and those who participated in any phase of the PB process. Real names are used for research team members, elected officials, and Denver nonprofits that implemented these PB processes.
3. The first PB process implemented in the United States because of a grassroots campaign occurred in Greensboro, NC in 2015 (Russell and Jovanovic 2020). Similarly, the PB processes in Denver I analyze here were of a grassroots nature. They were implemented independently of any governing institution (e.g., school or city government).

4. Most often, PB is implemented by municipal governments, but in the case of K–12 schools and postsecondary institutions, students work with school administrators/staff. In North America, PB has been implemented in an elementary school in New York City; a high school district in Phoenix, AZ; and in several colleges and universities (Participatory Budgeting Project, n.d.-b).

5. For example, Boston runs a youth-only PB process (called "Youth Lead the Change"), with people aged 12–22 years old deciding every year how to spend $1 million to improve their communities (City of Boston 2022).

Chapter 1

This Machine Has a Soul

Participatory Budgeting Comes to Denver, Colorado

By mid-December 2018, Auraria PB concluded its campus-wide vote, coinciding with the end of the semester. For just shy of two weeks, student volunteers had encouraged other students on campus to cast a ballot in the PB process. Volunteers tabled at popular spots around campus and encouraged students to cast votes in person or online. As described in the last chapter, I volunteered to work the table several days and encouraged passersby to cast a ballot. As I was leaving one day, Jeremiah explained to me that he was not sure how to convert the physical, paper ballots into a digital version to tally the results. I suggested that I could create a digital survey form that matched the ballot, and then I could enter all the paper ballots into the form, thereby creating a digital tally. Jeremiah thought it was a good idea, and because I wanted to be as useful to the Auraria PB organizers as possible, I offered to make the digital survey form and do the data entry for the paper ballots. Jeremiah was most appreciative, and we scheduled the following Tuesday to exchange all the PB ballots, prior to a Cole Has a Soul steering committee meeting that was happening that evening.

Jeremiah and I agreed to meet at my typical hangout spot prior to Cole meetings: a café a few blocks outside the neighborhood. Unfortunately, though, on the night of our meeting, the café had closed early, and so Jeremiah and I had to meet next door, at the café's sister establishment, a bar and hamburger restaurant. Jeremiah arrived about 15 minutes late and handed me a one-foot-tall stack of 612 paper ballots that were bound together using elastic hair ties. The bundle of ballots weighed nearly 20 pounds, in part because they were printed on legal-size cardstock. Each ballot was two-sided: one side had the ballot, and the other side had a voter survey questionnaire that we had developed. I began to question my sanity in agreeing to enter, by hand, more than 600 ballots. Jeremiah then told me he wanted the results by Friday—just three days away. The deadline was non-negotiable, he explained, because he already had an event scheduled for that day to announce the vote results. My jaw dropped, and Jeremiah quickly responded that he, Kyle, and Michelle (the other Auraria PB coordinators) would be willing to meet up for a data-entry party to help process the ballots. Then, just as quickly as he brought the ballots into the restaurant, he left. The exchange lasted less than five minutes, and I now had the responsibility of tallying so many ballots and survey questionnaires in just three days.

For the remainder of the evening, I puzzled over how I could uphold my promise to Jeremiah. I did not want to burden Jeremiah and the others by asking them to help me; after all, I had offered to perform the data entry. However, I also now knew that I had over-committed. For that night and the next, I spent my evenings inputting ballot data, but by the end of Wednesday, I had processed less than 100 ballots, and I realized I needed help if I was to meet Jeremiah's deadline. I remembered Jeremiah's suggestion for a data-entry party and resolved Wednesday night to organize just such an event for the next day.

Early Thursday morning, I reached out to Jeremiah, Kyle, and Michelle and invited them to help me enter ballots that night at The Sink, a dive bar and restaurant in Boulder, Colorado. We could eat, drink, and while away the night counting ballots. Thursday also happened to coincide with the last day of class for the university at which I was working. After I emailed the Auraria PB coordinators, I then emailed the students in the courses I was teaching and told them they had one last chance to earn extra credit: they could process ballot data. I offered five points of extra credit if they worked a 15-minute shift and ten points if they did a 30-minute shift. Despite the short notice, six students spent two hours in my office processing ballots, some of them choosing to stay for more than an hour, even though they only had to work up to 30 minutes. The students seemed to have fun, often talking and laughing with each other while doing the data entry. By the end of the workday, nearly half of the ballots had been counted, and a couple of students told me that they appreciated the opportunity to contribute to the research project and help the Auraria PB organizers accomplish their goals.

With nearly 300 ballots left to count, I worried that our gathering that evening at The Sink would last late into the night. Only Jeremiah and Kyle were able to attend. With Jeremiah's permission, I sent another email to my students offering a final call for extra credit: They could join us at The Sink that night to help process ballots. Jeremiah had promised to pay for refreshments, and I hoped that the opportunity for food and extra credit would entice enough students to skip any last-day-of-class parties and instead spend the end of their semester in a dingy restaurant, counting ballots and eating fried appetizers. We needed all the help we could muster to meet Jeremiah's deadline.

Our "party" started at 6:30 that evening. Jeremiah, Kyle, my undergraduate research assistant Therese, and I sat down at a large table with our laptops and ballots to start the data entry. To my surprise, another four students responded to my invitation and joined us. The eight of us spent several hours entering data, sharing stories, and breaking bread that night. Again, the students volunteered to stay longer than was required, and we made relatively quick work of the remaining ballots. The undergraduate students learned about PB along the way, and we all came to know each other better. By the end of the night, we were hatching schemes for how to implement PB on campus in Boulder.

Because of our collective efforts, I was able to perform a final tally and analysis of the Auraria PB ballots that night at The Sink and shared the results with Jeremiah and Kyle. We then reconvened the next night at a sports bar near the Auraria Campus in Denver and announced the results to an audience of Auraria PB participants. Over those whirlwind three days, our team of students, researchers, and community partners ultimately processed a total of 751 hard-copy ballots, 158 online ballots, and 540 hard-copy voter survey questionnaires.

*****

In this chapter, I share the story of how This Machine Has a Soul (TMHS) came to be, and in the spirit of reflexivity, I write myself into that story. That is, the origin of TMHS is special and deserves an explanation, but I also provide a glimpse behind the methodological curtain of this ethnographic, community-based study to explain my contributions to that historic effort, such as the ballot counting party I just described. Future chapters will be dedicated to a detailed accounting of each PB process and the participants' perceptions of those processes, but here I focus on the TMHS coalition and the historic discourses of oppression into which TMHS sought to intervene.

THE GENESIS OF A PARTNERSHIP

TMHS was led by a coalition of three local nonprofit organizations—Warm Cookies of the Revolution, Project VOYCE (Voices of Youth Creating Equity),[1] and Project Belay—that co-authored a grant application for funds to implement two PB processes in Denver, despite those organizations' lack of any prior experience with PB. All three nonprofits had as part of their mission promoting social justice by encouraging civic participation among and providing empowerment opportunities for Denverites who were members of marginalized populations/communities, including youth and people of color. Once the grant application was approved by a regional arts foundation in 2017, organizers began planning to implement TMHS.

The eponymous "machine" of TMHS was a metaphor with multiple meanings for the organizers. In one understanding, the "machine" was the City of Denver—the infrastructure, the industry, the institutions, the politicians, and the economic elites—while the "soul" was the everyday citizens of Denver. In another meaning, because organizers viewed the local government's traditional processes for city budgeting and citizens' engagement in those processes as being opaque, machine-like, and soulless, they wanted to use PB to show local stakeholders that *this* machine—the PB process—possessed a soul powered by the everyday residents who are vital to the city's functioning. No longer being simply cogs in the machine of local government and the organ grinders of its budgeting process, TMHS was a call for a dialogic ethos that employed, in practice, a communication process that promoted ethical encounters among PB participants that did not assimilate or subsume their Otherness but, rather, cherished people's differences (Lipari 2004). As part of the grant, TMHS organizers paid artists to construct Rube Goldberg machines meant to symbolize the overly complicated and confounding process of resource allocation pursued by the City of Denver (Fendt 2019; Warm Cookies of the Revolution 2017a, 2017b).

The Denver community organizers planned for the implementation of the two PB processes for nearly a year before launching TMHS in May 2018 and concluding the process in December 2018. Rather than implementing a single PB process, organizers decided to spread PB's benefits to two diverse communities (the Cole neighborhood and the Auraria Campus), with each site allocating $30,000 to fund community improvement projects.

The three nonprofits created a loose organizational structure for TMHS. Warm Cookies of the Revolution, which calls itself a "civic health club" (Warm Cookies of the Revolution 2013, para. 3) and organizes creative, artistic events that make civic engagement fun, served as the overall coordinator of the two projects and housed the grant funds. Warm Cookies of the Revolution was founded in 2012 and led by its executive director, Connor, a white man in his 30s. Connor and his organization had received numerous awards for their creative approach to civic engagement, with Connor, through his work with TMHS to improve civic engagement in the city, named a top "Denver disrupter" (Gardner 2019). Connor hired Michelle, a 30-year-old white woman and a Colorado native, to serve as TMHS's project coordinator. She was charged with communicating across the two PB processes to provide support, but for reasons explained in subsequent chapters, she worked mostly with the team implementing the Auraria PB process. Although Michelle provided some coordination between the two PB processes, she and Connor encouraged Project VOYCE and Project Belay to develop their processes independently of one another, with each organization responsible for implementing and facilitating its process.

Project VOYCE, a nonprofit organization that promotes youth activism and civic engagement, oversaw the PB process on the Auraria Campus. At the time, that nonprofit was led by Camila, a queer Latina in her 30s who grew up in East Denver. Originally founded in 2006 by high school activists, by the time TMHS launched, Project VOYCE was a well-established and highly regarded organization among residents of East Denver, and Camila was a well-known local activist who, the year that TMHS concluded, was elected to the Denver City Council to represent her hometown district. Camila hired Jeremiah, a 31-year-old Black man, to lead the implementation of the Auraria PB process. At the time, Jeremiah was a full-time graduate student pursuing a master's degree in political science at the University of Colorado Denver (located on the Auraria Campus), but he previously had been a longtime youth organizer who had worked in Denver for various nonprofits.

Project Belay, a brand-new organization that incorporated officially as a nonprofit during the implementation of Cole Has a Soul (the name given to Cole's PB process), with a mission of supporting community transformation in Denver through participatory democracy, oversaw the PB process in the Cole neighborhood. The organization was comprised of three Black women who maintained their other full-time careers during the time they worked to implement this PB process: Nicole was 36 years old and worked for a statewide foundation; Maya was a 39-year-old private investigator who previously had worked for a Denver City Council member; and Tamara was 43 years old and worked for several other local nonprofits. All three women were longtime residents of Colorado, and Tamara lived in the Cole neighborhood. In contrast to Jeremiah being the sole facilitator/organizer of Auraria PB, Nicole, Maya, and Tamara shared the responsibility of organizing and facilitating Cole Has a Soul.

I gained access to TMHS when Connor (from Warm Cookies of the Revolution) invited me to serve as the evaluator for both Auraria PB and Cole Has a Soul. I had worked previously with Warm Cookies of the Revolution, having conducted an evaluation of its public programming. During a casual conversation with Connor in early 2018, he mentioned that his and the other two organizations would be implementing two PB processes in Denver starting that summer. When I told him that I previously had organized a successful three-year grassroots campaign to implement PB in Greensboro (see Jovanovic and Russell 2014; Russell and Jovanovic 2020), and that I had conducted an evaluation of that PB process for the city's government (see Jovanovic and Russell 2016), Connor asked me to conduct the evaluation of the Denver PB processes. Thus, I was granted access to TMHS because of my prior work for and relationship with Connor, my expertise as a researcher (in general and with respect to PB, specifically), my knowledge of PB, and my prior work as a community organizer advocating for PB's adoption.

SITES OF STUDY: THE COLE NEIGHBORHOOD AND THE AURARIA CAMPUS

As explained in the prior chapter, the nonprofit coalition (Warm Cookies of the Revolution, Project VOYCE, and Project Belay) that implemented TMHS selected the Cole neighborhood and the Auraria Campus as the two sites for the Denver PB processes, largely because of the working-class, non-white population residing in the Cole neighborhood and because the institutions on the Auraria Campus serve diverse, marginalized student populations. Organizers reasoned, therefore, that the PB processes might better advance social justice by incorporating the voices of, and materially benefitting, people from these oppressed communities.

The Cole Neighborhood

Denver's Cole neighborhood, known commonly as "East Denver" or the "East Side," is located in the northeastern outskirts of the city. Historically, Cole has been a thriving, working-class residential community for people of color. As of 2017 (the year prior to the implementation of Cole Has a Soul), the neighborhood was comprised of 52% Latine, 32% white (non-Latine), and 14% African American residents; 33% spoke a language other than English at home; 15% of adults were not fluent in English; and 25% were foreign-born (The Piton Foundation's Shift Research Lab 2017). A considerable portion of Cole's residents were young, with 25% being under the age of 18 (The Piton Foundation's Shift Research Lab 2017). Poverty was prevalent in the Cole neighborhood, with more than half of households (55%) earning less than Denver's median income of $60,000, and 25% of the total residents, 39% of the children, and 56% of the African American population living in poverty (The Piton Foundation's Shift Research Lab 2017). Compared to the seven-county Denver metro area, Cole residents disproportionately are people of color, immigrants, and those with low income (see table 1.1).

Since at least 2013, however, the racial composition of Cole's residents has been changing, with more affluent, white Denverites moving into the neighborhood in search of affordable housing, and developers replacing single-family properties with expensive townhomes and condominiums. Many Cole residents with whom I spoke during this research study were unhappy about what they described as the gentrification of their neighborhood. As Gabrielle, a Black resident, stated emphatically,

> My neighborhood has been gentrified, and . . . we've lost [its] flavor. I didn't have a say in any of these changes. Although they [local government officials]

Table 1.1. Cole Demographics Compared to Denver Metro Area Demographics

Demographic	*Cole (%)*	*Denver Metro Area (%)*
White (non-Latine)	32.23	65.57
African American	13.97	5.2
Native American	.04	.76
Asian American or Pacific Islander	0	4.28
Latine	51.58	22.26
Foreign born	24.54	9.81
Persons in poverty	25.34	10.59
Under 18 years old	25.59	23.2
Children in poverty	38.61	13.63

Source: The Piton Foundation's Shift Research Lab (2017).

> had meetings [about neighborhood development], . . . the damage had already been done.

According to Taylor, a white resident who had lived in the neighborhood for more than a decade:

> People have been living here for years. [Gentrification] takes away some of the character, and it tends to feel like your voice is being taken away. You've got all these new people coming in and building all these boxes [the architectural style of new houses]. It used to be a nice, little duplex; now it's all gone!

Jocelyn, a Black resident, explained the changes in the Cole neighborhood in the historical context of Denver's Black community having been located on the East Side:

> Long-term, Black and Brown families have left the area, and what has been a close-knit community is becoming dominated by young, white people. There have been more and more conflicts between newcomers and long-term residents. Most new residents have never lived in a racially diverse neighborhood. It seems clear the new residents lack knowledge and understanding of the history [of that neighborhood], and how these changes impact long-term residents. . . . Many Black and Brown people feel fatigued in efforts to address whites about the harm [being done via gentrification], [and] many whites have confusion around racism and don't know what to do to repair the harm.

Alejandro, a Latino resident, told a story that connected the changing demographics of the Cole neighborhood and the built environment to systemic power structures that marginalized some residents and privileged others.

> When we first moved here in 1982, I worked downtown. I drove up and down Brighton Boulevard [a heavily trafficked road in East Denver], and blew out

> shocks on that piece-of-crap road. It wasn't until another class—another race—of people, started moving into that area where the whole road became—I just drove down that road recently, and I was, like, "God, it was never like *this*." Thirty-six damn years, . . . and we got nothing. So when we talk about marginalized, we're talking about economically; we don't have the weight to affect some of the changes, and, politically, it falls in the same way.

For 36 years, Alejandro and his neighbors drove on and tried to convince city authorities to improve that stretch of road, but it was only after affluent white residents began to move into the area that the street was repaired, which showed Alejandro that, for all those years, the city could have repaired the road but chose not to because of who lived in that neighborhood.

Cole residents' perceptions of their changing neighborhood were in line with quantitative research that has been conducted about that neighborhood. Between 2013 and 2017, Denver experienced the second-highest rate of gentrification for any U.S. metropolitan area (Richardson, Mitchell, and Edlebi 2020). Of the 80 neighborhoods in the Denver metro area deemed eligible for gentrification, 27.5% became gentrified during those four years, including Cole, with most of the changes occurring in areas of Denver where, historically, residents disproportionately had been people of color because of racist housing policies that barred them from living in other parts of the city (Richardson, Mitchell, and Edlebi 2020).

In addition to the changing demographics and physical landscape of the Cole neighborhood, residents struggled with a legacy of environmental racism. The neighborhood borders an area deemed the most polluted ZIP code in the United States in 2017 (Svaldi 2017)—an area containing two Superfund sites and six brownfield sites. Talking about the Cole neighborhood's environmental degradation, Elton, a Latino resident, claimed, "Nothing really lives too long over here; man, not even the bugs live long here. . . . There's nothing over here. . . . It's really sad, because it's bordered by a toxic triangle." That "toxic triangle" includes a metal fabricator, a recycling plant, and a petroleum refinery that, in Elton's words, "was spewing out" cyanide.

In addition to the toxic triangle, heavily trafficked U.S. Interstate 70 cuts through East Denver. Camila, the Executive Director of Project VOYCE, explained the road's genesis and its contemporary impacts:

> In the 1960s, that urban interstate was put in one of the most poor, highly immigrant communities in Denver after other neighborhoods fought it. Our community couldn't fight back. Here we are more than 60 years later, and instead of righting the wrong that was done with the initial construction, we have city leaders and state leaders tripling the size of this mistake.

Government officials were "tripling the size of the mistake" by pursuing a plan to expand Interstate 70, despite a multiyear grassroots effort by local residents opposing the project because the expansion would exacerbate negative health effects and increase displacement.

At times, the problems of neighborhood gentrification and environmental racism coalesced. For example, at a Cole Has a Soul budget delegate meeting, participants expressed dissatisfaction about construction that had begun on the 39th Street Greenway, which, they believed, was encouraged by young, affluent whites moving into the area, and had resulted in loud construction noise, street closures in and around the neighborhood, and dust and debris that filled their homes, cars, and lungs.

Given the decades of marginalization of Cole's residents, many had experienced firsthand how frustrating local government decision-making can be, especially with regard to budgeting decisions regarding local infrastructure and community development (e.g., road improvements and housing options). They had little faith that local governing bodies would listen to them and address their needs, and they were angry about the many years that those officials had been unwilling to address residents' concerns. As Samuel, a local Latino artist, said:

> I used to be real heavy into those [local government] community meetings and thinking I could go and give my input, and they'd care, but I don't think they care. You go and tell 'em your input, and they just wanna see the cool ideas that you have, and they already scheduled to do what they're gonna do a long time ago.

Jocelyn, a Black Cole resident, worked at the neighborhood's St. Charles Recreation Center (referred to by local residents as just "St. Charles"), a beloved hub of community activity, which is owned and operated by the City of Denver, and had been suffering from years of underinvestment despite increased demand for its services. Jocelyn told me about a process that occurred several years earlier that involved government officials soliciting input from local residents to improve the center:

> We [St. Charles staff] had a whole big event where the kids presented their ideas [to improve the center], and the mayor came, but it never came to something. I've been here seven years, and we've done three big events where we got people to submit their ideas, told the City, and nothing ever happened, so the kids are kinda frustrated now.

Alejandro, the resident who blew out his shocks on Brighton Boulevard, shared a similar sentiment about local governing systems' unresponsiveness, saying, "The system is set up to tell you 'no' first, and you have to know what 'yes' is and what 'yes' looks like." Cole residents, thus, had limited influence on governing decisions that affected their community.

Nearly every Cole resident with whom I spoke rattled off a list of desired community changes that had been ignored by local government officials, including opposing the Interstate 70 expansion, adding new stretches of sidewalks and making all sidewalks compliant with the 1990 Americans with Disabilities Act, improving neighborhood playground equipment, and increasing the number of bus stops in the neighborhood. A Latino resident illustrated what many Cole neighbors viewed as a common occurrence:

> The highway [Interstate 70] was always gross, and we always had the idea, like, "Yo, can we paint this? Can we make it better? Can we make it more beautiful? Can we do something with it?" and it was always, "No, no, no, get out of here. What are you talkin' 'bout? Get out of here. Nobody cares about your neighborhood; nobody cares about your community. We're not gonna spend money on that." Really? There were no funds for any of that stuff?

Many Cole residents, thus, saw their concerns as not being heard by local government officials, and although some residents knew that they had to fight to get public funds allocated to improve their community, the constant fight for even the smallest improvements was exhausting. Many residents believed that there had to be another way to have their needs met than the marginalizing, standard forms of citizen input (e.g., attending and speaking at Denver City Council meetings, and contacting elected government representatives).

Given these historic legacies of systemic oppression of residents, the ongoing crisis of neighborhood gentrification, and local residents' legacy of activism to resist domination, TMHS's organizers believed that Cole was a fitting site in which to conduct their PB experiment. These organizers believed that Cole residents could (re)assert control of their neighborhood by using PB to (re)direct public funding to meet the needs of this oppressed community and, thereby, advance social justice.

Cole Has a Soul Participation

As I explained in the prior chapter, this book focuses on PB participants' discourse during their deliberations, rather than the projects that were funded. Yet, it is worth knowing who showed up to participate in PB, as well as their demands, for those demands reflect the needs of the neighborhood. Table 1.2 presents a summary of the demographic characteristics of Cole Has a Soul's steering committee members, idea submitters, budget delegates, PB voters, and Cole neighborhood census data. The data is drawn from survey questionnaires I co-designed with my community partners. Six of the eight steering committee members completed a questionnaire (75% response rate), and all

Table 1.2. Cole Has a Soul PB Participants' Demographics

Characteristic	*Steering Committee (N = 6)*		*Idea Collection (N = 23)*		*Budget Delegates (N = 5)*		*PB Voters (N = 73)*		*Census*
	%	*n*	%	*n*	%	*n*	%	*n*	%
Age									
Under 18	0	0	4	1	0	0	5	3	22
18–24	0	0	0	0	0	0	11	6	4
25–34	17	1	39	9	20	1	25	14	25
35–44	17	1	9	2	20	1	37	21	20
45–54	33	2	17	4	40	2	9	5	10
55–64	17	1	22	5	20	1	11	6	8
65 and over	17	1	9	2	0	0	4	2	6
Gender									
Female	83	5	74	17	60	3	72	42	49
Male	17	1	26	6	40	2	26	15	51
Non-binary	0	0	0	0	0	0	2	1	N/A
Education									
Less than a high school diploma	0	0	13	3	0	0	9	5	27
High school diploma, GED, or equivalent	0	0	4	1	20	1	7	4	20
Some college, no degree	17	1	13	3	0	0	12	7	19
Associate's degree	0	0	0	0	0	0	9	5	N/A
Bachelor's degree	17	1	35	8	40	2	28	16	N/A
Graduate or professional degree	67	4	35	8	40	2	35	20	N/A
Annual household income									
Less than $10,000	0	0	14	3	20	1	11	6	N/A
$10,000–$24,999	0	0	14	3	0	0	9	5	N/A
$25,000–$49,999	50	3	24	5	40	2	18	10	N/A
$50,000–$74,999	17	1	10	2	0	0	16	9	N/A
$75,000–$99,999	17	1	14	3	20	1	7	4	N/A
$100,000 or more	17	1	24	5	20	1	38	21	N/A
Race/ethnicity[a]									
American Indian or Alaska Native	0	0	0	0	0	0	3	2	.07
Asian	33	2	4	1	17	1	6	4	.07
Black or African American	33	2	19	5	50	3	17	11	16
Hispanic or Latine	33	2	8	2	0	0	23	15	47
Native Hawaiian or Pacific Islander	0	0	0	0	0	0	0	0	N/A
White	0	0	62	16	33	2	46	30	34
Other	0	0	8	2	0	0	5	3	2

Note: According to census data, 34% of Cole residents have a college degree (e.g., associate's, bachelor's, or graduate/professional degree).

[a] Totals in this category may exceed 100% because respondents could select more than one option.

of the budget delegates completed a questionnaire. Of the approximately 199 individuals who submitted a project idea,[2] 23 completed a questionnaire (11.6% response rate). Because community partners did not provide me with the total number of votes cast in the Cole Has a Soul PB process, a response rate could not be calculated, but 73 PB voters completed a questionnaire.

Based on the number of project ideas and ballots submitted, more than 200 people participated in Cole Has a Soul, with African Americans, Asian Americans, and whites represented proportionally to the Cole neighborhood's census demographics; Latine residents underrepresented; and women overrepresented. Participants also disproportionately had low incomes, with 60% of budget delegates and half of steering committee members reporting household incomes below $50,000. Cole Has a Soul successfully incorporated people of color in high-involvement roles (i.e., steering committee members and budget delegates) and, in general, represented proportionally the Cole neighborhood's household incomes, whereas white people were overrepresented in low-involvement roles (i.e., idea submitters and voters), and women were overrepresented throughout the process, with that finding in line with findings from studies of North American PB participants' representation of local communities (Hagelskamp et al. 2016). Young people and Latine residents were underrepresented throughout this PB process, which is consistent with findings from studies of PB processes across North America (Hagelskamp et al. 2016). Finally, 14% of Cole Has a Soul PB voters reported that they were not eligible to vote in the most recent U.S. federal election, which means that this PB process engaged a sizable portion of Cole's residents who were excluded from that (and, probably, other) democratic processes. Overall, organizers were relatively successful in garnering the participation of Cole's historically marginalized populations in the Cole Has a Soul PB process, especially people of color (in high-engagement roles), women, and those with low incomes.

The projects on the Cole Has a Soul ballot included a park beautification project with the theme of peace, love, and unity; a restorative justice project to address the harms of gentrification; a farmers' market; a micro-grant program for neighborhood residents and nonprofit organizations; a grant program promoting collaboration across nonprofits in the neighborhood; youth empowerment programming; an electronic community billboard; and an outdoor pop-up movie theater. The winning projects from Cole Has a Soul were the farmers' market, youth empowerment programming, and the pop-up movie theater.

The Auraria Campus

On the other side of town from the Cole neighborhood, the Auraria Campus is located in downtown Denver and is comprised of the type of sleek buildings that dot the Denver skyline and are commonly constructed on urban college campuses. The Auraria Campus, as mentioned previously, is home to three institutions—Colorado Community College (CCD), the University of Colorado Denver (UCD), and Metropolitan State University (MSU)—that disproportionately serve first-generation, nontraditional-age, and working-class students of color (see table 1.3). In total, more than 43,000 students attended those three higher educational institutions at the time of this project, with, in 2017, 44% attending MSU, 33% attending UCD, and CCD students accounting for 23%. The campus is administered by the Auraria Higher Education Center (AHEC[3]), which oversees parking, maintenance, janitorial services, and new construction on campus, as well as the student center, bookstore, library, dining facilities, parking facilities, and classrooms that are shared and accessible to all three institutions' students.

Project VOYCE members implemented PB on the Auraria Campus because of that organization's mission to promote youth activism, and they wanted young people to benefit from the PB process. Project VOYCE members also viewed young people as often being a marginalized population because of, for instance, not being granted access to governmental decision-making processes (e.g., people under 18 cannot vote).

That lack of decision-making access was especially salient to Auraria Campus students, who believed that they had little to no influence on decisions that campus administrators made about the campus. For example, in 2018, the year that Auraria PB was implemented, UCD—the wealthiest institution on the campus—opened a new, multimillion-dollar wellness center, despite many students' objections that the center would exacerbate inequalities among the three institutions' students. Whereas all campus students could use the previous recreation center, only UCD students could use the new wellness center. When Auraria PB was implemented, many students on that campus were still licking their wounds after losing the battle against the construction of the wellness center.

Table 1.3. Auraria Campus Demographics Compared to Denver Metro Area Demographics

Demographic	*Auraria (%)*	*Denver Metro Area (%)*
White (non-Latine)	50	65.57
African American	7	5.2
Native American	1	.76
Asian American or Pacific Islander	7.4	4.28
Latine	26	22.26
Other race	9	N/A
Traditional age students (under 25)	61	N/A
Nontraditional age students (> 25)	39	N/A

Source: Figures derived from 2017 U.S. Census data and 2017 campus censuses.

The history of unilateral actions taken by Auraria Campus administrators caused students to distrust them, which was expressed during Auraria PB organizers' contested deliberations about whether to include AHEC administrators and staff members in the process. That issue appeared early in the process when, at a July 2018 steering committee meeting, Barbara, a white undergraduate student, raised the issue of whether campus administrators should be excluded from voting in the PB process. She expressed her skepticism when she asked, "I mean, is one dean gonna come down and manipulate all our votes?" Kyle, a white graduate student, responded, "They do, though!" and then described the wellness center's development process as having been "manipulated" by AHEC administrators, alleging that they "paid off" the three institutions' student governments to support the center. Although I was unable to verify Kyle's claim, many students at that meeting seemed to agree with the distrust expressed about campus administrators, which constituted a meaningful narrative for Auraria Campus students.

Students' distrust of campus administrators extended to their distrust of those institutions' students. For instance, during that same steering committee meeting, members discussed whether to appoint the three UCD students who had applied to be the three co-chairs for the PB process, or have one student from each institution serve as a co-chair. Committee members expressed the concern that a co-chair's allegiance to their institution might cause them to manipulate the PB process to benefit that institution, which would be especially problematic if all three co-chairs were students attending the same institution. Jennifer, a Black undergraduate student who served as a residential advisor in a dormitory, expressed a sentiment shared by several committee members:

> At the dorms right now, we have this horrible thing where they [administrators] said, "If you're an MSU or CCD student, you can't live there." If you're already living there, you're grandfathered in, but UCD bought out the housing, so future students won't be able to move in. I think we have to be vigilant [about students' bias toward their institution] if we go forward with three co-chairs [from the same institution].

To address the concern raised, steering committee members sought to promote a culture within the PB process of participants' allegiance to the Auraria Campus student body rather than to particular institutions. Their promotion of that culture can be summed up by the following exchange that occurred after Jennifer expressed the need to be "vigilant" about co-chairs not manipulating the process:

> *Barbara:* I was thinking PB isn't sponsored by all three of our schools, and that's why the students are coming together to make this happen. I'm not

planning on wearing my school swag when we promote this [process]. It's not like corporations, which is what these schools are.

Mari (a Latina undergraduate): I don't think it's that big of a deal that there's three co-chairs from the same school; it's more important that they're from different demographic backgrounds and can reach out to different groups.

Kyle: To go off what you both said, the people who are most committed to sectioning people off are the institutions. It's the student body who's most resistant to this [sectioning]. Even when introducing ourselves to potential PB participants, I think we should just call ourselves "Auraria students" rather than play into the rhetoric of our [particular] institutions.

PB steering committee members, thus, saw students of Auraria Campus's three institutions as desiring to come together but having difficulty doing so because AHEC administrators were dividing and creating hierarchies among students based on their institutional affiliation. One important goal of Auraria PB (which lasted from July 2018 to December 2018), therefore, was to promote unity among the campus's students by increasing their ability to influence campus affairs.

Auraria PB Participation

In total, approximately 1,300 people participated in Auraria PB, and, in every phase of Auraria PB, compared to Auraria Campus demographics, people of color and women were overrepresented or represented proportionately, and those with low incomes were overrepresented. Table 1.4 presents a summary of the demographic characteristics of Auraria PB's steering committee members, budget delegates, PB voters, and the Auraria Campus student population (referred to as "Census" in the table), drawn from survey questionnaires I co-designed with my community partners. Of the 15 steering committee members, 14 completed a survey questionnaire (93% response rate), and of the 29 budget delegates, 28 completed a questionnaire (97% response rate). In the voting phase of Auraria PB, 540 of the 918 students who cast a ballot completed a questionnaire, for a response rate of 59%, which was higher than the average voter survey response rate obtained in studies of PB processes conducted from 2014 to 2015 in North America (47%; Hagelskamp et al. 2016).

Because only six people who submitted a project idea in the Auraria PB process completed a questionnaire (2% response rate), meaningful demographic data about idea submitters could not be calculated. A definite count of the number of people who submitted an idea could not be obtained because those forms were completed anonymously and because idea submitters could

Table 1.4. Auraria PB Participants' Demographics

Characteristic	*Steering Committee (N = 14)*		*Budget Delegates (N = 28)*		*PB Voters (N = 540)*		*Census*
	%	*n*	%	*N*	%	*n*	%
Age							
Traditional age (< 25)	43	6	64	18	74	382	61
Nontraditional age (≥ 25)	57	8	36	10	26	124	39
Gender							
Women	50	7	64	18	59	297	50
Men	50	7	36	10	37	187	50
Non-binary	0	0	0	0	4	21	N/A
Annual household income							
Less than $10,000	57	8	14	4	25	117	8*
$10,000–$24,999	14	2	25	7	17	80	13*
$25,000–$49,999	14	2	32	9	29	136	22*
$50,000–$74,999	0	0	14	4	10	48	17*
$75,000–$99,999	7	1	4	1	9	43	12*
$100,000 or more	7	1	11	3	9	44	29*
Race/ethnicity[a]							
American Indian or Alaska Native	10	2	0	0	5	29	1
Asian	5	1	10	3	6	37	7
Black or African American	5	1	13	4	11	62	7
Hispanic or Latine	40	8	26	8	29	171	26
Native Hawaiian or Pacific Islander	0	0	0	0	2	9	.40
White	35	7	49	15	44	256	50
Other	0	1	3	1	3	17	9

[a] Totals in this category may exceed 100% because respondents could select more than one option.
* Because Auraria Campus censuses did not provide household income, these statistics are drawn from 2017 Denver County census data.

submit more than one form. However, information about their institutional affiliation could be gleaned from the idea submission form that they completed because submitters were encouraged, but not required, to indicate their institutional affiliation on the form. I counted each of the 400 idea submission forms as unique individuals. As a result, the affiliation of 51% of idea submitters was unknown, with 26% attending MSU (which enrolled 44% of Auraria Campus's students), 19% attending the UCD (which enrolled 33%), and 4% attending Community College of Denver (which enrolled 23%).

Approximately one in five Auraria PB steering committee members was ineligible to vote, and approximately that same proportion of Auraria PB voters did not vote in the most recent U.S. federal election, signaling the capacity of that PB process to include people who were excluded by those in power or excluded themselves from participating in that (and probably other) democratic process. Overall, Auraria PB, thus, successfully incorporated, in every phase of the process, student participants from marginalized racial, class, and gender populations.

The Auraria PB ballot contained 12 projects, organized into four categories, and voters could select up to four projects. Projects in the category "Access, Services, and Social Justice" included a textbook rental pilot program and a tri-institutional Native and Indigenous retreat. In the "Arts, Clubs, and Events" category, projects included a concert on campus, a campus world record day,[4] a modern languages panel series, a campus mural installation, and a tri-institutional internet radio station. In the "Campus Spaces and Shared Resources" category, projects included improving Wi-Fi reception in the library and increasing the number of microwaves on campus.[5] Finally, in the "Sustainability, Wellness, and Transportation" category, projects included a bus shelter, an Auraria Campus Kitchen,[6] and a tri-institutional bike-share program. In order from first to last, the winning projects were the textbook rental pilot program (16.4% of votes), the Campus Kitchen (15.8% of votes), improvements to Wi-Fi in the library (14.1% of votes), a concert on campus (9.3% of votes), more microwaves (7.4% of votes), a campus mural installation (6.7% of votes), and the tri-institutional Native and Indigenous Student Retreat (6% of votes).

Over time, my partnership with the organizers of TMHS grew into a robust relationship rooted in solidarity. In the beginning, however, I faced some skepticism and reluctance to grant access to the sites of study. This reluctance may have been because I was invited into the collective through Connor, who did not consult with the other members of Project Belay and Project VOYCE. Instead, Connor exercised his authority as the fiscal sponsor of TMHS to inform the other members that I would be evaluating the PB processes, and he encouraged them to work with me. Connor vouched for me to the other members, but they did not know me, and they may have been somewhat resentful to have an outside evaluator imposed upon them.

I quickly established rapport with Jeremiah and the organizers at Project VOYCE who were implementing Auraria PB. Jeremiah and I knew many of the same people involved in the broader network of PB advocates and researchers, and so we quickly established a common ground of trust. Additionally, Jeremiah believed my status as an "outside," university-based evaluator would lend credibility to his efforts to convince Auraria administrators to implement PB permanently. Although Jeremiah was a longtime community organizer, at the time of this study, he was a graduate student at the University of Colorado Denver, and all of the Auraria PB participants were either undergraduate or graduate students. Simply put, they were accustomed to being around university researchers, and so they were relatively receptive to my presence, treated me as a cultural insider, and frequently regarded me as an invited expert who possessed authoritative knowledge about PB that could benefit them in their efforts to implement the process on their campus.

As the opening vignette illustrated, Jeremiah and I worked closely to ensure the PB process was implemented successfully. In addition to counting all the ballots together, I met monthly (sometimes more frequently) with him and Michelle (TMHS's project coordinator) to discuss the progress of the research and share preliminary findings. Jeremiah sometimes called me on the phone to seek my advice about challenges he was facing with the PB process, and he tapped me to represent Auraria PB to student and faculty groups by asking me to give several presentations to campus groups that explained the PB process and encouraged attendees to participate in Auraria PB.

On the other hand, the organizers from Project Belay who implemented Cole Has a Soul, initially, were much less open to my involvement in their PB process. One reason may have been Connor's imposition of my presence without their consultation. Another reason, though, may have been their perception of me as a cultural outsider. I resembled many of the affluent young, white professionals who were gentrifying the Cole neighborhood: I was a 30-year-old white man from the U.S. South, a university researcher who was going to *study* them, and who had been living in the Denver area for only one year at that point. At the beginning of the partnership, Project Belay organizers frequently excluded me from email chains and group chats; they often failed to notify me about upcoming meetings and events, and if they did notify me, it was at the last minute, sometimes with just a 30-minute advance notice. The gulf between us was significant, and it presented a challenge to the implementation of this research study, the research partnership, and the successful implementation of Cole Has a Soul.

CHALLENGES IN THE RESEARCH PARTNERSHIP

Every interaction between ethnographers and those they study is socially situated and, therefore, is "an engagement in social relations as well as social relationships" (Fiske 1991, 333). Ethnographers' social relationships in the field are influenced by many discourses that, simultaneously, can constrain and enable communicative possibilities at any moment (Bakhtin 1984; 1986; Bourdieu 1990; Foucault 1972). Two particularly important discourses that can affect research partnerships are race and gender (Vakil et al. 2016), and, as I explain next, both of these discourses were salient in my work with Project Belay.

The Specter of White Masculinity

As explained earlier in this chapter, historically, Cole was home to a significant Black and Latine population in Denver, but in recent years, more affluent, white residents have moved into the neighborhood, creating conflicts between them and longtime residents of color. Throughout Cole Has a Soul, I was the only white man who regularly attended steering committee members' and budget delegates' meetings. As explained earlier, these groups were comprised mostly of middle-aged, working-class women of color. Thus, noticeable identity differences existed between Cole Has a Soul participants and me.

Given the typical discursive invisibility of whiteness for those who inhabit it (Ahmed 2012; Martin 2014; Nakayama and Krizek 1995; Owen 2007; Warren 2001), and the reluctance of hegemonic U.S. culture to address issues of race, Cole PB participants and I rarely remarked on my identity. However, two instances in October 2018 that occurred at budget delegate meetings illustrate how my race and gender may have subtly influenced the partnership.

The first instance occurred in early October, at the fourth budget delegate meeting, which was held in the usual location of the St. Charles Recreation Center and attended by Nicole (a Project Belay PB coordinator), three of the five budget delegates, and me (the only white attendee). The budget delegates were deliberating about which submitted project ideas could be developed into full-fledged proposals, with one idea suggesting a neighborhood community garden. Because budget delegates had little experience with community gardens, they discussed, if the project received enough votes to win, partnering with and paying a local nonprofit organization that specialized in community gardens to build and run the Cole garden. The budget delegates knew that the nonprofit's executive director was a white man, but Nicole explained that most people who participated in the organization's gardening programs were Spanish-speaking women. The conversation proceeded as follows:

> *Nicole:* I just know them because they are the only organization that does that work building community gardens.
>
> *Jason (to Nicole):* What's your experience with them [the organization]?
>
> *Nicole:* White saviorism. [laughter]
>
> *Vincent:* Okay, Nicole, tell it like it is!
>
> *Nicole:* But I think the women who participate in the programming care a lot about food security, and they see that as one avenue to get what they need, even if they have to experience some exploitation [i.e., being treated as charity cases].

Jason: Okay, I can just build raised [garden] beds, so if we can avoid that exploitation, then let's do that. I don't want to make anyone uncomfortable [laughter], so I won't use those words you [Nicole] said.

Vincent: No, it's cool. White saviorism is definitely a thing. I'm fine.

Although Jason did not identify any specific attendees who might be made uncomfortable by the words "white saviorism," I perceived him as referring to me—the only white person in the room—and, seemingly, chastising Nicole indirectly for, potentially, making me uncomfortable. I sought to redress Nicole's potential face threat and to allay Jason's concern by letting them know that the phrase "white saviorism" did not make me uncomfortable.

That incident, however, suggested that Jason had censored himself because of me being white. Although the meeting's atmosphere after that exchange remained friendly and congenial, I questioned my initial perception of Jason saying that, because I was white, the phrase might make me uncomfortable, and wondered whether he was implying subtly that I was performing white saviorism through this research project. This was the first explicit evidence I had that my whiteness affected committee members' interactions, and I will never know whether and to what extent other Cole Has a Soul organizers and participants may have altered their messages to accommodate their potential perceptions of my sensitivities to explicit talk about the effects of hegemonic whiteness.

Several weeks later, on Halloween, at one of the budget delegates' last meetings (to finalize project proposals to be placed on the PB ballot), attended only by Nicole (the facilitator), three budget delegates, and me (the only white attendee), my whiteness, again, was discussed explicitly. The budget delegates were discussing a project to organize a farmers' market in the Cole neighborhood, which Nicole proposed be located on the large grassy park area in front of St. Charles. Nicole asked whether Jocelyn, a Black budget delegate who worked at St. Charles, thought that St. Charles administrators would approve that location:

Nicole: The objective of the proposal is access to fresh and nutritious food, to encourage growth to the local food system. This proposal aims at providing a farmers' market for Cole, for a season. For location, I put, "In front of St. Charles," but I didn't ask your [Jocelyn's] permission! [laughter]

Jocelyn: I'm sure it will be fine. The new park will be built soon, so . . .

Jason: When is that gonna start?

Jocelyn: I'm not gonna lie; I don't know yet. I'll tell you once I get all the details, but it's gonna be nice trees, new parks, and stuff.

Jason: Wow, these white folks can get stuff done when they want to! [laughter] I mean, where they been these last few—Sorry, Vincent, I'm just cracking jokes.

Vincent: No, it's fine! I'm not offended.

In this instance, Jason started to make a joke about white people but cut himself short when he thought that I might be offended because of my whiteness. After saying that I was not offended, Nicole simply moved on to a discussion of the next project proposal. I did not feel any tension in the room, and it seemed that Jason apologized more as a reflexive act of politeness than because of anything I had done to communicate offense in the moment.

The rest of the meeting maintained a convivial atmosphere, marked by laughter and friendly ribbing among budget delegates and Nicole. Nevertheless, my presence likely cut short the budget delegates venting their feelings about the local government's racist, neoliberal policies that, for many years, had neglected and divested from the Cole neighborhood. In their view, it was no coincidence that, suddenly, Denver city officials were building a new park in front of St. Charles, at the same time that white, affluent residents were moving into the neighborhood.

After the meeting finished, Jason left quickly, saying that he wanted to have time to trick-or-treat with his young children. Although, typically, I lingered after meetings to help clean up, debrief with organizers, and engage in casual chatting, I decided to leave quickly, too, because Jason's comments had increased my awareness of how my race might have influenced committee members' interactions. I thought that, perhaps, Nicole, Jocelyn, and Shirley would appreciate a reprieve from this researcher's white, male gaze.

In her book on institutional diversity work, Sara Ahmed (2012), a queer feminist of color, described the "pleasures" of entering spaces that were a sea of "brownness" (35, 36) rather than a sea of whiteness. Ahmed described going to a conference that, predominantly, had white attendees, and going to a Black caucus meeting that an activist of color had organized, with ten people in the room, four of whom identified as white. Ahmed described her feelings about the meeting's organizer not asking those white attendees to leave:

> I was very uncomfortable. I had expected this time and space to be a chance to talk to other people of color. It felt as if the one space we had been given—to take a break from whiteness—had been taken away. (37)

After, one by one, all of the white attendees had left the caucus meeting before it ended, Ahmed wrote, "When the black caucus became itself, such joy, such relief! Such humor, such talk!" (37). Ahmed concluded that whiteness can be occupying in many ways, with political labor required to create spaces for people of color that provide relief from whiteness. Although the well-meaning white caucus attendees (who left quietly before the meeting ended) were characterized by what Ahmed called a "caring whiteness" or a "sorry whiteness" (37), their mere presence was stifling.

Ahmed's (2012) view of those white caucus attendees maps closely onto my experiences during the budget delegates' meeting, although there are some important differences. First, Project Belay's PB organizers had granted me permission to attend their events, and budget delegates knew in advance that I would be attending many of their meetings. Second, although the budget delegates were a multiracial group and included a white member, the two interactions that I described above offer evidence that my presence still may have been occupying and stifling, and that my rapid departure after their meeting on Halloween may have been another example of "sorry whiteness." I did, however, try to demonstrate my solidarity with the budget delegates' activist work, and I am glad that Nicole and Jason, at least, felt comfortable enough to say their jokes and address my whiteness explicitly, even if those interactions were cut short.

Developing Politicized Trust with Cole Has a Soul Participants

The ethics of CBR emphasize researchers' reflexivity, expertise, humility, dignity, action, and relationality (Tuck and Guishard 2013). Combining these ethical principles can contribute to feelings of solidarity among researchers, community partners, and research participants (see, e.g., Minkler 2004; Stoudt et al. 2019; Su 2019). Those who conduct CBR also endeavor to preserve their community partners' dignity. CBR "does not commodify or appropriate, instead it builds on the existing strengths and talents of community collaborators while assisting in the cultivation of new capacities and skills" (Tuck and Guishard 2013, 19). CBR also commits scholars to engaging in action beyond collecting and analyzing data and publishing results in outlets read predominantly by academic audiences. Scholars should share research findings in ways that are accessible and useful to their community partners and many others, such as by giving oral presentations about research findings to community partners; offering concrete, practical recommendations for practitioners; and/or submitting policy proposals to elected government officials (Tuck and Guishard 2013).

Finally, community-based researchers should not simply seek to establish trust with their community partner(s) but also be trust*worthy* with regard to their work in the community by taking time to understand the sociopolitical complexities of the communities with which they work, addressing issues of community representation and authorship, and reciprocating on communities' terms (e.g., providing services that respond to communities' needs and not just pursuing researchers' interests; Tuck and Guishard 2013). One component of demonstrating trustworthiness is to establish *politicized trust*, which "requires not only a personal working relationship but also a political or racial solidarity" (Vakil et al. 2016, 199) between researcher(s) and community partner(s). In conducting social justice research with underprivileged communities, trust and solidarity cannot be developed simply by researchers having good intentions or in a single instance; politicized trust requires researchers' ongoing commitment to cultivating mutual trust and racial solidarity due to the fragility of such trust (Vakil et al.).

I strove to be worthy of my community partners' trust through my research, regular presence at their meetings, and contributions to their efforts to successfully implement PB. Despite perceiving myself, and being perceived by many associated with Cole Has a Soul, as being an outsider, many participants appreciated my presence as an evaluator and believed that my work could help their efforts.

A joint meeting of steering committee members and budget delegates, held on October 24, 2018, marked a significant turning point with regard to Cole Has a Soul participants welcoming me into the PB process. After seven participants had arrived (four budget delegates and three steering committee members), Tamara (a Project Belay PB coordinator) asked everyone to introduce themselves, and she began that process by saying, "I'm Tamara and work with steering committee members, mostly, and some folks on the evaluation team, like Vincent. Woop!" I blushed at Tamara's joyful acknowledgment of me and the evaluation team, and I felt more welcome and included than I had at previous meetings.

After discussing several project proposals, attendees talked about how to make local politicians, especially Cole's Denver City Council representative, Aldus Brooks, aware of the PB process. Tonya (a highly respected Black elder and steering committee member) suggested that a select group of Cole Has a Soul participants could meet with and tell Brooks about the PB process. Attendees supported Tonya's idea and recommended inviting Brooks to the upcoming PB voting event, but in the following conversation with Tamara, Tonya reiterated the importance of, first, going to see Brooks:

> *Tonya:* I want a committee to go to him first, to tell him what we want, because they're doing a lot of community development. Susan [a Latina steering committee member] can support me on this, but the last neighborhood association meeting was *big*! People didn't want money; they just wanted to live a decent life.

Tamara: Right. A life of dignity.

Tonya: How do we live a life of dignity in this neighborhood? With all this construction in the neighborhood, the neighborhood doesn't have to be this dirty. You see people throwing stuff outta their cars. I think we can get from these two tables [of PB participants] a committee to go talk to Brooks before this vote comes out, but we also need to say these issues [e.g., food insecurity and youth violence] have been addressed [through the PB project proposals].

Attendees then discussed who from the PB process would meet with Brooks, and Tonya and Jocelyn expressed their interest. I added that I would like to attend the meeting with Brooks, not because I was a Cole resident but to share data collected by the evaluation research team, as well as to talk about who participated and what ideas were proposed, and I ended by saying that I wanted to support their efforts however I could. Attendees, subsequently, approved me attending the meeting with Brooks.

Tonya, Tamara, and Shirley (all Black women) were most excited about scheduling the meeting with Brooks and shared ideas about what they wanted to accomplish during that meeting. However, Tamara then said, "We [Project Belay] can go with you, but I think it will be more powerful to have all of you going. Tonya is the long-time resident and expert, . . . [and] Vincent can have that academic hat on, when appropriate." Tamara, thus, stepped back from attending the meeting to ensure that it would be resident-driven, with me being included because of my importance as an academic.

After that meeting concluded and I went home, I documented in my fieldnotes how I felt about being included in Cole Has a Soul:

> After tonight, I think I'm going to start saying "we" when I talk about Cole Has a Soul to the group. I've been saying "you" and keeping myself separate from the group, to acknowledge my outsider presence. However, after tonight, I feel more connected to the group. Tamara made it clear that she values my presence and sees me as part of the group. The group allowed me to join the meeting with the council member, and I've been here for several months, so I think the group sees me as having earned a place at the table. I'm glad to feel accepted into the group.

After that meeting, my identification with Cole Has a Soul participants, thus, shifted from "them" to "us," because I now saw us as working in concert to make the PB process successful. Although the proposed meeting with Denver City Council member Brooks never materialized, I interpreted my inclusion in that meeting as signifying that by committing to action, emphasizing relationality, and redoubling my efforts to value the diversity of community members' expertise, I had established politicized trust with Cole Has a Soul participants.

Despite those early challenges to establishing trust with Cole Has a Soul participants, by the end of the PB process, they appeared to see me as an integral partner. Specifically, when I attended the final Cole Has a Soul event, where the last votes were collected and winning projects were announced, Tonya encouraged me to cast a ballot, but I deferred, saying that I did not meet the eligibility requirements of living and/or working in the Cole neighborhood. Tonya disagreed and said that researching the Cole PB process constituted working in the neighborhood and had earned me the right to cast a ballot. Tonya's statement was another significant moment when I felt accepted by Cole PB participants, especially because she was such a well-respected community elder and gatekeeper.

A final example of navigating challenges experienced in my partnership with Cole Has a Soul occurred when I interviewed Amara,[7] an Indian American steering committee member. We spoke after the PB process had concluded, and when I asked at the end of the interview if she had any last thoughts, questions, or concerns to share, Amara responded:

> I do wanna thank you for your participation in this [the PB process]. I think the experience you brought to the group was really helpful. I think there were moments where we really needed that perspective from somebody who has gone through the PB process, and I think that is something to keep in mind for the future. . . . Also, I wanted to thank you because I think you being at the table and participating made a difference.

In the final analysis, despite challenges that I experienced in this research partnership, especially because of my identity as a white, male researcher who did not live in the Cole community, my community partners and I established mutual rapport, respect, and trustworthiness (Tuck and Guishard 2013). I strove to walk the tightrope of dialogical performance, holding in tension both commitment to and detachment from the research sites and PB participants, as well as identification with and differences between my community partners and me (Conquergood 1985).

NOTES

1. VOYCE is an acronym pronounced as a word (rather than each letter spelled out). In this case, VOYCE is pronounced vois, the same as the word *voice*.
2. Idea submission forms were anonymous, and people could submit more than one form. Each form submission was counted as an individual participation.
3. Another acronym that is pronounced as a word rather than spelled out. AHEC is pronounced ā-hĕk.

4. This project would have funded an all-day event where students tried to break up to five world records (e.g., the world's largest game of rock, paper, scissors; the world's largest limbo dance; etc.).

5. The Auraria Campus had several microwaves in dining areas available to students that they used to heat up meals brought from home. The microwaves were popular, with long lines of students often waiting to use them.

6. At a Campus Kitchen, students use donated kitchen space and food to prepare nutritious meals for students and community members at low or no cost.

7. Amara requested to be indentified as Indian American instead of Asian or Asian American.

Chapter 2

Auraria Participatory Budgeting

Students' Struggles for Justice

One of the most contentious moments of deliberation in the Auraria PB process occurred in July 2018, when the steering committee met to determine who would be allowed to participate in the process. Committee meetings were always held in the same conference room in the Tivoli Student Union on the Auraria Campus. Because the 90-minute meeting occurred in the late afternoon, I brought two dozen donuts for the ten committee members who attended, plus Jeremiah (Auraria PB's lead coordinator) and a representative from Project VOYCE. Committee members discussed and made decisions about important aspects of the Auraria PB process, including who could serve as steering committee members and their responsibilities, as well as general process rules (e.g., who could propose project ideas). Conversations about who should be allowed to participate focused on several issues that recurred throughout the Auraria PB process, including the inclusion of campus community members, equitable participation in the process, and the roles of campus staff members.

Jeremiah started the discussion of Auraria PB participation eligibility by asking members, "During the PB process, who should be able to submit ideas and who should be able to vote?" Andrea, a Latina undergraduate student, proposed that only campus students should be allowed to participate, but Jennifer, a Black undergraduate student, suggested that, perhaps, campus staff members also should be included, because "they work here." Kyle, a white graduate student, asked, "Who falls under 'staff'?" and then said, "I don't want administrators to come hijack this process." Barbara, a white undergraduate student, said that she was confused and did not understand why campus administrators should be excluded from the process and then asked, "I mean, is one dean gonna come down and manipulate all our votes?" Kyle laughed and replied, "They do, though!" He told a story about the new wellness center on the Auraria Campus that only UCD students could use, claiming that UCD administrators had "paid off" student governments to support the center's construction, and mentioning several other closed-door machinations in which, supposedly, those administrators had engaged. Although I was unable to confirm Kyle's claims about UCD's administrators, he sounded confident and well-informed, and several committee members nodded their heads in agreement with what he said.

That moment led to the following exchange between Mario, a Latino undergraduate student, and Kyle:

Mario: I think it should be currently registered students and full-time staff [who are eligible to participate in Auraria PB]. I think they care tremendously about the campus and the students.

Kyle: I think we should also think about the kind of staff, [as] I would have a problem with security having a vote, but I would be excited if the janitorial staff got a vote. I don't want security folks voting on this process.

Mario: I meant full-time staff, like janitors and teachers.

Jeremiah: Mario, do you think we should allow staff but not allow administrators?

Mario: No, administrators shouldn't be allowed to participate in PB because they would be too biased.

With Jeremiah's facilitation, committee members reached a consensus that campus students and some staff members (e.g., faculty and custodians) could participate in Auraria PB. They then discussed the issue that Kyle had broached about whether to allow campus security officers to participate, with the following interaction occurring:

Barbara: So, for staff, who are we excluding, then? Security and administrators?

Kyle: Hell yeah! [lots of laughter around the room]

Jeremiah: Does anyone want to allow security officers to vote?

Barbara: I don't understand why we want to exclude security officers. They only make, like, $12 an hour; many of them are part-time; and I've heard they aren't treated the best. I'm just wondering where the vitriol is [coming from], and why we don't want security. I know why we don't want administrators.

Jennifer, the only Black woman in attendance: The reason I said "No" to security [participating] is because the magic word here is "law enforcement"; they're enforcing the laws that come from administrators.

Jennifer, perhaps in response to Kyle's facial expressions that seemed to signal he wanted to say something, invited Kyle to share what he was thinking, with the following discussion occurring:

> *Kyle:* They [security officers] just piss me off—the amount of money that gets dumped into security. It would feel weird to have them be a part of the process.
>
> *Jennifer:* A lot of our support base is going to be students, and many millennials don't feel comfortable with the relationship between law enforcement and youth.
>
> *Andrea:* I was just gonna say, "I don't feel comfortable with people being allowed to vote who don't have a relationship with the students." Faculty members are allowed in because we have a relationship with them versus [the lack of relationship with] security [personnel].
>
> *Kyle:* The relationship between students and security personnel is adversarial.
>
> *Barbara:* I just don't wanna shit on the cops.
>
> *Kyle:* But do we want to shit on the cops? [laughter]
>
> *Mario:* I just think there's a stigma between cops and students, . . . [and] by not allowing [security personnel to participate in PB] and continuing that same stigma, we're not helping the situation. Somebody said that they only want people involved in the [Auraria Campus] community [to participate in the PB process]. I disagree that the officers don't have relationships with students; I have relationships with several of them, and I know some of them by name. I don't think there should be a distinction [made] between students and officers . . . [although some officers,] unfortunately, make some bad decisions. I don't think that if officers put in their vote, they would vote based on their interests.

Because the meeting was approaching the end of its scheduled time, Jeremiah asked if committee members wanted to vote on allowing security officers to participate in the PB process. Because many members said that they wanted to continue deliberating about that topic at their next meeting, no vote was taken, and Jeremiah adjourned the meeting.

Although committee members' deliberations about who would be allowed to participate in Auraria PB were characterized by lively disagreements, I saw no animosity expressed among members. Indeed, despite this being only the second meeting of the steering committee, I saw members forming friendships, with Mario inviting everyone to join him at a nearby pub after the meeting concluded; Jennifer and Mari sharing a long embrace before leaving; and Kyle and Barbara sitting for a while and talking about whether to include campus security guards in the PB process, with Kyle expressing his opinions in an animated manner, and Barbara seeking to learn more about his views.

At the steering committee's meeting the following week, members, again, deliberated about allowing campus administrators and security personnel to participate in Auraria PB. I suggested that PB phases could vary with regard to who was allowed to participate (e.g., the committee could allow anyone to submit a project idea but restrict PB voting to specific campus populations). After additional discussion of participation eligibility in Auraria PB, members decided that any campus member could submit a project idea (including administrators and security personnel) but that only students could serve as budget delegates and cast a vote to fund projects. That decision was motivated, in part, by the practical issue that running the PB process without campus institutional support would make some PB phases challenging in terms of verifying whether only authorized categories of campus staff members were participating in the process. The decision to allow only students to vote was based on committee members' belief that staff members and administrators already had a disproportionately high influence on funds spent to improve the campus, and that restricting eligible PB voters to students would send the message to the campus community (especially administrators) that students deserved some control of that spending.

*****

The highlighted interactions that occurred during this second steering committee meeting illustrated many themes that recurred throughout Auraria PB, including participants' concerns about the process being inclusive and equitable (e.g., diverse student participation), campus staff and administrators hindering and/or supporting the process (e.g., administrators "hijacking" it), and PB facilitators' significant role in coordinating the process. This chapter explores those themes, as well as how Auraria PB participants strove throughout the process to reimagine student activism on campus by promoting fun and friendships. I begin by explaining how Auraria PB's facilitators' discursive moves promoted participants to employ an instrumental approach to implementing the process.

COORDINATORS' INSTRUMENTAL APPROACH TO IMPLEMENTING AURARIA PB

Auraria PB was coordinated by Jeremiah, Michelle, and Kyle. Kyle, who played a major role in the meeting described earlier, began as a steering committee member, but by September 2018, when it was clear that Jeremiah needed additional support implementing the process, Project VOYCE hired Kyle part-time to assist Jeremiah. The significance of Jeremiah's contributions to Auraria PB cannot be understated. Multiple participants reported to me in interviews and during casual conversations that his leadership, organization, and motivation resulted in the process's successful completion. For instance, during her interview, Michelle described Jeremiah's "impossible task" of implementing the PB process in a short timeline, saying, "I told Jeremiah he couldn't do it. I was, like, 'There's no way you can do this in four months,' and then he proved me wrong. I was, like, 'Oh my God, this is a miracle.'" Numerous budget delegates and steering committee members shared that they completed their work because Jeremiah had put so much effort into supporting the process that they did not want to disappoint him and cause the process to fall short of achieving its goals.

When I interviewed Jeremiah, he said that he "initiated and coordinated the whole PB process at Auraria," describing some of his duties as being "the central hub of communication and action planning," and "the point person for everybody, from school administrators, to student government people, to the steering committee, to the budget delegates." Much of Jeremiah's work involved ensuring that PB participants had the information needed to complete their tasks, coordinating communication among campus stakeholders, scheduling steering committee and budget delegate meetings, and navigating the campus's bureaucratic red tape to enable Auraria PB to hold in-person events to solicit project ideas and to cast ballots.

Jeremiah agreed with PB participants' perception of how essential his role and work as coordinator were for accomplishing the Auraria PB process, saying:

> I think that an indispensable part of why this [PB process] was successful was because it was my job to make it successful. . . . I think there's got to be a paid coordinator whose job it is to *support* the students [who served on PB committees], and I think it's important that the coordinator understand themselves as working *for* the students, not the students working for them. . . . If there hadn't been someone like that in my role, I think this thing [Auraria PB] wouldn't have been possible, especially in the timeline we did it.

Although Michelle and Kyle assisted Jeremiah, much of the responsibility for coordinating Auraria PB fell on Jeremiah, and he was aware of that pressure during the process, noting during his interview:

> There were a couple points where we were so enmeshed in collecting ideas that when it came time to pivot and start recruiting budget delegates, and start the proposal development phase, I realized there was a week where, if I had gotten sick, the whole thing would have fallen apart because it was so much work.

Given Jeremiah's significant contributions to Auraria PB, his influence deserves attention, especially his instrumental approach to PB implementation, which, in the context of public deliberation, "assum[es] that the ultimate goal of democracy is to make legitimate and efficient political decisions" (Kim and Kim 2008, 52). Although committee members certainly, at times, engaged in relational communication (which I describe later), their discourse during meetings was overwhelmingly task-oriented, which, as explained in the next chapter, differed significantly from Cole Has a Soul participants' relational approach to deliberation and PB implementation.

Jeremiah's instrumental approach was evidenced in his facilitation of steering committee members' decision-making about the PB process. Jeremiah encouraged committee members to view themselves as being the process's decision-makers, saying at the first committee meeting, "We all work for you guys; you're the deciders." However, Jeremiah's high task orientation often resulted in him facilitating the committee's deliberations in ways that led to decisions Jeremiah preferred, with him, rather than committee members, then completing tasks associated with those decisions. For example, when the committee was discussing plans to set up a table on the campus to solicit the submission of PB proposal ideas, Jeremiah facilitated the conversation by asking the following questions:

> How do y'all see us actually staffing the tables? Ten to two is a four-hour block. How many people could be standing behind the table [and for] how long? I can imagine us creating a shift sign-up sheet. How long would those shifts be? What support would you need to be able to talk articulately about PB [to those passing by the table]?

After the meeting, rather than having committee members make the shift sign-up sheet, Jeremiah simply made it. Jeremiah also worked some hours at the table, and he and Michelle stocked the table with flyers, candy, and a banner to attract the attention of passersby.

As another example of Jeremiah's instrumental approach leading him to complete steering committee members' tasks, at a committee meeting in August, members were discussing recruiting budget delegates for the upcoming project proposal phase of the PB process. When Andrea suggested that a flyer could help recruit budget delegates, Jeremiah responded, "Okay, so Michelle and I need to design another flyer." Jeremiah did not even ask whether a committee member would design the flyer; he simply took immediate responsibility for completing that task.

Jeremiah's high task orientation in implementing Auraria PB, certainly, aided the process of completing necessary tasks, but that orientation also led to him not emphasizing relational aspects of the process, such as PB participants forming relationships with each other and with other students on campus.

For instance, by mid-August 2018, when the steering committee was preparing to implement its outreach plan and Jeremiah emphasized that its success depended on members working the table and spreading the word about Auraria PB, he did not mention that those tasks provided an opportunity for them to get to know other campus members and, potentially, expand their social networks.

However, Jeremiah's take-charge approach to facilitating steering committee meetings and task accomplishment changed when Auraria PB moved into the project proposal phase, with budget delegates conducting research to determine the feasibility of submitted project ideas and then developing them into project proposals that included estimated cost, design, and timeline for completion. Specifically, Jeremiah rarely attended, and when he did, he did not facilitate, budget delegate committee meetings; instead, coordinators decided that delegates should elect committee co-chairs to lead their work. That decision, in part, was made for a pragmatic reason: In contrast to the steering committee, which was comprised of 14 members and met weekly, Auraria PB had 27 budget delegates who served on four committees that met at various times of the week, making it almost impossible for Jeremiah, Michelle, and Kyle to attend all of those meetings.

The sheer number of budget delegate committees, thus, necessitated that they (not the coordinators) complete their work. Coordinators offered budget delegates support (e.g., an orientation/training session that included giving them a thorough training manual), but as Jeremiah said at the first meeting of one of those committees:

> We'll be here at the next meeting or two, but at some point, it's just gonna be y'all, and that's why these [suggested practices offered in the training manual] are all tools. We'll show you how to use them, but it's up to you all to implement them and figure out how to make them work.

The need for budget delegates to complete their work became clear as the deadline for placing projects on the ballot approached. In late October 2018, the Campus Spaces and Shared Resources budget delegate committee was not on track to submit project proposals in time for them to appear on the PB ballot (November 2018). Because of those co-chairs' absence, committee members had not compiled a summary of their potential projects, which was required to obtain campus administrators' approval of the projects, and was due in a week and a half. Jeremiah attended a meeting of the committee to motivate them to complete their work. However, rather than stepping in to complete that work for the budget delegates, Jeremiah encouraged members to take responsibility for their projects, saying:

> I really need you guys to step up and help your other teammates get organized, too, because I want to do more to support you all, but I'm running a completely

> different project for the other half of my job, and I'm going to Mexico in two weeks, and facilitating a conference next week.

When budget delegates explained to Jeremiah that campus staff members were not responding at all or in a timely manner to emails requesting information needed to develop delegates' PB projects (e.g., cost estimates), and asked for his advice, he recommended that they push staff harder than they had, saying:

> Just call them. Don't feel bad about bugging them; you, literally, pay their salary. You want to do a thing that will give them money, so you're not interrupting or being rude. . . . You can tell them you're with Auraria PB and that you want to help give them money. If the person isn't there, try to find out when they'll be in the office. Don't let them say the person will get back to you; find out when you can initiate, again.

At the time, I wondered if Jeremiah was asking too much of these college students, telling them, on top of their other life and school responsibilities, essentially, to go as often as possible during the next week to pester campus staff members until the budget delegates received a response.

In that moment, when it was possible that this budget delegate committee would fall apart, Jeremiah motivated members to engage in a final push to complete their important task work, regardless of the conflict(s) that their behavior might cause between campus staff and students. The budget delegates followed his advice and, by the deadline, submitted their summary of projects.

As these examples show, coordinators' instrumental approach significantly influenced the Auraria PB implementation process, especially with regard to who completed the required work. Although coordinators' approach may have led them to deemphasize some relational aspects of the PB process (e.g., development of committee members' relationships and minimal concern about managing conflict with campus staff members), because promoting social justice was an important goal of the process, as discussed in the next section, Auraria PB committees spent substantial time discussing two tasks that were crucial to achieving that goal: including diverse campus members in the process and distributing funds equitably.

AURARIA PB PARTICIPANTS' SOCIAL JUSTICE CONCERNS FOR EQUITY AND INCLUSION

From the start of Auraria PB, the coordinators and steering committee members wanted the process to be inclusive of and achieve equitable results for people from oppressed communities, with those goals subsequently taken up by budget delegates and even expressed by those who submitted project ideas and voted for project proposals. At the first steering committee meeting, for instance, Jeremiah said, "We want [this PB process] to be intentionally inclusive [of oppressed community members]," and at the second meeting, a week later, when committee members were discussing their rule-making process, he said, "I actually want to encourage us to think about how we can promote inclusion in determining our rules."

However, as the narrative that opened this chapter revealed, at times, steering committee members' discussions about who should be included in the PB process were contentious because their goals of being inclusive and promoting equity conflicted, similar to conflicts between principles of equality and equity in public deliberation scholarship that I discussed in the introductory chapter of this book. That narrative of the committee's discussion about whether Auraria Campus security personnel and administrators should participate in the PB process showed that Barbara and Mario, in line with the notion of "formal equality," or an equality-seeking ideal (Moscrop and Warren 2016), argued for including security personnel because they were campus stakeholders who, in some cases, as Mario said, had formed relationships with campus students.

In contrast, Kyle's and Jennifer's view that administrators and security officers should be excluded from the PB process because their location in the campus hierarchical power structures gave them a disproportionate amount of campus policy-making power (e.g., compared to students), adhered to an all-affected-interests principle (Fung 2013; Moscrop and Warren 2016; Young 2002). Kyle's and Jennifer's expressed views implicitly promoted committee members' consideration of how including those campus members would negatively affect campus students, especially students of color, because of the historic legacy of white supremacy that continued to inform policing practices. Ultimately, the committee's decision that any campus member could submit a project idea but only campus students could serve as budget delegates and vote in the PB process balanced committee members' competing desires for Auraria PB to be both inclusive and equitable by adhering to formal equality for the submission of project ideas (i.e., any campus member could have a good idea to improve the campus) and, simultaneously, ensuring equity in decisions made about projects (e.g., whether they appeared on the ballot and were funded based on the number of votes received).

Although only campus students could serve as budget delegates and vote, the steering committee placed no age restrictions, citizenship requirements, or stipulations about criminal records for casting a ballot, which expanded participation in this process to those who are often excluded from other democratic processes. For example, when Auraria PB students were out tabling to encourage passersby to vote in the process, one student initially declined to participate because he was on parole. Jeremiah then informed the student that he was indeed eligible to vote in Auraria PB, resulting in that student casting a ballot. Jose, a Mexican American undergraduate student who served on the steering committee, also voted, and after the process concluded, he told a room full of PB supporters, "I'm on DACA [Deferred Action for Childhood Arrivals[1]], so the fact that I was able to vote at all was great." In fact, 8% of Auraria PB voters who participated in my survey reported that they were not eligible to vote in official government elections.

Another moment that reflected steering committee members' desire to include historically marginalized populations in the PB process occurred when they selected the committee's co-chairs. Jeremiah had unilaterally pursued a policy of having six steering committee co-chairs (with two from each of the three campus institutions), but those who had volunteered to serve as co-chairs included only one student from MSU, three students from UCD, and two students from the Community College of Denver (CCD). At a committee meeting in July 2018 to decide whether to move forward with those co-chairs, members wrestled with issues of inclusion and representation. Specifically, those co-chairs overrepresenting UCD, which, potentially, was problematic because, compared to the two other campus institutions, UCD had only the second-largest student population, was the wealthiest institution on campus, and had a reputation among the students of being somewhat exclusionary (e.g., its policy of allowing only UCD students to use the new wellness center).

Notably, the steering committee rejected framing co-chairs as representing the higher education institution that they attended. Because Barbara was the third possible co-chair from UCD, committee members thought that she, if any UCD co-chair, should step down. However, the following interaction showed that committee members viewed the co-chairs as representing not their institution but all Auraria Campus students:

> *Barbara:* I was thinking PB isn't sponsored by all three of our schools, and that's why the students are coming together to make this happen. I'm not planning on wearing my school swag when we promote this [PB process]. It's not like corporations, which is what these schools are.
>
> *Andrea:* I don't think it's that big of a deal that there's three co-chairs from the same school; it's more important that they're from different demographic backgrounds and can reach out to different groups.
>
> *Kyle:* To go off what you both said, the people who are most committed to sectioning people off are the institutions. It's the student body who's resistant to this [division]. Even in our introductions, I think we should just call ourselves "Auraria students" rather than play into the rhetoric of our institutions.

Jennifer subsequently agreed that the committee co-chairs should not view themselves as representing their school but as addressing the needs of "neglected" community members, saying:

> Whatever the co-chairs' makeup ends up being, as long as it reflects the composition of our student body and students in the community, so I agree that it would be okay, as long as we know that you're reflecting the specific population that's been neglected.

Later in the meeting, Jennifer elaborated on populations she perceived as having been neglected:

> If we're going to have three co-chairs from UCD, then those town halls [for collecting PB project ideas] better be inclusive. We have disabled students, Latino students, and students living on SNAP and food stamps, as well as students struggling with housing insecurity.

These deliberations reflected nuanced consideration of power inequalities, with committee members resisting a discourse of student PB participants' identification with particular institutions and, instead, perceiving themselves as being "Auraria students." Committee members believed that this shift in identification would enable the co-chairs to represent all campus students, and especially, "neglected" students. Ultimately, members reached a consensus about moving forward with the three UCD co-chairs, but only after those co-chairs (and all committee members) expressed their commitment to including in the PB process as many campus members from marginalized populations as possible, no matter which institution they attended.

Another way that steering committee members worked to make the PB process inclusive was through targeted outreach to encourage campus members' participation (Ryfe and Stalsburg 2012). In August, committee members pledged to contact and encourage numerous campus groups and organizations to participate, especially those that represented marginalized populations, including the Black Student Alliance, the Native American Student Association, the Disability Services Center, a sustainability club, a democratic socialist organization, and first-generation college student groups. These invitations (or "greetings"; Young 2002) to participate demonstrated Auraria PB organizers' and steering committee members' commitment to including students from marginalized, neglected communities.

The steering committee's efforts to promote inclusion through targeted outreach generated impressive results. As explained in the previous chapter, for the most part, people who either submitted project ideas or served as budget delegates reflected Auraria Campus students' demographics. When I interviewed and asked Jessica, who submitted a project idea, what she thought was most powerful about the Auraria PB process, she noted the proactive, welcoming invitation to participate, saying:

> Just the fact that you guys do perform outreach, especially for this mad-dash campus; it's one of the only key ways to ensure that anyone can recognize what Auraria PB is. You see [promotional materials about Auraria PB] a million times, it gets into your brain, and then you know you can have a say if you choose to participate.

For Jessica, the numerous invitations to participate in the PB process sent the message that she could exercise power with respect to spending money to improve the Auraria Campus. Auraria PB's outreach, thus, emphasized students having a direct say in how money was spent on campus, rather than decisions being decided solely by administrators who did not represent students' interests. This strategy of emphasizing students' empowerment through participation in Auraria PB, as explicated below, reflected the value of equity that was woven throughout the process.

Equity and Social Justice

Auraria PB organizers, of course, did not want to be inclusive just for the sake of appearances; they wanted the process to result in equitable, socially just outcomes. Auraria PB participants' concern for equity was a prominent focus of committee deliberations and manifested in how the process was structured and how participants worked to realize that core commitment. I discussed earlier in this chapter how some issues of equity came into conflict with the process's goal of inclusive participation by people from oppressed communities; here, I focus on how participants constructed discursively the meaning of "equity," and whether and how they saw the PB process as advancing social justice.

First, Auraria PB participants worked to make the process rules equitable with regard to who could exercise power. To return to the chapter's opening vignette, during that steering committee meeting, Barbara explained the committee's decision that any campus member could submit a project idea but only campus students could serve as budget delegates and vote in the PB process:

> We just assumed that if it was a bad idea that an administrator submitted, that's not gonna get voted for. I mean, it wouldn't. . . . We wouldn't even put it [the project idea] on the ballot, because it's not equitable. If it doesn't meet our criteria, it wouldn't even be a possibility, so we wanted to limit voting to just students, because of the difficulty in discriminating [whether eligible staff participated].

Committee members wanted only campus students to be budget delegates and PB voters because students had less authority than administrators to make decisions about campus spending, and because committee members planned to structure the project proposal and voting phases of the process to generate equitable outcomes.

Barbara mentioned that equity would be an important criterion that budget delegates employed to vet project proposals, which proved to be the case. The budget delegates' training manual explained how they should vet project ideas to narrow the list of those placed on the ballot, encouraging them to "discuss community needs," defined as:

> The things and conditions that make possible for every person to live a dignified life and achieve their potential. Community needs are the things that make it possible for a community to be healthy, to thrive, and to live in peace. Everyone in our community should be able to meet their needs, which include clean air and water, healthy and sufficient food, adequate housing, health and health care, quality education, social and income security, and dignified work. (Auraria Participatory Budgeting and Participatory Budgeting Project n.d., 12–13)

To address these needs using the PB process, the manual encouraged budget delegates to prioritize projects that addressed the "deepest and most urgent needs, . . . [to] give disadvantaged and marginalized people a voice and increase their participation, . . . [and to] prioritize projects that benefit the most disadvantaged communities" (Auraria Participatory Budgeting and Participatory Budgeting Project n.d., 13). Thus, from the outset, budget delegates' work was framed as emphasizing the collective good, with special attention to advancing projects that promoted equity for marginalized communities that needed the funds most.

According to the training manual, after discussing community needs, budget delegates were supposed to use a "project evaluation matrix" to score and decide which project proposals should move forward in the process. Budget delegates rated every submitted project idea (using a four-point scale) with regard to four questions: How much need does this community have? How much need is there for the project? How much impact would this project have on the community? How feasible is the project? Notably, three of those questions were about projects meeting "community needs," with only one being about projects' feasibility. Thus, the project evaluation matrix guided budget delegates to assign considerably more weight to projects' ability to meet community needs than to their feasibility, encouraging delegates to focus on projects' promotion of equity rather than their cost-effectiveness and practicality. That framing was a significant departure from neoliberal, technocratic approaches to budgeting that emphasize projects' affordability and efficiency, an ideology that too often creates and sustains inequalities, because, typically, projects that would benefit oppressed populations are cost-prohibitive and/or difficult to implement because of the deficits that they are intended to decrease (Baiocchi and Ganuza 2017; Forester 1999; Leighninger 2006; Nabatchi and Leighninger 2015).

PB coordinators made clear at the start of budget delegates' work that the process needed to achieve equitable, socially just outcomes. For example, during their orientation session, Jeremiah employed the examples of a prayer room and accessibility issues on campus to illustrate the importance of budget delegates using the project evaluation matrix to develop project ideas that benefitted oppressed campus populations:

> Let's say there isn't a prayer room [on campus], then we would give that a high need score. There are lots of Muslim students on campus, and they pray, and they would like to do it in a private place that's dedicated to praying. [In terms of] wheelchair access, . . . how big of a deal would it be if you could get into an important building you couldn't get in before? This is a philosophy of . . . all of us in this group: We want this [Auraria PB] to be intentionally inclusive. So, we wanted to split this category into campus impact and community impact, so we don't wash out a wheelchair ramp or prayer room for Muslims.

Thus, although a project, such as a prayer room, might not generate a significant benefit for Auraria Campus's student population overall ("campus impact"), it would be highly beneficial for students who are religious, especially Muslims ("community impact"). Similarly, adding a wheelchair ramp to access a building might not significantly improve the quality of life for most able-bodied students ("campus impact"), but it would for disabled students ("community impact"). Therefore, Jeremiah encouraged budget delegates to take into account how proposed projects benefitted the needs of minority students (and staff) campus populations and not disqualify projects simply because they would not benefit the majority of students.

Auraria PB's goal of achieving equitable outcomes infused budget delegates' deliberations about proposed projects. For example, the Sustainability, Wellness, and Transportation Committee received several project ideas that addressed students' food insecurity on campus. After the initial discussion of those ideas, committee members decided to conduct research about establishing a food pantry on campus. They learned quickly that all three institutions had a food pantry, but all three pantries had many problems, including not being accessible (e.g., limited operating hours and locations), stigmatizing students who used them (e.g., requiring students to provide their student ID number to enforce strict limits on how many items could be taken per visit, causing students to feel guilty about taking what they needed to survive), and offering inadequate food choices (e.g., unhealthy options that catered to stereotypical notions of a "college students' diet").

Budget delegates wanted to create a single, tri-institutional food pantry that was open not just to students but to all campus members. During the next committee meeting, Michael, a white undergraduate student, asked, "Could we change it so that instead of being selective, the [three current] food pantries are open to everybody?" In response, Abby, an Asian undergraduate and committee co-chair, said that, although it was reasonable to scan people's campus identification cards, to have their contact information on file, the accessibility of those three food pantries was a problem. Abby noted that one institution's pantry was located on the second floor of the Tivoli Student Union, but to get to it, students had to "go to the third floor and someone will go with you, to let you into" the second floor food pantry. Kelly, a white undergraduate and the committee's other co-chair, added, "Yeah, it's really inconvenient, because someone who wants food probably won't ask for it. The extra barrier is not helpful." Hannah, another white undergraduate, concurred, saying, "The fact that each institution has its own pantry is pretty intimidating." After more discussion, Tanner, a Latino undergraduate, made a statement that summarized committee members' concerns about those food pantries: "The question is about how to make them more equitable." Members, again, agreed to conduct more research about those pantries before deciding whether and how to move forward with the proposed project of a single campus food pantry.

During their committee meeting the following week, budget delegates struggled with the many ideas offered about how, exactly, to make the proposed single food pantry more equitable than the campus's current food pantries. Realizing quickly that it would be exceedingly difficult to convince all three campus institutions to close their food pantries and work together to create a single campus pantry, delegates discussed establishing a fourth, more equitable food pantry on campus. Michelle wondered whether it was "possible to do something that's experimental, so you create something that's separate from the other schools' food pantries and on the honor system." Riley, a white graduate student who was passionate about solving the campus's food security issues, suggested that the best location for a fourth pantry would be in the library, which was centrally located on campus; accessible to all students; and, compared to all other campus buildings, had the largest window of operating hours. Michelle asked whether staff members would be needed to run the pantry. Hannah believed they would be needed to keep students honest, but Michelle pushed back, saying, "I just don't know why we can't have a room with food that people can take what they need, and, maybe, just write down what they took." Riley expressed support for that idea.

Shortly thereafter, David remarked that he wished it would be easy to stop stigmatizing students who, because of food insecurity, needed to use the food pantry, to which Riley replied, "I wish stigma was that easy to change. . . . I'm just really interested in you don't have to prove yourself [to get food from the proposed pantry]." David then said, "I'm hearing that the issue is equity, so maybe making it so people who need it [food from the pantry] the most get it." That remark prompted the following brief exchange that reflected differing approaches to making the food pantry equitable for people experiencing food insecurity:

Kelly: I think accounting for each person's needs complicates the proposed food pantry. We'd have to track people's income or financial aid status, which would just be a mess.

Riley: I think people just need more chances to trust each other.

Hannah: We could put a sign that says, "Take four items."

Michelle: Or how about just, "Take what you need"?

Although budget delegates did not make decisions about these specific issues regarding the proposed fourth food pantry, they agreed to move forward with the proposal and come to the next meeting prepared to discuss where to locate the pantry in the library.

Members of this budget delegate committee agreed that the proposed fourth campus food pantry should be more accessible than were the campus's current food pantries, but they disagreed about how to achieve that goal. All members seemed to think that locating the fourth food pantry in the campus's library would maximize the pantry's accessibility, but Kelly and Hannah wanted to restrict the number of food items that campus members could take per visit. Members wrestled with questions about surveillance of and the accountability of those who used the new food pantry, including how to ensure that only campus members who needed food would take it but not take "too much" food. They also discussed having staff members run the pantry and having users swipe their campus ID card for entry, but those ideas moved them closer to the perceived stigmatizing practices employed by the campus's current food pantries. To not stigmatize those who were food insecure, Riley and Michelle wanted to trust affected campus members to take what they needed from the pantry without surveillance. They and other committee members thus challenged the dominant discourse that questioned campus members' food insecurity need for, and wanted surveillance of them in, the food pantry (De Souza 2023); instead, they promoted a vision of social justice that enabled campus members experiencing food insecurity to obtain, with as few barriers as possible, food and other needed supplies.

Auraria PB voters also demonstrated the desire to allocate the available money equitably, such as when they voted to fund the Tri-institutional Native and Indigenous Student Retreat—a $5,500 project that, according to the Auraria PB ballot, would "provide critical opportunities for the students to gain social, emotional, and academic support, cultivate community, and connect with mentors"—even though Indigenous students constituted only 1% of the campus's student population. Additionally, the food pantry project evolved into a $4,000 Campus Kitchen proposal that, according to the Auraria PB ballot, promised to be "a student-run organization that partners with others on campus and the broader community to recover food that would otherwise be wasted and transform it into healthy free meals for students instead." That project came in second place, with approximately 16% of the votes, and received funding. The project that received the most votes was the Textbook Rental Pilot at the Auraria Library that allowed students to check out required course textbooks as regular library books, reducing the amount of money that students spent on textbooks—a welcome benefit for those with low income who struggled to afford tuition, textbooks, and other necessary supplies to attend university.

Certainly, not everything in Auraria PB worked to advance social justice. For example, one submitted project idea was to buy a drone that would fly around the campus with an umbrella to shelter people from the rain. Although Jeremiah described that project as being "highly feasible," it was not placed on the ballot because it did not address a pressing campus community need. Other projects that made it onto the ballot included a concert on campus, a campus world record day (with students trying to break five world records in a single day), and a campus mural, with the concert and mural both receiving enough votes to be funded. Although those projects, compared to others, were not as deeply rooted in advancing social justice, overall, Auraria PB students accomplished their goal—discussed explicitly during committee meetings—of having the process result in many equitable outcomes that addressed the material needs of oppressed students on the Auraria Campus. After all, other winning projects included the Native and Indigenous student retreat, the Campus Kitchen to address food insecurity on campus, and the textbook rental pilot program intended to increase affordability for students.

PREFIGURING CITIZENSHIP: FRIENDSHIPS, FUN, AND ACTIVISM

Auraria PB participants perceived their involvement in the process as an opportunity to reimagine student activism on campus. They believed that by practicing a more participatory and deliberative form of activism than what had occurred on campus before, they could model for other students ways to promote systemic change. The PB participants were frustrated by their student governments and campus administrators, who did not seem to do enough for students from oppressed populations. Indeed, as I explain later, Auraria staff and administrators presented significant barriers to the successful implementation of PB. Auraria PB participants chose to prefigure alternative forms of activism on campus by promoting widespread student participation in funding decisions, all the while trying to ensure they had a good time. In contrast to the rote, stuffy, formal campus engagement channels (e.g., student government), Auraria PB participants wanted to make campus engagement fun, and they formed friendships along the way.

First, promoting students' widespread engagement on campus was a major goal of the Auraria PB process and was emphasized, for example, when PB participants conducted outreach to encourage students to participate in the process, as well as when they touted the process's benefits to gain campus administrators' support. At multiple steering committee meetings, Jeremiah stated a common refrain about how PB promoted student engagement: "We're building a more effective way of engaging students than student government. I hope we use this [PB] to democratize spending on campus." At the orientation sessions for budget delegates, Jeremiah claimed, "We're not doing this [PB] on a hope that it will generate better engagement; we know that it will, and we're here to prove it." When I interviewed Ashley, a steering committee member, and asked her why she joined the steering committee, she said, "I have always been passionate about community engagement, . . . [and] the [recruitment] email mentioned that it [PB] would be an opportunity to become more involved in the Auraria community." Similarly, Paul, AHEC's campus planner, said in an interview that he supported Auraria PB because of its ability to engage students:

> Having students, faculty, and staff participate in our structure is more challenging on our campus. . . . It was exciting to see a new concept in student engagement in the administration of the campus. I'm always interested in new, exciting ways to engage people for planning around neighborhoods or campuses.

Paul added that some of Auraria PB's strengths included "student engagement" and "student participation."

Auraria PB participants also emphasized the process's ability to engage students when they made the case for the process to be adopted permanently on the Auraria Campus. When I interviewed Jessica, who submitted a project idea, and asked her if Auraria PB should be made permanent on the campus, she responded, "I would say absolutely yes, because it is a relatively safe way of being an intro to civic action." Similarly, in September 2019, a year after Auraria PB concluded, when some PB participants attended a meeting to persuade student governments and administrators to make PB permanent on the campus, Luke, who had been a budget delegate, argued that the campus was divided and that PB could bring students together:

> There's a huge grouping of the CU Denver students, and then, a whole separate bunch who are the MSU or CCD students, and one of the best things about PB, in my opinion, is that it can really bring all those institutions together into kind of a cohesive bond of democratic processes.

Later in that meeting, Emma, another former budget delegate, touted PB's ability to engage students:

> I know a lot of us here are within student governments or student orgs, or working some way engaging students on campus, so I know we all agree that it's really important for our students to be engaged and feel like they can be heard, and know that they have an actual say on our campus, which is exactly what PB does for students.

Thus, participants viewed promoting student engagement as central and one of the most beneficial aspects of the PB process.

Importantly, participants perceived "engagement" in PB as functioning differently from other forms of campus engagement, as reflected in their desire to "come together" and form relationships. Although, as explained earlier in this chapter, Auraria PB organizers primarily employed an instrumental approach to implementation that emphasized participants' efficient decision-making more than them forming relationships, participants did see relationship building as a vital means for promoting "engagement" on the campus.

As mentioned a number of times in this chapter, many PB participants viewed the Auraria Campus as being divided by institutional affiliation, and they believed that engaging in PB could bring students together into an integrated community. During her interview, Ashley, a steering committee member, said that Auraria PB provided her with opportunities to work with and "develop a sense of community" with students who were different from those she knew. Despite numerous other responsibilities in life, Ashley explained that she made time to participate in Auraria PB:

> Throughout the duration of the Fall semester, I was enrolled in 15 credits, held an off-campus job, and held an on-campus work-study position. Although my free time was very limited, I knew that an opportunity like this [PB] would allow me to meet other passionate and engaged members of the Auraria community.

Other steering committee members echoed Ashley's sentiments about the importance of Auraria PB in facilitating interactions among disparate student groups. For example, at the first committee meeting, as an icebreaker, Jeremiah asked members to share what excited them about the PB process. Mario, a CCD student, said that he was excited "to make a difference" and that he looked forward to "making connections with like-minded individuals." Barbara, a UCD student, said, "I'm excited about seeing the tri-campus come together; that's never happened before." She then looked at Mario and said, "You're one of only four people I've met from CCD," and that she looked forward to getting to know him better, signaling her interest in meeting people outside her current social networks.

PB participants appeared successful at forming civic friendships with one another. As the process progressed, discussions during steering committee and budget delegate meetings were marked by frequent laughter, jokes, and sarcasm, with the latter having been shown to promote relational development in contexts that include casual conversations among friends (Tracy and Robles 2013). For example, Jeremiah and Michelle were strangers before the PB process began, but 3 months later, they engaged in the following friendly, sarcastic interaction during a steering committee meeting, when Jeremiah asked Michelle to create a flyer for an upcoming event:

Jeremiah: Would you be willing to take a stab at just drafting a shitty version of that [flyer] so I can help with—

Michelle: That's painful, Jeremiah. You just assume it's gonna be bad. [laughter]

Jeremiah: I just mean for you to not work that hard on it.

Michelle: Yeah, I can draft something up.

Jeremiah (sarcastically): Everything you do is terrible; I hate it.

Michelle (smiling): Yeah, no, it's good to be honest.

Jeremiah (smiling): I love you, Michelle.

Through their facial smiles and verbal sarcasm, Michelle agreed to help make the flyer, with Jeremiah and Michelle reaching that agreement in a way that referenced their friendship and its importance to both of them.

Other researchers have expressed concerns that PB is dull, often times asking participants, for example, to spend hours vetting project proposals, making it unlikely that a diverse group of participants can be recruited (Hagelskamp et al. 2016). At times, Auraria PB was dull, but the friendships that participants formed appeared to make those dull moments worth their time.

For example, at a meeting of the Sustainability, Wellness, and Transportation budget delegate committee in mid-October 2018, members were deciding which proposed projects could continue to be developed, with one of those projects proposing an increased number of bike racks around campus. Members decided not to move forward with that proposal because an AHEC staff member had told a committee member that the campus would install more bike racks if a campus member submitted that request via email. Jeremiah joked that he wanted to email AHEC and ask for a bike rack right in front of the Tivoli Student Union because of the amount of time he was spending there attending PB meetings. A budget delegate played along, saying that Jeremiah should ask for a reserved space on the bike rack, with his name on it, and another delegate said that Jeremiah should ask for the bike rack to be in the shape of a "J," to signify that it was his. Such moments of light-hearted discourse made whatever dull work was required less tedious.

A final component and value of engagement for Auraria PB participants was their belief that students' involvement in the process would spill over into political activism in other contexts. For example, Jessica, who submitted a project idea, described PB as an "intro to civic action," implying that participating students would engage in civic affairs beyond the process.

Several budget delegates, who I interviewed immediately after Auraria PB concluded, reported that the PB process equipped them and other participants to pursue social change in other arenas of civic life. For example, Riley said that she would encourage "people to get involved" in a future PB process for "various reasons," which included "get[ting] deeper exposure to how decisions are made on campus, and I think that that information helps everyone navigate institutions that they're a part of." Riley added that the process could help students to "map when and why we might be giving away our power." Interviewees perceived PB as providing an opportunity for participants to exercise their collective power, and, as Riley believed, that the process would foster students' critical thinking about other ways that they could exercise agency to promote social change. Ultimately, Riley saw the empowered public deliberation that occurred in PB as a life-or-death necessity, stating:

> I believe that if we don't get serious about practicing decision making with each other, there is no way that our generation is going to have a chance to create the large-scale changes that we need to ensure, or even have a chance at, a livable future for a lot of people. . . . I think that increasing access to this [PB] model is really a practice of survival.

Other budget delegates echoed Riley's statements about the PB process. For instance, in an interview conducted shortly after Auraria PB concluded, Luke said that the process "made me be more open to social change, making me realize more that I could be a driving factor in social change." Luke's desire to be more involved in promoting social change than he had been previously was a result of PB making him aware that he could make a difference. Emma also reported being more prepared to engage in activism on campus after participating in the PB process as a budget delegate, saying that "knowledge-wise, I do think I can have more of an impact on what happens on campus than I did beforehand."

As these sample quotes reveal, participants believed that students' participation in the PB process would promote their engagement on the Auraria Campus and beyond. Those who participated as steering committee members or as budget delegates said that the process helped to prepare them for and made them more confident about engaging in other social change efforts, and thus increased their political self-efficacy, the extent to which people believe they can participate competently in political conversations (Nabatchi and Staniševski 2008). This development came despite campus administrators', at times, significant resistance to the implementation of PB on campus.

CAMPUS ADMINISTRATORS' AND STAFF MEMBERS' RESISTANCE TO AURARIA PARTICIPATORY BUDGETING

None of the three Auraria institutions' higher administration ever formally endorsed Auraria PB. Because Auraria PB used private grant funds, Jeremiah and Michelle simply started the process without asking for campus administrators' permission, although Jeremiah consistently believed that administrators would not oppose PB because the money allocated would be spent to improve the campus. At the same time, as this chapter's opening vignette illustrated, many PB participants did not believe that campus administrators pursued students' best interests, and they feared that administrators and staff members might hijack, undermine, or dilute the PB process. At one steering committee meeting, Kyle summed up many Auraria PB participants' view that campus "administrators are more concerned with growing their own budget and less concerned with the real wants and needs of students." Jeremiah and the steering committee, thus, wanted Auraria PB to be run by and for students, keeping campus administrators and staff members at arm's length.

Of course, it is worth noting that Auraria PB could not have moved forward without the institutions' tacit approval. Indeed, some staff members' involvement was essential for implementing the process, with, for instance, budget delegates not being able to develop their project proposals without input from staff members across a range of offices.

Two staff allies, in particular, made invaluable contributions to the PB process: Paul, director of campus planning, and Andrew, a sustainability officer. Michelle acknowledged the importance of these allies in an interview that I conducted with her after Auraria PB concluded, saying:

> Part of the reason why the Auraria PB process happened—of course, Jeremiah was the mastermind behind it all—but if we didn't get lucky and have some key supportive people in key positions, it just would have stalled. Like, if we didn't have Paul, I don't even know what we would have done. Nothing. It would have stopped right in that phase.

As the director of campus planning, Paul had to approve all Auraria PB project proposals, with that approval affording them legitimacy in the eyes of other campus staff and administrators.

Nevertheless, Auraria PB participants saw the campus bureaucracy as their primary obstacle, and the internal and external messaging of Auraria PB expressed that the process was occurring despite administrators' resistance to it. When conducting outreach, PB participants often remarked that the campus's three institutions were funded disproportionately by students' tuition and that the students had little control over how that money was spent on campus. The PB process was an attempt to resist the totalitarian control of administrators by exercising collective agency over how their tuition dollars were spent.

PB participants often expressed their reluctance to work with AHEC staff members. For example, at an August 2018 steering committee meeting, members discussed how much involvement they wanted the campus staff members ("advisors," in this exchange) to have in the PB process.

> *Barbara:* So, we don't want any advisors helping out?
>
> *Mason:* They can help, but they're not, like, a key member.
>
> *Jeremiah:* Yeah, a big part of these [budget delegate] committees' work is to go out into the world and do research, asking how much does it cost to build these park benches, and can we even put a park bench there. They're always talking to people, but those people aren't members of the committee.
>
> *Michelle:* Those proposals have to be able to be implemented, so I imagine they'll have to be approved by AHEC. So, there's working with AHEC [staff members], but they're not on the committee.
>
> *Jeremiah (sighing):* So, there's working with AHEC.

Campus staff members, thus, were not members of the budget delegate committees, which limited their involvement to a supporting role. Additionally,

Jeremiah's final comment during that interaction about working with AHEC demonstrated his reluctance to work with campus staff (even in August, when Auraria PB was only collecting project ideas) and that he saw obtaining AHEC's approval to implement projects as a necessary inconvenience.

PB participants' lack of trust in and reluctance to work with AHEC's staff members continued into the project proposal phase. At the first Arts budget delegate committee meeting, Jeremiah used an icebreaker to ask what everyone was most and least excited about with regard to the PB process. Morgan responded that he was most excited about the possibility of installing more art on campus but said that the "least exciting thing is going through AHEC and seeing what it actually is going to allow, because I know about its bureaucracy." Morgan's comment was followed by heavy sighs from several budget delegates who shared Morgan's dislike for working with AHEC's staff. Later in that meeting, Morgan made a persuasive (and successful) appeal that he should be elected co-chair of the Arts budget delegate committee because he understood that although "there's a lot of bureaucratic obstacles to go through dealing with AHEC," his ability to navigate that bureaucracy would facilitate budget delegates' work.

When I interviewed Andrew, the AHEC sustainability officer who was an early and enthusiastic supporter of Auraria PB, and who worked with budget delegates to develop some of their project proposals, he described Auraria PB student participants as possessing an "air of defiance, which [the campus's] administration doesn't do a great job with." Andrew claimed that, during the project proposal phase, campus staff members "felt ambushed" by budget delegates' aggressive requests for information about projects' feasibility and costs, and perceived their responses as often being "misunderstood" because budget delegates did not recognize when staff members were making a "true commitment" to projects versus identifying projects as "just possibilities." Because Andrew believed that most campus staff members shared his enthusiasm about helping the PB process to succeed, he viewed PB participants' negative attitudes toward and defiant communication with and about staff members as unwarranted. Andrew said that Jeremiah and the other organizers needed to "build relationships" with administrators and staff members "to sustain" the PB process, rather than viewing them as "the opposition."

Andrew was most frustrated about not being permitted to be more involved in the process (e.g., being allowed to regularly attend budget delegate meetings and to deliberate with budget delegates) because he believed he had valuable expertise to contribute. As he explained:

> If I would change anything, I wanna be allowed to be more involved. I get the benefit of it [Auraria PB] being student-led and student-focused. I just think I could have helped more and made Jeremiah's life a lot easier. . . . The

> Sustainability and Wellness budget delegate committee gave me a list of 64 [project] ideas and gave me the floor for 10 minutes to say what's feasible and what wasn't. . . . I felt underutilized, I guess.

Andrew thought that PB participants "were just using us [campus staff] for what they needed," and he was frustrated with the PB coordinators for not keeping him informed about the process's developments. As he claimed, "No one communicated directly to me what [project proposals] won, for instance! They didn't even think to update me after the [vote] results came in, so how valuable was I?" Despite his perceptions of being "used" and "underutilized," Andrew still supported the PB process and was willing to help the student participants make it permanent on the Auraria Campus and said that PB organizers "should know they have more allies in the administration that can help."

However, despite Andrew's assertion that campus administrators and staff members wanted to be helpful allies of the PB process, PB participants perceived their antagonism toward those campus members as being warranted. Those students' distrust of campus administrators prior to Auraria PB (e.g., for making spending decisions that participants perceived as promoting institutions' reputations at students' expense) increased substantially during the process and was fueled by their frustration with campus policies that adversely affected Auraria PB (e.g., not getting permission to conduct outreach in some campus buildings) and supported their general view that administrators sought to prevent students from engaging in campus activism and from exercising collective power to determine campus policies. PB participants' antagonism toward campus administrators, thus, supported the finding that when policies are perceived to be problematic, people who implement them are targeted for confrontation by direct action activist campaigns (Minieri and Getsos 2007).

PB participants experienced numerous bureaucratic obstacles in working with campus administrators who prevented participants from contacting more students through outreach (e.g., not being allowed to table in more than one place on campus) and from developing some proposed projects (i.e., staff members not providing required information to move projects forward during the project proposal development phase). With regard to AHEC bureaucracy limiting Auraria PB's outreach, in August 2018, before the fall semester started, steering committee members decided that Auraria PB needed to be an officially sanctioned student club, which would grant process representatives the ability to reserve spaces on campus for their events, as well as the committee receiving $300 from the campus (provided to all student groups) to support its work.

The committee members decided to incorporate as a club through CCD, because doing so presented the fewest bureaucratic obstacles. However, after becoming a club, during a steering committee discussion of upcoming campus events where they could table to collect project ideas, Barbara pointed out that because the club was registered only with CCD, members could not attend any exclusive events hosted by the campus's other two institutions. For example, to reserve a table at a UCD-only event, Auraria PB had to be registered as a UCD club. The club was never registered with the other two institutions because it was not as high of a priority for the steering committee as was organizing and implementing the PB process, but not registering the club with MSU and CCD constrained PB participants' outreach possibilities.

Other bureaucratic obstacles could be seen as insignificant when treated as stand-alone events, but, collectively, over the course of the process, they hamstrung Auraria PB in meaningful ways. For instance, in December 2018, I volunteered to help steering committee members and budget delegates collect votes for Auraria PB, which was nearing its end. When Jeremiah arrived to work his shift soliciting votes, he talked with me about being fed up with the campus institutions' bureaucracy, venting his frustration about the semester's worth of obstacles with which he had struggled. In particular, Auraria PB's outreach had been hampered because, as Jeremiah explained, administrators had authorized setting up a table at only one place on campus, despite his efforts to obtain approval for multiple locations.

> I tried to get permission to set up a table in front of one of the buildings on campus, and I was appalled! The administrators wanted two weeks' notice and to set up a walkthrough of the building, just for us to sit in front of the doors and ask people to vote in PB!

As I listened to Jeremiah express his unhappiness with campus institutions' responses to Auraria PB's outreach efforts, I noticed that the ballots had a space at the top for voters to write the date, the university that they attended, and their student ID number, but the box for the ID number was marked out on all of the ballots. I knew that the steering committee wanted to collect ID numbers to verify that voters were campus students and that they did not cast more than one ballot, so I was surprised to see the ID box blacked out.

When I asked Kyle why the student ID box was marked out, he explained that because the steering committee could use ID numbers to view students' private information, such as home addresses and grades, AHEC determined that collecting those ID numbers violated the U.S. Family Educational Rights and Privacy Act. Kyle said that although AHEC's position was reasonable, he wished that AHEC had informed PB organizers before the voting process started. In contrast, Jeremiah was angry with and cursed AHEC for not telling him sooner about that issue, because Auraria PB had already collected some ballots that contained student ID numbers, and Jeremiah now had to take extra steps to keep those ID numbers confidential. He told me that throughout the semester, he had been angered and annoyed by all of the campus administration's bureaucratic red tape and stonewalling of Auraria PB and that if he had not been paid to organize it, he would have dropped the project.

One week later, PB participants gathered at a sports bar near the Auraria Campus to announce the winning projects and to celebrate the completion of the work done by steering committee members, budget delegates, and PB organizers. As attendees reminisced about what they had been through that semester, consumed appetizers, and toasted each other with frosty glasses of beer, some grumbled about the bureaucratic barriers they had faced. Jeremiah shared that a budget delegate had developed a proposal for a wine tasting on campus, but because campus staff never responded to email requests for needed information, the proposal did not move forward. Moreover, he said that one of the campus's student governments had tried to invalidate the entire PB process by claiming, without evidence, that "all the numbers were wrong" for the estimated costs of winning projects and the number of students who had been involved in the process. He also said that all of the posters around campus advertising the Auraria PB process had been taken down twice. When another partygoer asked whether those posters had received the necessary approvals from campus staff before being put up, Jeremiah insisted that they had, saying, "They [the posters] were legit as fuck. I feel good that we did as well as we did, given the challenges."

When I interviewed Jeremiah, approximately two months after Auraria PB announced the winning projects, and asked him what was most challenging about the process, he said the "barriers of the administration to having this thing [Auraria PB] move forward." He characterized campus bureaucrats as being "passive-aggressive," explaining that "they wouldn't tell me 'No,' but they would try to make it hard [to get approval]." Hence, although AHEC did not explicitly oppose Auraria PB, it erected many hurdles that made it difficult for PB participants to complete their work.

Jeremiah said that, at the beginning of the PB process, despite their lack of understanding of the process, the campus's student governments were opposed to it and claimed that it was a scam. Jeremiah explained the substantial amount of distrust and skepticism expressed by student government members, staff members, and administrators about the PB process, and that he grew tired of constantly having to "prove ourselves and verify that we were legit." Despite being a seasoned organizer, Jeremiah was surprised by the high degree of resistance, saying, "I thought they would resist; I just didn't think that they would do so much [to hamper the PB process]."

Riley, the budget delegate who worked on the food pantry project that became a Campus Kitchen, was also surprised by the extent of resistance to Auraria PB. During my interview with her after the PB vote results were announced, Riley said that, because of her prior work organizing campus students to engage in activism, she did not have lofty expectations about administrators' support of the PB process, but was surprised by the extent of administrators' "dishonesty that seemed to happen throughout the process . . . telling the student delegates one thing and then saying something else behind closed doors."

PB participants, thus, struggled with campus administrators often moving the goalposts, sending conflicting messages, and/or outright lying about how the process could move forward, and they were frustrated that administrators, staff, and student governments were not more supportive of the process. Some campus staff members viewed Auraria PB as a temporary inconvenience that was likely to fail, and consequently, their lack of aid frustrated the students who took this PB process seriously.

Finally, it is important to note that not all PB participants had negative experiences with campus staff. As mentioned previously, Andrew and Paul, two campus staff members, expressed deep sincerity about wanting to help PB student participants and stated that working with them was the most rewarding aspect of the Auraria PB process. Additionally, Kyle told me in an interview that, when the PB process began, he shared other steering committee members' distrust of and frustration with administrators making decisions about the campus without PB students' input, but that the PB process "made me sympathize more with the administration. As much as I hate to admit that, these are people with concerns that I hadn't really recognized before." Prior to participating in Auraria PB, Kyle had been one of the students who, in his words, would "just barrage a bureaucracy with all sorts of demands, but when you are trying to implement those demands, you kind of get to sympathize with the [administrators] . . . and their concerns." During the PB process, Kyle thus found himself in a similar position to campus administrators, having to respond to students' demands when he implemented desired projects, and that experience made him appreciate challenges that campus administrators and staff members often face.

Ultimately, many Auraria PB participants viewed campus administrators' systemic barriers that prevented them from exercising collective agency as the most significant challenge to the process. Although steering committee members' and budget delegates' work was difficult and time-consuming, those challenges paled in comparison to the resistance of AHEC's bureaucracy to the process, which impeded PB students' efforts at many turns of the process, from performing outreach, to developing project proposals, to soliciting votes. Although some campus staff members were committed to and supportive of the PB process, PB participants grew increasingly frustrated with campus policies and rules that limited their ability to engage students on campus, and with those who made and enforced those rules. As a result of this frustration, and because Auraria PB opened their eyes to more just and democratic ways to allocate resources, a handful of former Auraria PB participants launched a campaign in 2019 to convince campus officials to make PB permanent on campus.

EPILOGUE: THE CAMPAIGN

As I explained in the beginning of this book, an important goal of the organizers of This Machine Has a Soul was that, after completing the Auraria PB process, participants would become an organized and motivated constituency committed to engaging in activism to make PB permanent on that campus. For instance, Jeremiah hoped that, following the conclusion of the PB vote in December 2018, during the spring 2019 semester, PB participants would launch a grassroots campaign to accomplish that goal, which, if approved by May 2019, would mean that the PB process could be conducted, again, the following academic year.

However, from the very start, that campaign to make PB permanent on the Auraria Campus was dogged by a lack of student participation, with only Jeremiah, Kyle, and two former steering committee members attending the first campaign meeting in February 2019. Despite the low turnout, Jeremiah expressed at that meeting his belief that the campaign would attract widespread student participation:

> This, in some ways, is gonna be political. We're probably gonna piss people off on campus. I love that stuff. I think it will be easy to get students feeling agitated about the campus screwing them over, and for them to come to meetings to tell the Chancellor to give them their money back. I don't think we can do PB on Auraria unless we've built a base of students who are down to engage, basically, in activism to move this agenda forward.

The four attendees subsequently organized a campaign recruitment event that was held on the Friday before spring break, but no additional students attended it.

Lacking grassroots support for making PB permanent on the Auraria Campus, the few former PB participants involved in the campaign decided that Jeremiah should run for president of UCD's student government, a powerful position from which he could advocate for the permanent adoption of PB. Jeremiah did run on a ticket with Tanner, a former PB budget delegate, as vice president, but Jeremiah's other responsibilities forced him to drop out of the race.

By April 2019, the campaign to implement PB permanently on the Auraria Campus was running on fumes, with only Jeremiah, Kyle, and me attending that month's organizing meeting. At that meeting, Jeremiah said, "I don't mean to sound so negative, but it's been really fuckin' rough. I'm the person talkin' to all these admin people, tryin' to sell them on doin' this [PB] again, and they're, like, 'You and what army?'" At that point in the campaign, Tanner had dropped out of the student government race and had not been in contact with Jeremiah for weeks. Hannah and Michael, two former budget delegates, had pledged to run the campaign's social media accounts, but they had not posted anything. According to Jeremiah, many former PB participants he contacted during that spring semester about the campaign had not responded to him, and those who did respond said that they were too busy to spend time on the advocacy campaign. Although Auraria PB may have equipped students with skills to engage in activism, many chose not to apply those skills to this campaign.

By May 2019, it was clear to Jeremiah and the others involved in the campaign that they would not achieve, before the end of that semester, their goal of making PB permanent on the Auraria Campus. They decided to postpone campaign work during the summer but pledged to reconvene when the fall 2019 semester started.

By the start of that fall semester, several positive developments had occurred for the PB campaign. First, some Auraria PB projects that had been approved in December 2018 had been implemented, including improvement of the library's Wi-Fi and the launch of the textbook rental program, both of which demonstrated the material effects of the PB process. Several former PB participants also had been elected to executive positions in campus student governments, including Tanner (who was elected to a different position in UCD's student government), Hannah, and Michael—all of whom had served on the Sustainability, Wellness, and Transportation budget delegate committee. Additionally, during the summer, Jeremiah had secured pledges of support for a second PB process from some campus administrators, including MSU's president and UCD's director of diversity, equity, and inclusion. Together, those institutions had committed $88,000 to fund a second PB process, if the campus's student governments approved that process, with Jeremiah already having secured the support of UCD's student government. However, it was not clear where the money for PB would be housed and what organization/office would control and allocate the funds to implement the process.

After continued negotiations with various stakeholders, the campus's student governments, in consultation with their staff advisor, who, from the beginning, had opposed Auraria PB, decided that to make PB permanent, first, all three student governments had to pass a resolution supporting the process. The body that represented and coordinated the student governments—the Student Advisory Committee to the Auraria Board (SACAB[2]), comprised of student representatives from each student government—then had to pass a resolution to create a PB implementation committee. Jeremiah and the other campaign participants perceived the requirement that all student governments pass a resolution supporting PB as just another campus bureaucratic obstacle put in place, at the behest of the student government staff advisor, to prevent the campaign's success, as they already had enough allies on SACAB to approve a PB implementation committee.

In September 2019, the final push to make PB permanent occurred. Jeremiah and other student activists had arranged a meeting of key campus staff members, administrators, student government representatives, and SACAB members. Several former PB participants planned to make a persuasive presentation that was intended to resolve any of those stakeholders' concerns about the PB process and to motivate MSU's and CCD's student governments to pass a resolution supporting the process, which UCD's student government already had passed.

In a meeting to prepare for that presentation, Jeremiah made it clear that, "This conversation with the student governments is likely to be the make-or-break conversation. If it goes poorly, PB probably won't happen, but if it goes well, we'll likely get a green light." To fill that meeting with PB supporters, Jeremiah invited campus librarians—allies of the PB process—to attend and talk about how well the improved Wi-Fi and textbook rental program were working. He also invited the co-executive director of the Participatory Budgeting Project (the most prominent organization advocating for and implementing PB processes in North America) to speak about PB's benefits.

On the day of the meeting, approximately 40 people attended. The student activists came with a well-prepared presentation that explained PB and asked the campus's student governments to commit, in total, at least $100,000 to implement a second PB process. That funding would be apportioned in an equitable manner, with each higher education institution contributing according to its percentage of the Auraria Campus's student population (e.g., MSU, with 45% of the student population, would contribute $45,000).

After the activists' brief presentation, during the question-and-answer period, several staff members and even some students in the audience expressed skepticism about implementing PB a second time. A staff member who oversaw campus events (e.g., concerts) insisted that their office could spend the money more efficiently than PB student participants would. Diana, MSU's student government president, expressed a desire for "representation" in the process based on funding, which caught the activists by surprise:

> MSU is open to [approving PB], but we need some clarification. Why is it $45,000 that's expected for us to do annually and then increase as the years go on? Currently, we're on a downward slope of enrollment. . . . In addition, we

> want equal representation for our dollars, so if we are contributing $45,000, whereas others are contributing less, we should have more representation.

When Jeremiah asked what "representation" meant, Diana responded that she wanted "actual students who represent MSU interests in proportion to the money that we're contributing." In other words, because MSU would contribute the most money to the process, Diana wanted more students from MSU than from the other two institutions "actually having a say in how this money is allocated," a condition that the PB activists could not meet because there was no way to control how many students submitted a project idea, volunteered to be a budget delegate, or voted in the PB process, much less restrict the proportion of PB participants affiliated with each institution.

The meeting ended without a firm commitment from the student governments of CCD or MSU to pursue a resolution supporting the permanent adoption of PB on the Auraria Campus. Although Auraria PB student activists had been motivated by a desire to tear down ideological barriers that separated students according to the institution that they attended, the skepticism expressed at that meeting by staff members and student leaders about the PB process was driven by the desire to protect their institutions' turf. Following that "make-or-break" meeting, because CCD and MSU student governments' support of the process could not be secured, the grassroots campaign dissolved, and PB was not made permanent on the Auraria Campus. Despite the earlier successes of Auraria PB's instrumental approach to PB implementation, organizers were unable to transmute that work into a widespread grassroots movement to make PB permanent on campus.

In contrast to Auraria PB, Cole Has a Soul pursued a starkly different approach to implementing PB that generated different outcomes. Those participants emphasized a relational/dialogic approach to implementing PB, which I explain next.

NOTES

1. Deferred Action for Childhood Arrivals (DACA) is a U.S. immigration policy that allows some individuals with unlawful presence in the United States, after being brought to the country as children, to receive a renewable two-year period of deferred action from deportation. Despite some protections from deportation and permissions to work legally, DACA does not provide a path to legal permanent residence or citizenship, and, therefore, recipients are not eligible to vote in federal elections.
2. Pronounced sā-kăb.

Chapter 3

Cole Has a Soul

People Power, Community Connection, and Relationship Building

On a warm August evening in 2018, members of the Cole Has a Soul steering committee met in a neighborhood community center—their first meeting in three months. The group had launched its PB process back in May with a neighborhood assembly, but a lack of follow-up by Project Belay's facilitators and difficulty coordinating committee members' summer schedules had prevented the committee from reconvening.

Tamara, one of the Cole Has a Soul PB facilitators, and I were the first to arrive at the meeting. After several others arrived, Tamara announced that dinner (pizza and salad) would be delivered soon. The meeting was scheduled to start at 5:30 pm, but by 5:40 pm, some committee members still had not arrived.

By 5:50 p.m., Tamara casually shifted the small talk occurring among the eight attendees to the business of the evening. The first item discussed was the door-to-door canvassing that they had been doing in the Cole neighborhood to collect residents' ideas about potential community improvement projects that could be funded through their PB process. For that canvassing, Elise (a 41-year-old white woman) partnered with another steering committee member who was not at this meeting, Tonya, a 70-year-old African American woman who was a longtime Cole resident, a well-respected community leader, and fluent in both English and Spanish. Elise explained the benefits of their bilingual dyad spreading the word about Cole Has a Soul:

> Having someone who spoke Spanish and someone who spoke English was really good. We'd go to the door together, and if it was an English person, I would speak, but when it came to needing someone who could speak Spanish, Tonya was pretty good. She felt confident answering questions . . . [and] she got some good ideas and conversation. I liked talking with people, but I was super

nervous at first. I liked hearing people's stories . . . finding out how long they'd been in the neighborhood, and what they liked and didn't like [about it].

Another steering committee member, Reyna, a 45-year-old Asian American woman who was married and had two children, then offered another reflection on the intersections of identity and outreach when she canvassed alone. Reyna said that she was received well by newer white residents of Cole but that she experienced difficulty at the house of a longtime Black resident. The following interaction between Reyna and Susan, a 55-year-old white Latina, then occurred:

Reyna: I think there were pockets of support for PB. I think you [Elise] and Tonya had a lot of success. Even that little corner you canvassed was largely white, and so it [Cole Has a Soul] was well received: "Yeah, sure, I'll go vote!" . . . I canvassed the same day I met with Tonya and Elise. Tonya was using terminology, such as "betterment of Cole," but I hit one household, and it [that phrase] was not well received. I think if Tonya had gone there, it would have been fine. I think there were some judgments about me because I'm new and young-looking. This guy just lit into me.

Susan: Isabelle [another steering committee member] told me about that [interaction].

Reyna: Oh yeah, I just tried to defend myself. I think I used the wrong terminology. . . so I didn't have much success [soliciting project idea submissions]. I tried to talk to as many people as possible to get ideas, for sure. So, I don't know. I don't regret it [canvassing], though. I think that's just one of the only ways to get out there and have this process work.

Susan: I was actually dreading having to do it [door-to-door canvassing]. I would actually knock on the door and then, like, back away! [Laugher] I ended up enjoying it. I was actually surprised at how many people came to the door and acted interested. Of course, there were some who didn't care.

Tamara brought that portion of the meeting to a close by saying,

I think what happens is this [PB] is just such a new and different approach [to public engagement]. Older residents remember the old ways [of public engagement], and we gotta work through the business-as-usual of it. I would imagine you have a deeper level of investment [in public engagement than does the city government]. You guys were out in some rain, knocking on doors; it's just not something we see anymore!

Some residents of Cole, thus, saw the PB process as being "new" and "different" from the "business-as-usual" way that the city government solicited residents' input about community improvement, such as posting an announcement in the local newspaper about an upcoming hearing that residents could attend. Some residents were not used to people coming to their houses, knocking on the front door, and asking them for project ideas to promote what these steering committee members called the "betterment of Cole." Committee members, thus, had some success using this new public participation process, but they also experienced challenges associated with trying to include diverse voices in their PB process, reflecting their values of promoting solidarity, relationships, and listening to previously unheard resident voices.

*****

In the previous chapter, I discussed the instrumental approach that Auraria PB facilitators implemented. This chapter explicates the relational approach that those involved in Cole Has a Soul employed to implement that PB process. Of course, the PB participants also included some task-oriented discourse, but as will be illustrated in this chapter, the relational approach was dominant. In this relational approach to public deliberation, "participants aim to cooperate, reach understanding, and do justice" (Young 1997, 385). From a relational perspective, deliberation is less about informed, rational, efficient, and legitimate decision-making (as was depicted in Auraria PB), and more about an intrinsic standard of morality (Christiano 1997). The dialogic, relational dimension of deliberation acknowledges affective components of deliberation, such as people's feelings about groups with which they identify, and alternatives to employing rational argumentation when participants communicate during deliberations, such as through storytelling (Foss and Griffin 1995; Young 2002). Stories, and their dialogic qualities, open pathways for understanding others and, thereby, can transform topics being discussed and the quality of contact among participants (Black 2008; Polletta 2006). Such dialogic moments in public deliberation can expand participants' minds, provide opportunities for them to hear and understand others' viewpoints, and liberate them from their private interests (Button 2005).

The opening vignette in this chapter illustrates that, in Cole Has a Soul, participants' relational approach to implementing PB privileged building relationships with one another, feeling connected to their geographic community, and "coming together"—a culturally significant relational form of public participation. Participants also viewed the PB process as being valuable for listening to previously unheard voices. Additionally, as the chapter shows, participants' deliberations focused on ensuring that the PB process promoted social justice by being inclusive of diverse community members' participation and achieving equitable outcomes. Participants also hoped to leverage their collective power to reimagine the community through Cole Has a Soul.

"COMING TOGETHER" AS SOLIDARITY

Cole Has a Soul participants believed that by engaging in this PB process of collaboratively exercising collective power to benefit the common good of their neighborhood, Cole residents would strengthen their relationships and "come together." For participants, "coming together" through this PB process would increase Cole neighbors' feelings of solidarity with one another, their feeling of being connected to the neighborhood, and their public participation. As an example of prefiguration, participants modeled "coming together" among themselves, striving to create the relational connections with each other that they hoped would spill out into the broader Cole neighborhood. The discursive act of "coming together" included greetings, invitations to participate in the PB process, expressing care for one another, and hosting celebrations. Finally, participants believed that, in addition to bringing Cole residents together, the PB process would increase the neighborhood's resiliency through the social and material capital resulting from the community improvement projects funded, with their relational orientation leading them to achieve that goal by emphasizing residents' local expertise and collective ownership of proposed projects.

"Coming Together"

In a video interview conducted by Warm Cookies of the Revolution, Sydney, a Cole Has a Soul participant, shared why she thought the PB process was important for residents of the Cole neighborhood, which had experienced years of divestment but now was being gentrified: "Community [members] coming together and not just saying what they want but actually implementing and doing something together . . . builds power, collectively, to be able to take more and more action." In an interview that I conducted after Cole Has a Soul concluded, Maya, one of the process's facilitators, remarked that the most rewarding aspect of the PB process was "seeing community [members] come together and rally together; just see[ing] those participants jump on board quickly and see[ing] people so excited."

One of the most vocal proponents of the perceived ability of this PB process to promote Cole community members "coming together" was Jocelyn, an African American budget delegate who worked at St. Charles (the local public recreation center, which was a significant cultural and community hub for the Cole neighborhood), and who had founded and continued to run a small nonprofit organization that implemented restorative justice dialogue circles[1] in that community (mostly, for young people). At the first meeting of the budget delegates committee,[2] she explained that she was participating in this PB process because "I would like to be part of the change, bringing the diverse community together, [as] I feel, like, it has separated, and we need to bring that diversity together."

As another example, in October, budget delegates met with the steering committee to explain the decisions that they had made about which projects to place on the PB ballot. Jocelyn had developed what she called a "gentrification listening project," which would use restorative justice principles and practices to help Cole residents address the harm that they had experienced from the displacement of some residents because of the gentrification of their neighborhood.

When Tonya, a steering committee member, questioned whether and how Jocelyn's proposed project related to project ideas that Cole residents had submitted, Jocelyn said that her project addressed "the need [for Cole residents] to listen to each other. I agree with beautifying the community, but we can't enjoy it if we're not coming together to understand each other more." "Beautifying the community" was a euphemism for the proposed PB projects of physical infrastructure, and although Jocelyn wanted her neighborhood to thrive, she did not want it to come at the cost of decreased social cohesion among community members. She argued that because her gentrification listening project would promote community members' "listening" to and "understanding" one another, "across racial and class lines," it would help Cole residents to "come together" and, thus, was worthy of being included on the PB ballot, which it was.

Cole Has a Soul committee members' discourse, thus emphasized their belief that by exercising collective power and increasing Cole residents' listening to and understanding of one another, their PB process would result in community members "coming together" to increase feelings of solidarity. Importantly, as explained below, "coming together" included dialogic encounters among participants that helped them get to know one another (or know them better than they did prior to this PB process) and form relationships that included friendships.

Relationship Building among Cole Has a Soul Participants

Cole Has a Soul participants remarked during committee meetings and in interviews that developing friendships with other participants was one of the most notable features of the process. Participants developed their relationships by engaging in communicative practices that included greetings and invitations (Young 2002), demonstrations of care for the Other, and moments of celebration. Indeed, the most significant encounters that participants experienced during the process were not when they engaged in task-oriented deliberations but when they interacted using these and other forms of relational communication to model the feelings of solidarity they hoped Cole Has a Soul would promote throughout the neighborhood.

For example, during the individual interviews that I conducted with Susan, Tonya, and Jason (all steering committee members), they each said that getting to know others in the Cole neighborhood was the most rewarding aspect of the PB process. Susan said that the most rewarding part of the PB process was "making those connections with fellow committee members," and that she was happy she participated because "I did make connections in my community [with people] I didn't know before." Tonya said that she had "bonded with most of the steering committee members. I could call one of them right now and say, 'Let's go have tea.' It's been a fun, serious, little group." Similarly, Jason expressed that the most rewarding part of the process was working with fellow budget delegates (all of whom were women): "I guess, just working with that group. I like that group of ladies. Seeing the project through, up to this point, with that group of people." Jason said that he benefitted from the PB process because of those "new relationships" he had formed, explaining that "I got closer with people in the group. . . . I had seen them around the neighborhood, but I got more of a sense of who they were, [which] I liked."

The desire to get to know their neighbors motivated participants to join and remain in the PB process. For example, initially, Susan was reluctant to join the steering committee because of prior time commitments to the Cole Neighborhood Association, but as she explained, "What put me over the edge in deciding to sign up was seeing the other people in the room who were volunteering, and wanting to make deeper connections with them." Tonya also explained that she remained involved in the PB process because she developed relational connections with other participants:

> We liked each other, and I liked the committee members. I liked the [PB] organizers [from Project Belay]; they were cool [and] they were easy, [which] just kept me coming [to PB meetings and events]. It was relationships, and I believe it kept them [the other steering committee members] coming, too.

Interviewees' statements about the importance of getting to know their neighbors as motivating their participation in Cole Has a Soul were reflected in their communication during PB committee meetings, which included telling stories about each other, their work, and neighborly actions they were doing for one another. For instance, at one steering committee meeting, where members prepared to pass the torch to budget delegates, who then developed submitted project proposals, Tonya expressed her feelings about the steering committee's work coming to an end:

> I wouldn't have known most of you guys had I not been in Cole Has a Soul. I ran into Elise again [at a community event], and we had already started Cole

> Has a Soul, and she could introduce me as her friend. . . . Because this group has bonded, it would be a shame to dismantle [it].

At a December steering committee meeting, near the end of the Cole Has a Soul PB process, Tamara told a story that demonstrated how the goodwill established among committee members continued to be expressed outside of their meetings: "I came into my office the other day and had a piece of cake on my desk from Shirley [a budget delegate] for a really small thing that I helped her out with. I was, like, 'You need anything else?!' [laughter]." That piece of cake was not the only baked good that PB participants shared with one another to signal their relational connections.

At an August steering committee meeting, when Tamara asked members to report their experiences canvassing the neighborhood to collect PB project ideas, Tonya and Elise shared a story about picking cherries from the tree of a Cole resident. As they explained, when Tonya and Elise approached that resident's house, Elise noticed that a cherry tree in the front yard was laden with cherries ripe for harvesting. After speaking with the homeowner about the Cole Has a Soul PB process, Elise asked if she could use the cherries to bake pies. The homeowner, an older adult, welcomed Elise's request because he was unable to harvest all of the cherries, and, consequently, many would rot. Elise picked as many cherries as she could, made several cherry pies, and delivered one to the homeowner and gave a few to Tonya. After Tonya mentioned during the steering committee meeting that Elise had gifted her those pies, Elise jokingly chimed in, "That's our secret!" The room erupted with laughter, and many attendees remarked that the wonderful thing Elise had done exemplified Cole Has a Soul's goal of enhancing relationships among Cole's residents.

Cole Has a Soul participants' relational approach to engaging in this PB process was also evidenced during the October meeting where budget delegates met with the steering committee to discuss the final project proposals that would appear on the PB ballot. Except for Jason (who was both a steering committee member and a budget delegate), budget delegates and steering committee members did not know each other; consequently, at the start of the meeting, Tamara asked everyone to introduce themselves. When it was Jason's turn, he said, "I'm Jason. I think—" and Shirley, a Black, 62-year-old woman budget delegate, interrupted him and asked, "You think you're Jason?" Amidst the laughter, Jason said, "For now!" leading to more laughter.

During their time working together, Jason was often the butt of Shirley's jokes. Jason and Shirley were strangers when the process began, but by the time this meeting occurred, near the end of the PB process, they had become comfortable enough to joke and laugh with one another, even in a room filled with people Shirley did not know, engaging in a culturally significant, relationally oriented language game called "signifying," which is common among African Americans (Alim and Smitherman 2012).

Ultimately, many who were involved in Cole Has a Soul believed that building relationships among participants needed to be at the center of PB processes. For instance, during an interview that I conducted immediately after Cole Has a Soul concluded, Reyna, a 45-year-old Asian woman who served on the steering committee, said:

> I think relationship building should be at the forefront of PB. If we're going to do things different than the City and County of Denver, then we need to act like it and make sure we're doing that. We have a unique opportunity to go out and talk to neighbors. I don't think current Denver City Council members are hitting the streets like we are and talking to people. I think that [behavior] should be in the forefront of another PB group or organization. We really need to make relationships and connections, and I think we would see PB go a lot farther and gain some speed and recognition from local government.

Cole Has a Soul participants' relational approach to engaging in the process led them to view forming relationships among participants as a central, not a secondary or supplemental, characteristic of successful PB processes, with those characteristics differentiating PB from other, dehumanizing forms of public engagement that city governments sponsor. Deliberations during this PB process thus functioned as a form of prefiguration, as participants strove to create the kind of public input and decision-making process they wanted to see in their city.

Although those involved in Cole Has a Soul lauded the centrality of relationship building among PB participants, Reyna, a steering committee member, thought that the amount of time steering committee members and budget delegates spent getting to know their group's members may have hindered the PB process. Specifically, she believed that relational emphasis prevented those participants from engaging in more robust outreach about the PB process. Reyna claimed that if steering committee members "had gone out into the community to build community, we would have still built relationships and seen each other's strengths. I [thus] think we could have done relationship building a different way."

Greetings, Demonstrating Care for the Other, and Celebrations

Some of the most poignant moments that occurred during Cole Has a Soul did not revolve around participants rationally considering evidence to make decisions or wrestling with how to accomplish the process's goals of including marginalized populations and achieving equitable outcomes but, instead, involved participants communicating their empathy and support for one another and expressing their joy about working together.

Many moments throughout Cole Has a Soul illustrated participants' use of the communicative practice that Young (2002) called "greeting" (explicit verbal and nonverbal mutual recognition and conciliatory caring for the Other), but one instance, in particular, serves as an exemplary illustration. In October, I arrived 10 minutes early to a budget delegate meeting and saw Tamara, who would be facilitating the meeting rather than Nicole, who had facilitated all other budget delegate meetings, preparing the space to serve the dinner that Project Belay always provided for evening meetings. As we interacted, Tamara shared that she felt disconnected from PB participants because she had not attended any meetings since August. However, she looked forward to reconnecting with the budget delegates that night. As Tamara wiped down the tables to provide a clean eating surface for PB participants, I noticed that instead of the typical seating arrangement of four separate tables, each with four chairs, Tamara had pushed the tables together because, as she explained, she wanted to serve the food in a "family style, like in Georgia, North Carolina, and South Carolina. You know, like, family."

Tamara's attention to arranging the meeting room before attendees arrived communicated an important greeting of welcome, with Tamara drawing on her cultural knowledge of Southern U.S. hospitality to design that physical space in a way that would encourage budget delegates to see their group relationship as being similar to that of a family. This example was indicative of the many times that Cole Has a Soul participants employed greetings that, in contrast to traditional forms of greeting group meeting members (verbally welcoming them, asking them to introduce themselves, and using icebreaker exercises to help them get to know one another), explicitly acknowledged and appreciated fellow participants' humanity.

The humanizing aspects of Cole Has a Soul also manifested in the numerous moments when participants expressed their care for each other. In particular, when PB group members disclosed personal life challenges that they were experiencing, other members often expressed empathy for their situation and validated their humanity. For instance, at a steering committee meeting in August, Reyna arrived about 10 minutes late and, almost immediately, began talking about an intergenerational family communication challenge that she was experiencing, with the following interaction occurring:

> *Reyna:* It's good to see everyone; it's been a while! Sorry I'm late. Let me just share. [Laughter] My parents live with me, [and] we're trying to reach some understanding about how to communicate between generations, like with my kids.

Tamara: It's called a "sandwich," and you're the meat. [Laughter]

Susan: That changes as you age. Eventually, you'll be the bread!

Elise: You might be a piece of lettuce next. Work your way up. Mayonnaise. Like, you just get spread all over everything.

Reyna: Yeah, it's really tough. My dad was at the library trying to print something out, and he wouldn't ask for help because he was ashamed to ask. It's, like, "Look, I don't know everything, either. You've gotta get over whatever your shit is." Sorry, I traveled all weekend, and I just wanted a day to myself without anyone asking me questions.

Tamara: Thank you for being here.

As this interaction exemplifies, although Reyna entered the meeting late and members were discussing task-related business, in line with their strong relational orientation, members put their work on hold, created space for Reyna to share the personal life problems she was experiencing, and expressed, through humor and explicit appreciation, their care for Reyna.

Moreover, immediately following the interaction described above, Tamara highlighted Reyna's accomplishments, with the following interaction occurring:

Tamara (addressing the group): Reyna was in Huntington Beach with, like, nine children. Somebody brought home the gold [medal] in box lacrosse.[3]

Reyna: Yeah, Tamara's daughter.

Tamara: And somebody got silver [implying that Reyna's daughter won that medal], so you [Reyna] were holding a lot of space. Thank you for being *here*. I was, like, "God bless, Reyna." I would let my kids go anywhere with Reyna. . . . Sometimes, our parents don't get what we do, and the kids definitely don't. I'm sending love your way, and, maybe, we can enjoy happy hour together later. Well, we're here.

Although the phrase "Well, we're here" transitioned members into their PB business, the interactions described above—and many other interactions—showed the care that these PB committee members offered one another, whether it was by baking and delivering pies to another member, leaving a slice of cake at a member's office, reminding each other to pick up their children from school, offering emotional support when members shared their personal problems, or ensuring that the food provided at meetings met members' dietary needs (with, in one case, Tamara reordering dinner because she had forgotten to get Elise a dairy-free alternative).

Participants' relational approach to engaging in PB was also evidenced by and at events that they organized to celebrate the PB work they had accomplished. For example, the steering committee organized an event to announce and celebrate the PB vote results. That event was held in St. Charles's gym, which committee members decorated with colorful balloons. Music played over loudspeakers, and food was served, including a large, homemade sheet cake baked by one of the steering committee members. That event also featured a raffle, with several small children, including Isabella's son (Isabella was a steering committee member), reading aloud the winning raffle numbers. When Isabella's son read a raffle number that awarded a gift card to Nancy, another steering committee member, Isabella joked that her son needed to pick her number next, to which Nancy replied playfully, "No, he just gave a gift card to his new auntie!" with attendees erupting in laughter. Later at that event, when Shirley's teenage daughter and Tamara's teenage daughter started to perform the electric slide in the middle of the gym, someone changed the song to the "Cupid Shuffle" (a popular line dance), and Shirley, Tonya, Susan, and the teenagers danced along as audience members cheered.

Finally, members of PB groups, especially toward the end of the process, often celebrated their work and what they achieved. For instance, in December, after Cole Has a Soul vote results were announced, Nicole led a meeting of budget delegates and steering committee members in a conversation about what the process had done well and how it could be improved, with the participants involved in the following exchange identifying what went well:

> *Tonya:* We got the voices of the community, and we had celebrations; it wasn't all work.
>
> *Tamara:* Like, throughout?
>
> *Tonya:* Yeah, this: just sitting and laughing and talking and building on the relationships.
>
> *Shirley:* Doing crafts.
>
> *Nicole:* We did arts and crafts! That was fun.
>
> *Tonya:* We were dancing!

In line with their approach to implementing Cole Has a Soul, participants highlighted the relational strengths of the process.

Community Building

An important aspect of Cole Has a Soul participants' "coming together" to promote solidarity was their belief that the process would help Cole residents build community connections across the neighborhood. Participants remarked frequently in meetings and during interviews that engaging in the PB process would increase Cole residents' sense of connection to and responsibility for each other.

For instance, Jocelyn, a champion of restorative justice, often argued for including on the PB ballot projects that incorporated restorative justice because they would "build community," and that her gentrification listening project (explained previously) was "a restorative project, so it would restore the community." Although that project did not secure enough votes to be implemented, in line with PB participants' relational approach, a primary criterion for putting projects on the PB ballot was their perceived ability to build community among Cole residents.

Participants viewed PB as a way to improve their neighborhood, both materially (through projects implemented) and relationally (relationships developed during the process). For example, when I interviewed Jamie, who attended the Cole Has a Soul kickoff event and submitted a project idea, she described Cole residents as being "eager for someone, anyone, to listen and help them make a better community." At a steering committee meeting in August, Tonya made a statement that confirmed the PB process was reaching disenchanted residents:

> People who we talked with have a recognition of us. They won't remember our names, but it would be too bad if we faded totally out of the picture [after the process concludes]. I can't tell you one name, but I could walk to a lot of houses that I visited, because I fell in love with a lot of people.

The relational connections that Tonya formed with neighbors may not have been deep, but walking the neighborhood's streets and visiting residents' homes to collect project ideas had generated a sense of love for her neighbors and neighborhood.

However, at least two participants thought that the PB process did not develop Cole residents' sense of community as successfully as they had hoped because they were unable to reach a critical mass of residents. Susan remarked in an interview after the process ended that "the community outreach was the struggling point. We did go door-to-door a few times, and although that was successful, we were only able to cover a small piece of the neighborhood, and, still, a lot of voices were missed." Similarly, when asked in an interview how the process could have been improved, Tonya claimed, "Maybe less time [spent] on planning and more time being in the street. I think being in the street was critical, and we didn't do as much of that as we should have." Susan and Tonya believed that the PB process did not engage as many Cole residents as it could have, which limited its effects on building community in that neighborhood. They remarked that steering committee members and budget delegates may have spent too much time interacting with each other and not enough time interacting with Cole residents who did not serve in those roles. Nevertheless, participants' desire to promote feelings of community connection among Cole residents pervaded Cole Has a Soul, and, as explained below, two prominent ways that participants worked to build community were by emphasizing residents' local expertise to inform the development and collective ownership of PB projects.

Local Expertise and Collective Ownership

Many PB participants remarked that they needed to build a sense of community in Cole because of the history of divestment and discrimination directed toward the neighborhood. The many years of government officials underfunding infrastructure and social programs in the Cole neighborhood (e.g., roads not maintained and, despite increased demand, decreased funding for afterschool programs at St. Charles) contributed to residents' perceptions that politicians viewed the neighborhood as being insignificant. Prior to the gentrification of Cole that I described in chapter 1, poverty and violence had started to increase in this historically working-class neighborhood, which was eroding trust among many of the residents. PB participants blamed racist, capitalist power systems for the unfavorable changes in the Cole neighborhood, and they deeply distrusted government institutions that had done little to help residents. That distrust was exacerbated by government policies that incentivized property developers to build in the Cole neighborhood, bringing in new and displacing longtime residents. Because participants perceived the PB process as offering an opportunity to lift up the talents and expertise of Cole residents, as well as to establish collective ownership of important aspects of their neighborhood, they saw PB as a valuable departure from the "business-as-usual" approach that city government used to manage the Cole neighborhood.

Indeed, many PB participants had little faith in government institutions' ability to meet their community's needs. As a Latino resident interviewed in a video produced by Warm Cookies of the Revolution shared:

> The people are the machine of the city. I think the people keep the city going. . . . I think there is no city without the people, so I think the city needs to refocus its attention on the people of the city and not [on] the money of the city.

Alejandro also remarked in another video, "I don't expect soul and heart to live in those places [government entities], 'cuz I don't know how they were created to do that. . . . We are the ones who have the hearts and souls."

Shirley, a budget delegate, expressed a similar statement at the joint meeting of budget delegates and steering committee members, saying, "They [the City of Denver] should just give us the money instead of hiring people to do the work, because they're not doing it with the heart that people in the community are doing it." Thus, Cole residents perceived the local government as not caring about them, but residents saw their hearts and souls as making the city, which is why PB, potentially, could be a powerful process for them.

For example, in a video produced by Warm Cookies of the Revolution, Camila (executive director of Project VOYCE) remarked that PB could preserve the unique cultural values of the Cole area and promote residents exerting collective control of the built environment:

> When you're growing up, and you're building these value systems, they're largely influenced by the souls of people you're interacting with, the souls of ancestors, because you've carried on value systems in communities. I think that this [PB] is a way to preserve those values, to make them come alive in choices that we're making about the spaces that we live in and the future we want.

Because Cole residents perceived themselves as having little control over what happened in their neighborhood, as well as their values not being shared by the people in charge of making those decisions, they were excited about participating in a process that allowed them to decide how to improve their neighborhood.

Many Cole Has a Soul participants knew that Denver city officials were considering implementing a citywide PB process funded by tax dollars and were looking to Cole Has a Soul as a potential model. Participants expressed reservations about future PB processes being co-opted or watered down if the city implemented PB. Nicole, a facilitator from Project Belay, told a meeting of steering committee members and budget delegates that City of Denver officials implementing PB was "scary" because "they may not be thinking about getting so many people involved, and I'm worried about the City taking this process and doing something else." In an interview that I conducted after Cole Has a Soul ended, Amara, an Indian American steering committee member, expressed a similar concern:

> I think we need to really take a critical look at how our city functions already, and just being careful that it remains a true PB process with community. That's why I would like to stay involved. I'd hate to see this [PB] adopted by the city and then tokenized where they [city officials] say they have a PB process, but it's not a true process where community has a say.

When I interviewed Jason and asked how he felt about the lack of city support for Cole Has a Soul, he responded that it was a "good thing . . . [because] we were allowed to come up with our own plan and implement it without some biases they may have had to enact it." Jason said that, overall, he was "happy" that Cole residents implemented the PB process without support from the City of Denver.

Jason's comments highlight an important cultural belief that was shared among PB participants: Although Cole residents did not trust the City of Denver, they had exceptional faith in their neighbors to take ownership of and use PB to benefit as many community members as possible. Sydney explained this focus on self-reliance and communal care in a video produced by Warm Cookies of the Revolution:

> We don't want things done for us; we want to do things together. We want to build together, create together. We don't just want a plot for affordable housing for the projects; we want the neighborhood to be affordable together. We want to build that community together. We don't just want it done *for*; we want to do *with*, and we want to be part of implementation the whole way.

PB participants, thus, wanted to be free of city government's interference with the process, not to pursue selfish ends but to pursue the collective good, especially because, for many residents, neoliberal government policies about community development had failed in the Cole neighborhood.

As such, throughout the PB process, participants often emphasized residents' local expertise, an important discursive shift that framed neighborhood members as being capable and talented rather than as needy, underdeveloped, or underserved—the perspective of many wealthy developers, nonprofits, and city officials.

Indeed, the focus on local control and collective ownership for the common good often manifested during budget delegates' deliberations about potential PB projects. For example, when I asked Taylor to describe how budget delegates eliminated projects, she said that one of the first steps was that "We ruled out things that were clearly the City's purview." Budget delegates, thus, wanted to develop projects that did not need approval from the local government to be implemented.

However, budget delegates struggled with how to design several project ideas about the beautification of Cole's parks, as those parks fell within the local government's jurisdiction. Jason suggested doing trash pickup, but then said, "That's a [City of Denver] Parks and Rec thing, too," leading to the idea being eliminated. When they discussed landscaping, Taylor said, "I [think that] the plants are the City's deal," which led to not moving forward with that project.

Ultimately, budget delegates settled on painting park benches and tables to beautify the neighborhood's parks. They proposed inviting students from the local schools to create and paint art related to themes of peace, love, and unity. At a budget delegate meeting, Nicole summarized the values that were motivating the group:

> Estimated impact [of the parks beautification project] is just a few things. One is that . . . Cole residents will take ownership of creating art together. Residents will be guided to reflect on how the themes relate to Cole and asked to take action to improve Cole. . . . Youth involvement will foster pride and community connection.

Thus, budget delegates moved forward on the proposed project because it promoted Cole residents' "ownership" of public resources; in this case, a park.

LISTENING TO THE UNHEARD

Another significant theme of Cole Has a Soul was that participants wanted to listen to residents' voices that, previously, had gone unheard by local officials. The PB process was viewed as a way for residents to communicate with community members and project a unified voice externally to people in powerful positions. Many participants' comments related to "being heard" spoke of PB as standing in contrast to the "business-as-usual" approach employed by local government.

For example, Taylor, a white, 48-year-old budget delegate who had lived in Cole for more than 20 years, talked about the value of PB in the context of the gentrification that was occurring in the neighborhood, saying, "A lot of people feel like new people are taking over. They want to have a voice about what their neighborhood needs because they live there." PB offered an opportunity for people to make their voices heard by government officials. In the words of one Black Cole resident, "I want them to be able to see: Yes, we were here. Yes, we did fight, [and] we said something."

Other PB participants also expressed the historical neglect of the community by powerful stakeholders who did not listen to residents' expressed concerns. Gabrielle said that Cole residents had always been highly engaged but that people in power were unwilling to listen to them:

> People's involvement has always been there, but if you only get . . . one group making decisions, then all the people's voices cannot be heard. You would think [that because we live in] a democracy . . . everybody should have a voice, but what I've come to find out . . . is that's not true; decisions are being made in the boardroom without all the people.

The Cole Has a Soul PB process, thus, offered an opportunity to ensure that residents' voices would be heard, a significant departure from the so-called "democratic" processes in which residents had participated previously.

During Cole Has a Soul, occasionally, concern about residents' voices manifested during participants' deliberations. At a steering committee meeting, Tonya said that idea collection was more challenging than she expected because she struggled to figure out "how do we get the voices we never seem to reach." At the PB process's kickoff idea collection event, Tonya delivered a brief speech to encourage attendees to submit project ideas by emphasizing the importance of listening to the previously unheard. As she said:

> This is the voice of the people. This is the language and voice of the people. No matter what ends up getting implemented, this is the voice of the people. . . . This is your resident voice, and we know you have a lot to say. Share your thoughts with us; don't hold back.

After Cole Has a Soul ended, during an interview I conducted, Tonya reflected on how listening to the unheard transformed into the exercise of collective power:

> All of the concerns that the people I talked with had, I can lean on the PB process to get to the council[person] and say, "This is through the PB process. This is what we learned the people want." I'll be heard quicker than if I just come out as a resident and said, "Well, this is what I think people want." [Instead,] I can say, "This is what the people want because they told me face-to-face." PB gave me the power to do that, and the documentation.

By pooling together residents' voices, Tonya believed that Cole Has a Soul legitimized residents' concerns in the eyes of elected city officials. The PB process provided the evidence needed to ensure that neighborhood residents spoke collectively to elected officials about their community needs.

The Necessity of, and Challenges with, Engagement and Participation

Importantly, PB participants recognized that making voices heard through PB required residents' "engagement" or "participation" in the process, which necessitated significant labor on the part of residents. Participants believed that residents' engagement in PB could increase their community engagement in other arenas of public life. A Black woman in the neighborhood recognized that PB was just one small way to address larger systemic problems when she said, "We may not be able to change everything, but we can chip away at it." Alejandro, commenting about the work required to engage in PB, said, "We call it 'participatory government' because if you don't participate, you don't get crap, and we have every right, every day, to go and shake those foundations." Thus, Cole Has a Soul may have been hard work, but it possessed the potential to shake the foundations of dominant power systems in the City of Denver.

Cole Has a Soul participants dedicated much time and energy to "engage" in the PB process. As Reyna explained, "We kinda had set out doing something different than what government does, . . . [which required folks] to pound the pavement and talk to people." In an interview that I conducted with Amara, she said that the purpose of the steering committee was to "get [the] community engaged" in the process. At one meeting, Tonya shared that she had spoken with more than 200 people to encourage their participation in Cole Has a Soul.

Participants believed that engaging in PB would generate spillover effects of residents' increased knowledge of and capacity to engage in public participation. For example, during my interview with her, after Cole Has a Soul concluded, Maya (a facilitator from Project Belay) said that "community folks got engaged and understood the power and the process of budgeting, and there was some knowledge attained." Nicole, another facilitator from Project Belay, also believed that PB would generate a "better engaged citizenry," saying in an interview I conducted with her:

> To be able to support communities in having a deeper understanding of all the complexities of policy making and budget decisions is a win, and it's a win for deeper democracy. It's a win for a better engaged citizenry.

Reyna confirmed that view when she expressed in an interview that she had developed communication skills from canvassing to collect project ideas:

> I don't think those are bad skills to know, to be able to talk to people and see where they're coming from. It might be uncomfortable, but it would be a worthwhile skill to have in any job you do.

However, a significant number of Cole Has a Soul participants remarked that the process did not engage as many people in the neighborhood as they had hoped. When asked how participants could have improved the process, Amara said that they should have developed better "ways of engaging the community . . . [to] get more people involved in understanding what the process is and doing more community engagement around the PB process, rather than just the idea collection." She hoped that organizers of future iterations of PB would "really get people to want to be involved at a different level than just another project out there." Additionally, at a steering committee meeting that occurred after the process ended, Reyna remarked that if they were to implement PB again, she would want participants to "spend a lot more time engaging in large events to get to know more residents."

Even the quality of engagement among steering committee members and budget delegates was not as robust as some of those PB participants had hoped. Susan, who observed that some steering committee members had dropped out of the process as it progressed, explained that this lack of commitment was the result of fatigue with the process:

> I was feeling burnt out; I'm sure others were, too. It felt like a lack of commitment on people's parts. . . . It was disheartening that there was so little, minimal engagement from everybody by the Fall and Winter. People were obviously losing steam.

She remarked that, in the future, organizers ought to define "more clearly the expectations of steering committee members, and that we need you to be committed to attending meetings and participating at all stages and staying engaged."

Some examples of what Susan described as "burn out" among Cole Has a Soul participants came to the fore when Cole Has a Soul's organizers hosted their celebration to announce the winning projects. Although, as explained previously, that event was full of dancing, laughter, and goodwill among attendees, there was an undercurrent of exhaustion that marked the event. For example, Jocelyn was supposed to announce the vote results at the event, but she never showed up and did not notify anyone about her absence, causing Reyna to fill in for her at the last minute.

At another point during the party, Elise sat next to me and expressed her frustration with the PB process, saying that she volunteered to be a steering committee member because she thought Cole Has a Soul would promote public art in the neighborhood; although she had made peace with the fact that no public art was going to be created through this PB process, she was annoyed by the lack of communication from Project Belay facilitators about when meetings were to occur and how the PB process was progressing. She also had done much of the planning for this party/event and thought that she had not received enough support from fellow steering committee members and from Project Belay's organizers to accomplish the event as successfully as possible. She said that she had stuck with the PB process only because of her personal rule that when she committed to doing something, she stuck with it to the end. However, she did not want to continue to be involved with implementing funded PB projects, and a week later, she emailed committee members and announced that she was withdrawing from the committee.

Despite their burnout by the end of the process, many participants strove for the PB process to be inclusive of diverse, marginalized community members' participation and to result in funding equitable community improvement projects.

SOCIAL JUSTICE CONCERNS OF EQUITY AND INCLUSION

Participants' concerns that the PB process be inclusive revolved, primarily, around issues of accessibility of the process, conducting outreach about it, and using the process to address the needs of young people living in the Cole neighborhood. Additionally, as explained below, participants wanted the outcomes of the process (the projects funded and implemented) to promote equity in that neighborhood, a value that manifested most significantly during budget delegates' deliberations.

Inclusion

First, Cole Has a Soul organizers and participants strove to engage Cole residents in the process. Those PB participants, for instance, decided that anyone who lived, worked, prayed, or studied in the Cole neighborhood could submit a project idea, serve on the steering committee, or cast a vote. Moreover, the age limit for voting was set at just 10 years old.

Concerns about inclusion also manifested through the outreach conducted by Cole Has a Soul participants. The group did not perform intentional, targeted outreach but, instead, opted to canvas as many neighborhood residents as possible and relied on network recruitment to solicit project ideas and votes. Due to the disproportionate number of Cole residents of color who were also of low income, the steering committee and budget delegates reached people from oppressed groups, despite not making a plan to target them specifically.

The PB organizers and participants were especially pleased with the door-to-door canvassing they conducted to collect project ideas from residents. In a video produced by Warm Cookies of the Revolution, Nicole (one of the organizers from Project Belay) even highlighted that they had performed more than one round of canvassing for project ideas: "We did another round of canvassing, going door-to-door to try and reach those folks and hear their voices." Jason, a budget delegate and steering committee member, reported in an interview, "I thought the canvassing did really well going door-to-door to get suggestions."

Due to these outreach efforts, as chapter 1 demonstrated, the process was effective with regard to including people of color in high-involvement roles (i.e., steering committee members and budget delegates) and, in general, represented proportionately the Cole neighborhood's household incomes, although women were overrepresented at every phase of the PB process. Additionally, 14% of Cole Has a Soul PB voters reported that they were not eligible to vote in the most recent U.S. federal election, which means that this PB process engaged a sizable portion of Cole's residents who were excluded from that (and, probably, other) democratic process(es).

Concerns about inclusion also manifested during deliberations among budget delegates to design projects. For example, one project idea was to install a bike-share dock. At the time, the City of Denver had a public bike-share system called "B-cycle." The system used docks, meaning that a user would have to pay to unlock the bike from an automated rack of B-cycles, and then return the bike to another dock once they had finished using the bike. That summer, corporations had deposited other mobility options around the city, including dockless scooters and bikes. However, the Cole neighborhood did not have a B-cycle dock, nor were dockless mobility options typically found in the neighborhood.

This fact was even a joke among budget delegates, with Shirley asking at a meeting, "Did anyone find stuff out about bikes that don't come to our neighborhood?" which was met with laughter from the other budget delegates. The budget delegates knew that mobility options were limited in their neighborhood because of the legacy of racial capitalism, and Shirley's comment pointed out the absurdity of that system, for the bikes and scooters were mostly located in spaces populated by affluent, young, white residents and tourists.

The idea for a B-cycle station was eliminated fairly quickly because it would have required working with the City of Denver. Instead, budget delegates focused on organizing neighborhood bike rides as a way to foster community, promote exercise, and offer activities for the many young families in the neighborhood. Channeling the value of inclusion, the group discussed using PB money to buy bikes that residents could use on these community bike rides. This was to include neighbors in the events who may not own a bicycle, perhaps due to financial constraints. Jason proposed purchasing 30 bicycles, but Shirley was skeptical, saying, "Well, if we have 30 bikes, and 32 people show up, we're gonna have two folks cryin'." For Shirley, the idea could not be inclusive enough because the group would not be able to purchase a significant number of bicycles without excluding some people. Ultimately, this project idea did not move forward because of these concerns about inclusion.

A final example of how concerns about inclusion manifested in Cole Has a Soul was the level of youth involvement. Young people did not participate meaningfully in the PB process, nor was there a concerted effort among the

PB organizers to garner their participation. Nevertheless, many of the Cole Has a Soul participants wanted the process to benefit youth in the community, which demonstrated concerns for including absent Others in the process. Participants wanted to address the issues facing young people in the neighborhood (e.g., gang violence, police violence, poverty, and food insecurity), even if young people did not attend many of the Cole Has a Soul events. For example, during my interview with Taylor, she said, "I think a lot of youth in this neighborhood are disenfranchised. They need something to enable them to overcome that or to make that a positive in their lives." Additionally, during her interview, Reyna shared that many Cole residents were worried about young people in the community, saying, "I know that when I did canvassing, a lot of people said, 'It's for the kids. We should do something for the kids.'"

As a result, one of the projects that was placed on the ballot for Cole Has a Soul was the "Youth Empowerment" project. At a cost of $10,000, as described on the PB ballot, the project was intended to fund "youth-serving organizations" that supported "youth empowerment in the Cole community." Organizations could apply for a grant to support their youth programming, with desired projects, according to the project description, including "motivating youth to be innovators and entrepreneurs," "conflict resolution training," "training in team dynamics," and promoting a "sense of responsibility to self and others." The project description also listed estimated impacts of the project:

> Youth are heard, validated and supported as they learn skills to assist in their personal transformation and development. The lessons learned will last a lifetime and can be used on an ongoing basis. Community leaders will emerge, be activated, and make an impact beyond this proposal. Youth will leave the experience with a more positive attitude and sense of self-worth, thus building their self-esteem and improving [their] overall quality of life.

Ultimately, the Youth Empowerment project came in third place in terms of votes (behind the pop-up movie theater and a community garden project) and was funded.

Despite the Cole Has a Soul participants and organizers emphasizing the inclusion of as many Cole residents as possible in the PB process, not all of their efforts were successful, which was acknowledged by organizers and participants during meetings and in interviews. For instance, as the results presented in chapter 1 showed, participation by Cole's Hispanic population lagged at every stage of this PB process. Although two Hispanic women served on the steering committee (but rarely attended meetings), PB participants' efforts to include Hispanic residents seemed insufficient. For example, at the few large public events that Cole Has a Soul hosted (e.g., the kickoff and the announcement of the vote results events), Spanish interpreters were available for anyone who was not fluent in English, but I only saw one attendee make use of the interpreter.

Two of the steering committee members acknowledged in interviews I conducted that the process fell short in attracting participation from Hispanic neighbors. Susan believed the process could have benefitted from having more long-term residents on the steering committee and "more consistent representation of the Spanish-speaking community." Tonya wished more people had voted in the process and that "more Spanish representation would have been good" because when she canvassed to collect ideas, "I bet 75% of the people I talked with were Spanish speakers."

The process may have benefitted from conducting creative, targeted outreach to Hispanic residents, but the steering committee did not pursue such a strategy. For example, Michelle (from Warm Cookies of the Revolution) made several recommendations for conducting outreach, but PB participants did not implement them. Specifically, Michelle suggested that they make a PB *paletero* cart, and by the end of the process, she still wished they had pursued that strategy, saying in an interview that I conducted with her, "I still wanted that *paletero* cart, one of those ice cream carts that roll around, [offering] a free ice cream and a handout [with information about] the next [PB] meeting." At a steering committee meeting, Michelle proposed, "I think when the [project] proposals are finished, we could have artists come in and pitch the projects. And arts could be good for doing outreach."

No one explicitly rejected these ideas, but they were not implemented. At a budget delegates' meeting in October, the group discussed an upcoming vote kickoff event:

> *Tamara:* Let's talk about the look of the event. Do we want artists there? This is an opportunity to use a creative approach. If we want artists to do something, we can ask them to help design a yard sign or something. It doesn't have to be that day.
>
> *Shirley:* We don't need all that extra fluff, I'm tellin' ya!

Shirley's comment reflected an attitude among many Cole Has a Soul participants, although they may not have used language as strong as Shirley's. Efforts at creative, targeted outreach to encourage participation in PB were seen as an unnecessary hassle.

In retrospect, Tonya, a steering committee member, wished they had engaged in more robust outreach overall, not just to Hispanic residents and/or young people. At a steering committee meeting in December after the conclusion of the PB process, Tonya remarked, "I just don't think it [community contact] was planned out well enough. There was no strategy." When I interviewed Tonya several months later, she said, "The most important piece of this [PB] is outreach." She then told the following story that illustrated the participants' shortcomings in contacting Cole residents:

> Even when we were voting that last day at St. Charles, I decided to do this quick effort of going down the street [to solicit PB votes]. I knocked on a door, and I told them about voting [in PB], and this guy said, "We already mailed in our ballot." He was talking about the [U.S. federal midterm] election. He was just up the street and didn't know anything about the PB process! How did that happen? Making sure we got every house in Cole—and Cole is such a little box, we should have been able to get every house twice. In the beginning, middle, and end [of the PB process], maybe three times, but we didn't. That's what I would advocate for: more time to do the outreach, even if we [needed] a committee on the steering committee that was just for outreach.

Steering committee members did not have a coherent strategy for conducting outreach to Cole residents about the PB process; instead, they relied on members contacting people in their social networks to promote the process. Unfortunately, the committee was comprised of only eight people, and it was impossible for them to reach, through their personal networks, the nearly 5,000 people who lived in the Cole neighborhood at the time. Even the canvassing, which committee members viewed as being successful, was not especially coordinated, with only a handful of members volunteering to canvass and no plan for how to reach as many houses as possible in the time available.

Equity

Another important value for Cole Has a Soul participants was that they wanted the process to incorporate, promote, and advance concerns about equity. This value was explicitly stated by several of the PB organizers from Project Belay. For example, in a video produced by Warm Cookies of the Revolution, Nicole described equity as the "foundation of everything":

> Equity has to be at the foundation of everything. If we don't intentionally create a process that's bringing in the most marginalized, they won't come. . . . The people who are able to be engaged the most are the people who have the most privilege, and that's a major issue. And so I would really love all of us, not just this process, but as a city, as a community, to really think about what it means to start with equity first and then go from there.

Camila (from Project VOYCE) also believed that lessons learned about equity through the PB process could generate systemic benefits. She believed

PB could "help local governments make decisions that are more equitable" and that PB was a tool "that local governments can use to create healthy, equitable cities."

Similar to Auraria PB, deliberations about the role of equity in Cole Has a Soul appeared, predominantly, during budget delegates' deliberations about project proposals. In September, at one of the first budget delegates meetings, Nicole was the facilitator and led the group in a discussion about the role equity would play in their deliberations, starting with a definition:

> *Nicole:* So what is your understanding of equity? What does it mean to you?
>
> *Jason:* I don't know. Everybody havin' an equal share. Representation for everyone.
>
> *Taylor:* I think equity is about access. Equality is everyone gets the same piece of pie, but equity is that everyone is close enough to get a piece of the pie.
>
> *Nicole:* "Equality" and "equity" are often used interchangeably. Equality is all about people getting the same thing, but not everyone has the same needs.

In this brief exchange, Jason expressed a view of equity that was similar to equality, reflecting the liberal democratic ideal of treating all people the same. However, Taylor and Nicole suggested that equity would ensure each person was given their due according to their circumstances. The discussion continued:

> *Nicole:* I use the language of "oppression" versus "privilege." I'm not sure that's your language. How do we want to take this [equity] lens and look at the [project] ideas through this lens?
>
> *Taylor:* I like the idea of oppression versus privilege, but I think there is some overlap. I think we can ask, "Is this [project] idea going to have a strong impact for the marginalized rather than just the privileged, predominantly?" I think one factor is how marginalized—
>
> *Nicole:* I hear what you're saying. It's more consideration—
>
> *Taylor:* Yeah, maybe more weight towards those who tend to be marginalized than not.

At this point, Nicole introduced concepts of "privilege" and "oppression," which Taylor appeared comfortable discussing. Incorporating the idea of oppression linked budget delegates' ideas of "equity" to systemic issues that resulted in people's material needs going unmet. Later, Nicole sought to illustrate how concerns of equity could influence the group's deliberations about project ideas by using a submitted project idea of a public pool as an example:

> *Nicole:* We can think about this [equity] in terms of impacts, too. We can think about a pool, for instance. I'm not sure we can assume who came up with that [project idea]. But can we assume a pool is gonna help folks on the margins more than like a program around health or swimming?
>
> *Taylor:* And it's not just who it serves but how it reduces the margin between oppressed and the privileged. So some of the programmatic things [project ideas] might do that.

Finally, having defined equity and illustrated its value, Nicole steered the group to consider how the equity component of project ideas would fit in with their other considerations:

> *Nicole:* Let's write down some things we can keep in mind [when deliberating]. Like I would like us to keep in mind, who is experiencing the most disadvantage? I don't wanna prescribe what we're gonna do, but thinking about equity, are we willing to say whether a project will impact people who are more privileged or people who are more oppressed?
>
> *Jason:* I think equity should be a component, for sure. . . . What other parameters are we gauging them [project ideas] by?
>
> *Taylor:* So maybe equity comes after feasibility.

In contrast to Jeremiah at Auraria PB, who distributed a training manual to budget delegates with a project eligibility matrix that had all of the components already defined, Nicole pursued an emic approach to determining the criteria for evaluating project ideas. She walked the group through defining "equity" and illustrating its value. However, as Taylor's comment demonstrated, the group decided to weigh "feasibility" more heavily than "equity" in their deliberations about whether to move forward with a project idea. Although putting feasibility ahead of equity may have eliminated some projects that would have been difficult to implement but would have benefitted oppressed community members, plenty of the budget delegates' deliberations addressed equity.

At that same meeting where Nicole guided budget delegates in defining equity and developing their evaluation criteria, the group began an initial round of eliminating project ideas. Someone had submitted an idea for a public mural at the Tramway Nonprofit Center located in the Cole neighborhood. Jocelyn said, "I don't think it's going to be some value to the neighborhood."

Taylor agreed, saying, "I think there are more pressing issues [than public art]." Nicole countered, "I don't want to throw out art altogether. We can use it in programming or something. What about an art fair?" The project idea of an "art fair" was already on the list of submitted project ideas, and Jason responded, "That feels like something more people can participate in. Keep it." Concerns about equity manifested in similar ways throughout the evening.

On the submitted idea of "food trucks," Jocelyn asked if "food truck" referred to mobile grocery stores. Jason and Taylor responded they thought it referred to "taco trucks," which were not equitable, so the idea was eliminated. However, the group approved a farmer's market idea, saying that the nearby Five Points neighborhood had one, and the group believed a farmer's market would better address food insecurity than inviting food trucks into the neighborhood.

Later, the group discussed an idea for "halo cameras," which would increase the number of security cameras in the neighborhood in an effort to reduce crime rates. Nicole believed the halo cameras clearly violated the group's equity criteria because they increased surveillance of innocent people and further fueled the racist prison–industrial complex. However, budget delegates were unsure, suggesting that reducing crime would benefit the community. I shared a story about the same project idea that occurred in the New York City PB process. After conducting some research, the budget delegates in New York learned that halo cameras do not prevent crime; they simply aid in the apprehension of suspects after an alleged crime had occurred. In response to this, Kevin said, "Strike it!" and Nicole added, "And yeah, in terms of restorative justice, we don't want more of our kids in jail. We want them supported."

Immediately following the conclusion of Cole Has a Soul, both budget delegates whom I interviewed expressed that the emphasis on equity in the process made an impact on them. Jason described the process's focus on equity as "another good piece" of the process, especially the incorporation of what he called "underrepresented voices." More significantly, Taylor reported that exposure to the focus on equity in the PB process changed how she perceived social change:

> I thought about social change differently in that there was more of a communal element to it, much more of a grassroots feel. Maybe that's because the social justice I've been involved in wasn't grassroots. It [PB] felt much more of the people and by the people. . . . I think because it's just ordinary people that had no other common purpose. . . . In this case, these are just five strangers walking into a room! . . . It was a little rougher and not as streamlined, and that made it a more powerful experience.

For Taylor, including discussions about equity in their deliberations made the process less streamlined but also a more powerful experience than other advocacy groups/campaigns in which she had participated. This quote about PB being "powerful" connects to another important theme for PB participants: exercising their power to reimagine community.

EXERCISING POWER TO REIMAGINE COMMUNITY

Many Cole Has a Soul participants perceived the PB process as an opportunity to exercise collective power in their community, while simultaneously reimagining that community, as well as their relationships with each other and extant political systems. For instance, Michelle described the approach of Project Belay as one intended to aid in people's exercise of collective power: "The goal of Project Belay was to build capacity within the community to organize themselves." Thus, the organizers of Cole Has a Soul believed one of the purposes of PB was to empower participants, and they intentionally strove to offer opportunities for that to occur.

Among steering committee members and budget delegates, three of the five people I interviewed shortly after the conclusion of Cole Has a Soul reported feeling an increase in their political self-efficacy because of opportunities to exercise collective power by proposing project ideas, deliberating about which ideas to develop into proposals, voting on those proposals, and then implementing the winning proposals. Jason said his political self-efficacy increased because he "actually got to both suggest ideas that I thought would work and then vote on those proposals." He said that opportunity had never been offered to him before in public participation processes. Reyna also reported an increase in her political self-efficacy. She believed "the power was always there" in the community and that she would feel even more confident in her power to make social change once the projects were implemented. Amara indicated,

> By participating [in PB], it does make me feel like I have the power to have an impact in the community. . . . I feel like this process gave me an opportunity to have that kind of impact, a more direct impact than I would have [otherwise].

However, two of the interviewees reported no changes in their feelings of political self-efficacy. Susan reflected there was no change because of the one-time status of Cole Has a Soul:

> I don't feel like me, as a community member, I have more power to impact my community. This was an opportunity to be a part of that decision making, but I

don't feel like it's changed any long-term outlook. It hasn't made a permanent change.

Taylor reported no change in her political self-efficacy, but she expressed that PB helped her imagine alternative governance processes and what is required to pursue grassroots social change:

> I didn't know people could do PB before we started, so that was pretty exciting to me. [I learned] you don't have to just elect your representatives. There's a possibility that you could more directly make that decision. Sometimes it feels like there's a wide gulf between elected representatives and constituents. [PB] aims somewhere in the middle. . . . You're getting a better taste of how you can affect the world around you much more directly.

Thus, participating in PB may not have increased Taylor's sense of political self-efficacy, but it did expand her horizons regarding ways that she and others could engage in political affairs. It offered lessons in how she could affect her community through deliberative activism (e.g., increasing social ties between neighbors and funding projects to address social inequalities).

Two other interviewees remarked that the opportunity to exercise their power related to interacting with elected officials and drawing from the social networks they established through the PB process. For example, Maya explained how the value of "coming together" related to increasing people's political self-efficacy, saying, "I think people even got to know their neighbors [through PB], and folks may be a little more empowered about how to create a process to get things done in their community." For Maya, working on PB helped participants strengthen their social ties and increase their ability to "get things done," whether that was targeting government officials, developing advocacy campaigns, or simply leveraging community resources to implement community-run programs.

Finally, PB participants reported increased political self-efficacy because they identified power inequalities between local residents and government, and came to understand how residents could affect them. The organizers of Cole Has a Soul certainly were aware of the legacy of systemic oppression in the neighborhood. Camila even remarked that these systemic inequalities were part of the reason why they implemented PB in the area:

> Today, we have one of the highest concentrations of poverty, low levels of education, and high levels of immigrant and monolingual Spanish speakers in the community. It was a perfect target for a project like this because they [government officials] didn't expect for community to have the financial or political resources to fight back.

A meeting of budget delegates and steering committee members in December offered several examples of how the ethos of deliberative activism (a commitment to deliberative ideals of listening, reasoning, and readiness to transform) manifested as participants discussed how the PB process provided opportunities to reimagine residents' relationships with each other and their government. The meeting occurred after the vote results had been announced, and the purpose of the gathering was to identify the successes of the processes (what the facilitators called "roses"), challenges ("thorns"), and next steps for the implementation of projects and advocacy for PB. Reyna remarked that PB taught her that Cole residents no longer had to abide by government processes and policies:

> It's clear to me that we need to harness the power in the neighborhood. We've all abided by local government. We get out there and vote; we get the signatures [for petitions]. But I guess the rose for me is that, "Wow, this is another option for getting things done." And we just have to keep doing it better.

Tamara remarked that she enjoyed Cole Has a Soul because there was "shared power in the process." Tonya agreed that there was "shared power" and "shared vision" during the PB process. This sharing of power was contrasted with typical government input processes that left residents feeling as though they had no power. Finally, several of the steering committee members expressed interest in expanding the impact of their PB process by lobbying their city councilmember. Tonya and Shirley were sitting on either side of Elizabeth at a round table when this exchange occurred:

> *Tonya:* We need to see Councilman Brooks. We're at next steps, and we need his support—
>
> *Shirley:* No, he needs *our* support! You keep gettin' it backwards.
>
> *Elizabeth:* We need each other.

Shirley corrected Tonya for making a remark she perceived as reinforcing residents in a power-down position; instead, Shirley suggested that the residents were the ones with the power to make a change. Finally, Elizabeth, who happened to be sitting between Tonya and Shirley, reasserted a core value of deliberative activism, suggesting that the politician and the residents required the support of each other to improve their neighborhood. The PB process thus fostered conversations that critically assessed social power relations. The PB participants wanted to take care of their neighbors without government support, but they recognized that expanding the PB process offered an alternative pathway for social change, a process whereby elected officials and local residents could share power to advance social justice.

Thus, overall, Cole Has a Soul reflected a significant departure from the business-as-usual approach of public participation from local government. PB participants imbued the process with cultural values that likely arose from their social positions (e.g., race, class, and gender), with steering committee members and budget delegates consisting, primarily, of women and people of color, some of whom were low-income. The values of coming together, building relationships with one another, listening to the unheard, inclusion, equity, and exercising collective power provided a unique flavor to the PB process, one centered around dialogic encounter and personal development. However, by the end of Cole Has a Soul, questions remained about the process's success in promoting activism to advocate for PB, other spillover effects for participants' civic engagement, the durability of the relationships formed through the PB process, and its lasting effects for promoting social justice.

EPILOGUE: UNREALIZED POTENTIAL

At two points in the PB process, steering committee members and budget delegates expressed interest in meeting with Aldus Brooks, their Denver City Council representative, to lobby for the city's permanent adoption of PB, or at least for him to address the concerns that residents identified through the process. I detailed one of these moments, which occurred in October, in chapter 1. At that meeting, the group appeared motivated to reach out to their councilmember and flex their collective power by giving him a list of project ideas from Cole Has a Soul that they could not implement. They agreed to form a delegation that included Tonya, Jocelyn, Shirley, and me. Tamara, who facilitated that meeting, indicated that Maya would schedule a time to meet with Councilmember Brooks because she used to work in city council and had more experience and knowledge in dealing with those elected officials than other PB participants. However, that meeting with Councilmember Brooks never materialized. Maya did not get in touch with the delegation to coordinate, and the PB participants did not press the issue again, allowing the contact with Councilmember Brooks to fall by the wayside.

The second moment occurred at that final large meeting in December that I just described in the prior section of this chapter, when Elizabeth remarked that "We need each other." This time, some PB participants wanted to meet with Councilmember Brooks and/or with Denver's mayor, speak at a Denver City Council meeting, or even contact a Colorado state legislator. Tonya was most energized about these possibilities, and she was tasked with getting in touch with Councilmember Brooks. However, if Tonya contacted Brooks or any other elected representative, it did not result in a meeting with multiple PB participants, nor did any PB participants speak at a Denver City Council meeting. I was unaware of any of them contacting elected officials, and no organized advocacy campaign emerged. Instead, by January 2019, most steering committee members and budget delegates had dropped their involvement with PB. Having successfully launched the process and held a community-wide vote, they believed that their work was done, and, as demonstrated earlier, many participants were burned out from the work they had put into the process. A small group of former steering committee members and budget delegates continued to meet with Project Belay to implement the approved projects, but I was not invited to attend those meetings.

Therefore, no concerted grassroots effort emerged to advocate for the permanent adoption of PB, as the organizers from Warm Cookies of the Revolution, Project VOYCE, and Project Belay had hoped. Nevertheless, in 2020, Denver's mayor committed to piloting a PB process in the city, allocating $1.7 million of public funds (Fendt 2019; Sachs 2020; Weissman 2020). This tentative victory was the result, primarily, of Connor's lobbying of city staff members and elected officials. This Machine Has a Soul had generated some media coverage (Beaty 2018; Blackman 2019), and the effort was bolstered by Connor's and Camila's involvement, both of whom were well-established activists in the city (Gardner 2019), which increased PB's visibility. Connor met, mostly, one-on-one (occasionally, Jeremiah from Auraria PB accompanied him) with city staff members and councilmembers to convince them to adopt PB. Two councilmembers came out in support of the process, one of whom was Camila after she defeated Councilmember Brooks in a local election. However, I have no evidence that participants from Cole Has a Soul were an organized constituency whose political activism convinced local leaders to adopt PB. Nevertheless, Connor insisted that convincing the city to adopt PB was a collective effort, even if few people were involved in the political activism to make it happen. He even told me that he had shared my evaluation materials with some city staff members, expressing that, "We couldn't have done it without you."

My work in the Cole neighborhood ended shortly after the process concluded in December 2018. I remained involved in the grassroots effort to adopt PB permanently on the Auraria Campus, which I described in the previous chapter, but that effort fizzled out by the end of 2019. It was clear by then that the implementation of PB on the Auraria Campus and in the Cole neighborhood generated significantly different outcomes in terms of deliberative activism, cultural values that manifested during participants' deliberations, and short-term effects on political self-efficacy among the participants. These differences were due, in large part, to the varying approaches to implementing PB that the organizers adopted: an instrumental approach in Auraria PB, and a relational approach in Cole Has a Soul. However, I was still curious to know about the longer term effects of participating in PB. Would participants' experiences generate lasting spillover effects, in terms of their political self-efficacy and public participation rates? Would the relationships formed among participants during PB last? Would the implemented projects make a noticeable difference in their respective communities? Did participants still perceive PB as a tool for promoting social justice? And did the differing approaches to implementing PB play a moderating role in any potential changes? In the historic summer of 2020, I contacted former PB participants to find out.

NOTES

1. Restorative justice circles provide opportunities to address harmful behavior through a dialogic process that explores people's wounds, needs, and obligations to one another. Typically, participants include individuals whose actions caused harm to others, individuals who were impacted by that harmful behavior, and facilitators. In restorative justice circles, parties talk about the harm that was caused and settle on a plan to repair the harm.
2. Whereas Auraria PB had 29 budget delegates divided into four committees, Cole Has a Soul had only five budget delegates serving on a single committee.
3. Box lacrosse is an indoor version of lacrosse.

Chapter 4

Transformations

Changes in Participants' Capacities for Social Justice

COVID-19 ripped through the United States like a wildfire in 2020. What began as only a few cases reported on cable news quickly spread throughout the country, upending lives, careers, families, schools, and much more. In March of that year, the university where I was working abruptly canceled all in-person classes indefinitely, and shortly thereafter, Colorado entered a "lockdown," requiring all but "essential" workers to stay home. As the World Health Organization declared COVID-19 a global pandemic, many of my students scrambled to find flights to leave the state and return home before everything shut down. Grocery stores ran out of necessities such as cleaning products, toilet paper, and some foodstuffs. That spring, much of my surroundings appeared as a ghost town: neighbors huddled in their homes, streets were devoid of cars, downtown was empty of tourists, and university hallways and offices were dark and lonely. No one knew when, or if, the pandemic would end.

Not everyone, however, had the privilege of staying inside. Those essential workers, many of whom labored in low-paying, working-class sectors, were thrust into public spaces to grease the engines of capitalism. Health inequities in the United States existed before the COVID-19 pandemic, but the pandemic laid bare those inequities for all to see. People of color were disproportionately affected because of systemic oppressions that resulted in poorer health and healthcare than white residents, as well as people of color's disproportionate employment in frontline, essential occupations (Golden 2020). Nationwide, infection rates among African Americans were the highest of any racial/ethnic group, and they died at 1.4 times the rate of white people ("The COVID Racial Data Tracker" n.d.). Despite constituting 13% of the U.S. population, Black people were 15% of COVID-19 deaths where race was known ("The COVID Racial Data Tracker" n.d.).

In response to the crisis, a conservative U.S. federal government implemented social safety net policies unprecedented in the twenty-first century. Federal and state governments enacted eviction moratoriums, expanded child tax credits to combat poverty, increased unemployment reimbursement rates, provided free healthcare (for expenses related to COVID-19 prevention and treatment), and enacted the PPP, which, in name, tried to preserve workers' incomes, even though the program experienced rampant fraud (Dilanian and Strickler 2022; DiNardi 2022). The federal government even issued direct payments to citizens[1] to help them weather the fog of death surrounding them.

Of course, the fact that the United States has had more reported deaths from COVID-19 than any other country on earth (1.1 million, as of July 2023; Mathieu et al. 2020) demonstrates that the United States' pandemic response was wholly inadequate. Nevertheless, for the first time in decades, many U.S. residents realized that their government was capable of implementing universal policies that could benefit working people, instead of capitalists and industries of death (e.g., the prison–industrial complex, the military–industrial complex, the immigration–industrial complex, and so on). U.S. residents witnessed firsthand that government officials could have been sending working people direct cash payments at any point in time; they could have banned evictions at any point; they could have offered everyone free healthcare at any point. They simply chose not to. If all this was possible, many wondered, what else could be done to alleviate people's suffering?

Then, in the summer of 2020, Derek Chauvin murdered George Floyd, and "Black Lives Matter!" became the clarion call of uprisings across the world. In the United States, millions took to the streets to demand an end to the racist criminal justice system, constituting what may be the largest protests in the history of the nation (Buchanan, Bui, and Patel 2020). Revolution was in the air as people sought to advance a new, radical vision for society, including calls to abolish police, cancel rent, provide healthcare for all, eliminate student debt, free all prisoners, live in harmony with nature, and much more. Community organizing, activism, and mutual aid became daily activities for many U.S. residents. For a time, it seemed the people, united, might actually dismantle the structures of imperialism, racism, and capitalism and replace them with something that resembled a just society.

In response, police forces across the country rioted. They engaged in systematic violence against peaceful protestors, including the use of kettling, chemical warfare, and physical brutality. Police punched protestors, shoved them to the ground, deliberately shot them with tear gas canisters, and destroyed property. Fascist vigilantes joined the fray and coordinated with local police, sometimes shooting and killing anti-racist protestors (Levin 2020b). In Washington state, federal agents committed an extrajudicial killing of an anti-fascist protestor, with then-president Donald Trump describing the operation as "retribution" (Levin 2020a, para. 11).

The police repression in Denver (where I was studying PB) was as violent and illegal as in other major cities. Police officers targeted racial justice protestors with live ammunition, pelted them with beanbags fired from shotguns, and subjected them to chemical weapons such as pepper spray and tear gas—illegal to use in international warfare, but perfectly legal for domestic police action. The FBI, in a callback to its infamous Counter Intelligence Program (COINTELPRO) of 1956–1971, surveilled and harassed activists simply for their political speech and used informants to disrupt racial justice networks in Denver, Fort Collins, and Glenwood Springs (Aaronson, n.d.; Stafford 2021). A civil trial eventually found the City of Denver liable for the police violence, confirming violations of protestors' free speech rights and freedom from unreasonable force (Kasakove 2022).

Simultaneously, in Aurora, a nearby suburb of Denver, local activists were outraged by the police killing of Elijah McClain, a 23-year-old Black man who lived in Aurora. A peaceful vigil for McClain was disrupted by Aurora police, who charged the crowd and deployed tear gas and pepper spray on mourning families. Aurora police later arrested several protest organizers on trumped-up charges, which were eventually dropped. The activists were further vindicated when Colorado's Attorney General investigated the Aurora Police Department and found "a consistent pattern of illegal behavior" by police (Vera and Selva 2021, para. 13). The Attorney General's report also found that Black people in Aurora were more than twice as likely to be arrested as whites, and half of the people subjected to physical force were Black, despite African Americans being just 15% of the local population (Vera and Selva 2021).

Some of the people involved in PB threw themselves into the Black Lives Matter movement. An undergraduate research assistant for this project, along with some of the former Auraria PB participants, poured into the streets of Denver and Aurora and fought for dignity, justice, and a chance at a decent future. Some of them went out to the protests every night, for weeks. Again and again, night after night, they stared down state violence, choked on tear gas, and cared for their comrades. They took on leadership roles by helping organize protests, and they tried to steer the movement toward strategies that could secure lasting change.

I was struck by the students' willingness to put themselves on the frontlines, and I wondered to what extent their experiences with PB informed their decisions. This Machine Has a Soul had laid the groundwork for community building, imagining new futures, and social justice activism. I wondered, as social order churned in the summer of 2020, how the former PB participants were responding. Did the PB processes have any lasting effects on the participants and their communities? Did they learn anything through PB that was helping them navigate all this upheaval? To find out, I began contacting former PB participants and organizers.

*****

A significant appeal of PB is that it can function as a "school for citizenship" and a "school for democracy" (Cohen, Schugurensky, and Wiek 2015, 10). That is, as residents come together through PB to deliberate to improve their communities, they learn important democratic habits that they can then carry with them into civic life beyond PB (Schugurensky 2006). As such, the quantity and quality of learning that occurs in PB have seen intense scrutiny from scholars (e.g., Almasan 2017; Cohen, Schugurensky, and Wiek 2015; Goldfrank 2007; Gregorčič and Krašovec 2016; Lerner 2010; Lerner and Schugurensky 2007; Lüchmann 2009; Schugurensky, Mundel, and Duguid 2006; Schugurensky and Meyers 2008).

This field of research has found that PB participants tend to report increased local knowledge (about the geographic area and people who live in it), professional knowledge (technical expertise), activist knowledge (political know-how), and collective knowledge (shared by the group of participants; Nez 2016) of democracy/civics (Schugurensky 2017). Examples include participants' increased knowledge of the municipal budget, their neighbors, and their community's needs, including material inequities in their neighborhood, as well as environmental and social issues that affect community members.

PB participants also tend to learn more about democracy in general, reporting higher levels of knowledge about participatory governance structures and local government processes (Schugurensky 2017). They learn about government administrative processes, their elected government representatives (e.g., names and contact information), and about individual and collective rights. They also learn about power dynamics among various stakeholder groups and the ideological orientations of public actors. PB participants have reported increased knowledge about revenues and expenses, taxes, and trade-offs involved in most budgetary decision-making (Almasan 2017; Gilman 2016; Goldfrank 2007; Gregorčič and Krašovec 2016; Grillos 2014; Lerner 2010; Lerner and Schugurensky 2007).

PB participation has also resulted in changes to participants' political self-efficacy, opinions about democratic governing processes, and feelings of connection to their geographic community and residents (Cabannes 2004; Lerner and Schugurensky 2007; Lerner 2010; Pinnington and Schugurensky 2010; Schugurensky 2017). When PB participants have implemented projects that improved their communities, they have reported increased perceptions of ownership of and increased feelings of pride in their communities, with this finding being "particularly evident in marginalized and under-serviced communities" (Schugurensky 2017, 21). Furthermore, as PB participants engage with others living in their city or town, they tend to shift identification from their neighborhood to the city as a whole, which corresponds to the change in PB participants from focusing on narrow self-interests to being concerned about the common good (Schugurensky 2017). Participation in PB can change people's general attitudes about democracy, too, with evidence suggesting that, over time, PB participants reported greater appreciation for the time that it takes to do democracy well (Schugurensky 2017).

Learning in PB is not only about internal changes to self-perception and attitudes about the world. PB participants also learn and/or develop skills to engage in democratic society. Research has found that participants can increase their problem-solving skills and communication skills (e.g., public speaking and careful listening; Schugurensky 2017). They learn how to craft project proposals, prepare meeting agendas, promote projects through personal interactions and social media, evaluate the merits of competing projects, persuade and negotiate with others, make collective decisions, interact with government officials, critically analyze government documents, monitor government commitments, and even confront public officials when necessary (Schugurensky 2017).

Finally, participating in PB can result in changes to participants' democratic behaviors. During PB, participants have reported talking more frequently with neighbors about their community's problems, devoting time to finding solutions to those problems, and channeling those solutions into the PB process. They also contacted city officials to get information to improve project proposals; monitored the implementation of approved PB projects; and, at the end of the PB cycle, meta-communicated about the deliberative process to improve the next cycle's voting procedures, budget delegate participation rules, deliberation rules, and community outreach (Almasan 2017; Gregorčič and Krašovec 2016; Lerner and Schugurensky 2007; Lerner 2010; Lüchmann 2009; Schugurensky 2006).

These changes in democratic practice do not end with the PB process. Instead, research has found that after engaging in PB, compared to before, participants were more likely to report issues with public infrastructure to the agency responsible for fixing them and advocate for PB in city districts where it had not yet been implemented (Schugurensky 2017). PB participants also reported becoming more interested in politics than they were before participating in the process; paid more attention to political news and public budgets; joined community organizations and, to a lesser extent, political parties; volunteered; networked with neighbors; collected signatures for petitions; and attended public meetings (Schugurensky 2017). Thus, PB can offer "a pathway to politics for adults (particularly women and minorities) who were not exposed to prior political socialization in their social milieus" (Schugurensky 2017, 23).

However, as with many studies of PB, most of this research on democratic learning has been conducted in the Global South, where, as I explained at the beginning of this book, the material and cultural context for PB implementation and participation is significantly different than in the Global North. Nevertheless, if people learn citizenship through PB, I wanted to know: What had the Denver PB participants learned about citizenship? How did their PB experiences shape their perspectives and approach to public participation, as well as their perspectives of their communities, democracy, and social justice? And, finally, what does this say about the ability of PB to foster prefiguration—a radical reimagining of people's relationships to each other and governance processes?

This chapter offers insights from a second round of interviews with 14 former PB participants conducted between September and October 2020 (between 19 and 20 months after the two PB processes concluded in December 2018). The 14 interviewees included seven budget delegates (four from Auraria PB and three from Cole Has a Soul), five steering committee members (one from Auraria PB and four from Cole Has a Soul), and four PB organizers/facilitators (one from Auraria PB and three from Cole Has a Soul).[2] The interviewees spoke about PB's effects on their public participation rates, political self-efficacy, feelings of connection to their geographic communities, relationships with former PB participants, and perceptions of PB's relationship to social justice.

TRANSFORMATIONS IN ACTIVIST ORIENTATIONS

Most interviewees ($n = 9$; 64%) reported minimal to no changes in their public participation quantity and quality after, compared to before, participating in PB. The remainder ($n = 5$; 36%) reported engaging in drastically different forms of public participation because of their involvement in PB, including, as explained later in this chapter, being radicalized to pursue robust social justice policies.

Minimal Changes to Public Participation and Political Self-Efficacy

Seven of the nine Cole Has a Soul interviewees reported that participating in the PB process did not result in meaningful changes to their public participation quantity or quality. Notably, those seven respondents were already highly involved in public affairs before Cole Has a Soul, and they simply remained heavily involved in their community after the process's completion. Rather than saying that Cole Has a Soul changed their public participation practices, these interviewees said that PB "reinforced," "enhanced," and "restored" their approach to civic engagement, signaling subtle shifts but not drastic transformations.

For example, Taylor identified as an activist before participating in Cole Has a Soul but said that the PB experience deepened her understanding of that identity,

> I don't know if it changed anything. I guess I would say more "enhanced." During that time, I felt more strongly an activist identity, . . . but I think I had one before, and I have one now. It's just different is all. [A] different level of intensity.

Jason also said he always possessed "an activist's mentality" because "bein' a Black man in America, I kinda deal with injustices daily." Hence, as he explained, participating in Cole Has a Soul was just another way for him to "get involved with the community."

Already experienced activists, this group of interviewees reported that the process reinforced their views of democracy, feelings of political self-efficacy, and beliefs about social change. Susan reported that Cole Has a Soul was neither empowering nor disempowering for her, did not change her view of democracy in any meaningful way, and did not affect her perceptions of what was required to pursue social change. Instead, participating in the PB process "reinforced [her] understanding of how difficult [social change] is." Similarly, Taylor said that the PB process "underscored" and "reinforced" the idea that "You can't really make social change by yourself. . . . You can't be a lone voice in the wilderness and expect it to do much." Perhaps because of the process's emphasis on collective, organized social action, Taylor and Jason both reported that their PB engagement increased their faith in democracy.

Although the PB process did not change these seasoned activists' views of democracy and social change, some of them reported that Cole Has a Soul taught them lessons about activist communication. Shirley, a budget delegate, learned that activism could be fun, saying:

> It was fun workin' through the ideas and tryin' to get to what was most important. And those are exciting to me to even just work through. . . . But once you're workin' in the plan, and you're doin' it, and, you know, . . . it was a really fun activity.

Maya and Nicole, two of the coordinators from Project Belay, also reported lessons about activist communication. Nicole said that Cole Has a Soul showed her what was possible when people engaged in deliberative activism through PB:

> Before I learned about PB, I didn't know that it was possible that people could do that. People could actually vote on things with public dollars and create proposals. I didn't know that was possible, and, so, now, I know it's possible, and that feels like a really big, important win, in my mind.

Although PB expanded Nicole's view of how direct democracy and public deliberation could support activism for social justice, she acknowledged that systemic barriers remained:

> [I] still think our system is rigged. . . . My view of what is possible within democracy has widened, but . . . the reality of, like, the systems that oppress and, like, keep things in the status quo are still . . . there, and they're stronger than ever.

Thus, the majority of interviewees from Cole Has a Soul reported few, minor changes to their political self-efficacy and understanding of what types of social action were required to promote social justice. However, they remained clear-eyed about oppressive systems that could undermine their efforts to have residents exercise collective control over public dollars.

From Auraria PB, two interviewees reported minimal to no changes in their public participation after Auraria PB concluded. For instance, Hannah, a former budget delegate, reported few changes to her public participation after Auraria PB concluded. However, prior to participating in that process, Hannah was already highly engaged in civic affairs (e.g., she was a prominent member of the campus's sustainability club), which may explain why she described PB as "another step in the process of leading me in this direction" of increased public participation. For instance, after PB concluded, Hannah joined the University of Colorado Denver student government, later served on SACAB, and when I interviewed her, she was volunteering with an organization to mobilize voters to oppose a referendum that would restrict abortion access in Colorado.

Although participating in PB did not change Hannah's public participation rates, she reported that the process provided her with knowledge about the inner workings of the Auraria Campus administration. The process taught her how the campus worked, which administrators were in charge of which departments, and how student governments could influence the campus. After participating in the process, Hannah said that she had

> a lot more confidence in my ability to learn how everything operated, and once I learned it was down to a select few people, and I realized there was a committee [SACAB] that, basically, was directly connected to those people, I thought I was able to just jump into [SACAB] and go for it.

Hannah even emulated some aspects of the PB process when she served on SACAB, including implementing a similar idea collection process to identify students' priorities for improving the campus.

Thus, the majority of interviewees, overall, reported little to no changes in their public participation rates and political self-efficacy, including a majority of interviewees from Cole Has a Soul, and a minority of interviewees from Auraria PB. Other interviewees, though, did report drastic changes in their public participation rates and political self-efficacy.

Meaningful Changes to Public Participation and Political Self-Efficacy

From Cole Has a Soul, only Tamara (a project coordinator and facilitator) and Elise (a steering committee member) reported significant changes in their public participation after completing that PB process. Notably, neither Tamara nor Elise identified as activists before Cole Has a Soul, and they did not identify as activists afterward, either, despite expressing changes in their attitudes about public participation. Elise had little experience with public participation prior to PB, saying, "I didn't really do much [public participation] before Cole Has a Soul at all." Tamara had been heavily involved in the Cole neighborhood prior to the PB process, but mostly through service-oriented nonprofits and volunteerism.

When I asked Tamara if she considered herself an activist, she was demure, offering, "I wonder if I've paid enough dues to say that. . . . I'd love to be [an activist]. I feel like it's a title of honor, and I'm not sure I paid my dues." She explained that the title "activist" was aspirational for her: "A facilitator of change is what I hope to be. I wanna be an activist. I want my kids to be activists." Prior to Cole Has a Soul, Tamara had focused on small-scale community interventions to alleviate people's suffering, but she explained, "I [am] really very much interested in public participation on a broader scale as a result of being in PB."

As such, Elise and Tamara reported significant changes in their public participation in the time that had followed the conclusion of Cole Has a Soul. For Elise, Cole Has a Soul "reinforced that, like, you can get involved, and you can do things to sort of help the process and, like, make sure the process runs smoothly, or the way it's supposed to run." After participating in PB, Elise volunteered as an election judge (someone at a polling location who settles disputes between poll workers and voters about election rules, such as whether a voter can cast a ballot), which she perceived as a meaningful step up from her minimal engagement in community affairs prior to PB. She characterized the work of an election judge as "being a neighbor and, like, helping our neighbors." She explained, "I feel like a part of the community when I'm working as an election judge, and knowing that these people are my neighbors is kind of a good thing."

Tamara was a facilitator/coordinator of Cole Has a Soul, and the experiences of facilitators are rarely recorded in studies of PB (for an exception, see Baiocchi and Ganuza 2017). However, Tamara expressed what amounts to a transformation in her approach to public participation after the conclusion of Cole Has a Soul. Prior to PB, in her words, she "was a part of the machine." Her public participation was about performing community service *to* Others rather than *for* and/or *with* them, and her engagement ignored systemic causes of oppression. She said that PB "changed me as a facilitator of a process or of a conversation." It also "deepened" her understanding of democracy:

> Because if you asked me before [Cole Has a Soul], I would say, "Of course I live in a democracy. Of course . . . there's democratic processes and all." . . . Like so many other times in my life, I thought I knew something, then . . . there was a lotta learning I was in store for.

Coordinating the PB process even helped Tamara secure a full-time position as a community organizer, where she worked with a coalition of ten community-based organizations to promote youth access to the outdoors. As she said, "I didn't know I was gonna get hired full-time. I didn't know I'd be able to bring that [experience with Cole Has a Soul] in and leverage it."

Tamara's experiences in PB motivated her to pursue systemic reforms in public decision processes to make them responsive to the people's needs. She said, "Bein' in PB made me want . . . other folks who are used to controlling, manipulating, [and] tokenizing [residents] to stop their crap, and start actually engaging people." To illustrate her point, she told a story about her time serving as a board member overseeing Denver's parks and recreation facilities. She was most frustrated by board members' simple offerings of "Thank you for your comment" in response to residents' public comments:

> We say it to people all the time who show up and make public comment at the parks and rec board meetings. It's startin' to really, really annoy me. And plus, I made public comment like last month at a city council meeting, and they're just like, "Thank you for comin'." It's, like, "You're killin' me!" So I'm startin' to be a pain in the rear, probably, to the other [parks and recreation] board members because I'm like, "Okay, what happens to this?" Like, somebody wants car-free parks. They shouldn't have to keep emailin' me, and they are emailin' a lot. . . . Like, give us some resolve now, doggone it.

Tamara's experience with PB not only increased her desire to pursue systemic change; it also expanded the realms in which she performed her activism. As she explained, "Well, before [Cole Has a Soul], . . . I was not tryin' to do anything with a budget. I guess I would say I would accept the budget." However, the PB process illuminated for her the ways that budgets reflect cultural priorities and shape the material world. She realized, "There's something that goes with that budget, and it's about power and influence, and systems, you know. I think this project made me much more aware of how those pieces connect. Systems [and] budget implicate history, like context." In other words, Cole Has a Soul aided Tamara in realizing that funding decisions are connected to systems of power, which, in turn, explain the connections between historic oppressions and contemporary inequalities, and she was more attuned to influencing budgetary decisions in the arenas in which she worked.

Lastly, Tamara reported that Cole Has a Soul taught her the importance of working with other community members to advance social justice. This commitment now motivates her ongoing community work:

> We can know how to navigate [social] change, but if you're not transferring that capacity, that knowledge, over to other people, like, what are you really doin'? . . . For me, where I am in my life, in my career, too, it's like, if I'm not helpin' somebody else raise their capacity [for social change], I don't think I'm doin' anything. . . . It is not enough for me to be able to effect change [alone].

Prior to Cole Has a Soul, Tamara was a passionate volunteer, dedicated to serving people from oppressed and marginalized populations. However, after coordinating the PB process, Tamara transformed her approach to public participation from one of charity into something that more closely resembled activism (even though she was not willing to claim an activist identity): pursuing collective social action *with* and *for* the oppressed to address systemic reforms that affected material conditions, thereby contributing to social justice.

From Auraria PB, three of the five interviewees reported significant changes in their public participation after that PB process concluded. These participants reported that the process, as one of them said, "opened the curtain" to reveal power dynamics at play on campus, provided them with knowledge and confidence to engage in other political activism, and taught them what work was necessary to achieve social change. For example, Emma and Luke served as budget delegates during their first semester on campus, when they were barely 18 years old. Prior to their PB participation, neither of them had been involved much in activist work. Emma, who was born and raised in a small, rural, conservative, predominantly white town in Colorado, had served on her high school's student government, but, as she said, PB "was a completely new experience," and that she was "so glad to have been a part of something that's more realistic and inclusive of people in the real world." Moreover, after participating in Auraria PB, Emma worked with a state legislator on budgeting issues, attended social justice protests and demonstrations, and joined SACAB.

Similar to Tamara, Emma credited PB with expanding her vision of ways that she could engage in social justice activism; in particular, she said that "PB definitely opened up my views on how people can be involved in budgeting . . . and how impactful that is." Before her PB participation, she thought that budgeting issues were "over my head." The relationships that Emma formed during Auraria PB also expanded her notions of how to engage in activism because, as she explained, "people on our PB committee were running for student government, . . . and they gave me the push to actually run for a position [on student government]."

Most significantly, participating in the PB process made Emma aware of power inequalities on the Auraria Campus and what was required of her to pursue social change both on and off campus. She described herself as becoming "radicalized" after Auraria PB concluded, which she credited as having initiated that process:

> I also think, just in general, I've become more radicalized over the years. I would say it [PB] definitely has shown me how much power we don't have in our current system, . . . but it also showed me what can happen if people are actually given more power in any form of our democracy.

For Emma, the PB process allowed her "to see kind of behind the scenes onto what happens on our campus and how it's run . . . and, like, open the door for me to be able to be a part of that."

Emma emphasized that participating in PB and coming to understand the political machinations on the Auraria Campus did not dissuade her from activism but, instead, showed her what was possible if she would fight for social change. As she explained:

> It [PB] showed me if these systems are implemented, you can have so much say in it, but also, not to be a pessimist, it showed me how much people can fight against these changes being made. It showed me what people aren't able to do at this point, like what restrictions we have on us currently, but I'm not taking it from a pessimistic point of view. It definitely has inspired me to fight for more of these changes, and . . . it showed me what can be done, what the possibilities are.

Emma said that she had become a full-throated PB advocate who talked about it to anyone who would listen.

Similarly, Luke reported that participating in Auraria PB had profound effects on him. Since the conclusion of the process, he had joined a socialist political organization and become involved in community organizing around several social justice campaigns, including efforts to resist the City of Denver's sweeps against homeless camps. Luke claimed that "a lot of the social skills I've learned throughout the Auraria PB process are very applicable to my organizing now." Participating in PB helped him, as a socialist activist, to "engage in community and talk about shared experiences," making him "more comfortable engaging in a more politically active climate." Luke reported that PB helped him develop his "leadership skills" and "interpersonal skills," which, in turn, increased his confidence about engaging in social justice activism. As he said, PB "made me feel like I'm more capable of leadership, and that kind of was one thing that galvanized me to be more involved throughout the campus and . . . develop the confidence to organize on larger scales."

Similar to Emma, Luke reported that Auraria PB encouraged him to think critically about power arrangements on campus. He explained that PB exposed him to a process

> that is . . . much more democratic than the systems that we have in place now. . . . And it also kind of made me reflect on our current institutions, and how their democracy, in my opinion, is a really weak democracy.

Luke later elaborated that "weak democracy," to him, did not provide opportunities for widespread and meaningful participation from people who would be impacted by a decision/policy.

Ultimately, this critical reflection taught Luke what was required to pursue social justice. Luke had become disenchanted with electoral politics and saw participatory, deliberative processes, such as PB, as offering a way for people to exercise collective power in their daily lives. His time away from the PB process had increased his appreciation of it, believing that PB could "just benefit our political climate . . . as a whole." Luke concluded that "It [PB] gave me more hope," and it had taught him the importance of deliberation and communication in pursuing social change:

> It [PB] gave me just a more realistic approach to how change is implemented. It kinda helped show me how . . . change, you know, is a process, a deliberative process where you have to engage with others. You have to deliberate—communicate—your ideas. . . . And it's step by step that you make change.

Prior to PB, Luke had not been involved in any type of activism for social justice. However, he credited Auraria PB with setting him on a path that resulted, in just two years, with his identification as a socialist and participation in large-scale community organizing to promote social justice.

Finally, Kyle, a former steering committee member and coordinator for Auraria PB, also reported significant changes after his involvement with PB. Participating in PB did not change Kyle's frequency or type of civic engagement; he reported he was involved in social justice efforts before and after the process. In fact, Kyle did not want to identify as an activist, instead preferring the terms "resident" or even just "regular guy." In chapter 2, I remarked that, immediately following the conclusion of Auraria PB, Kyle reported increased empathy for campus administrators and staff. That empathy had nearly disappeared when I interviewed Kyle two years later. He told me that he now saw PB as a distraction, a pressure release valve that required students to dedicate their energies to the process rather than engaging in direct action to confront systemic inequities:

> It [PB] was just kind of like a misdirection. . . . Now I see that if the students were to be involved politically, on campus, I think that it should be in direct confrontation to the administration, rather than . . . trying to work with it.

Kyle reported that Auraria PB "showed me who my friends were, and who my enemies were," with most campus administrators and staff falling into the category of "enemies."

Although the PB process did not catapult Kyle into more fervent activism for social justice, he shared the sentiment of Emma and Luke that the process taught him about power inequalities on campus. Kyle said the process "gave me a more realistic assessment of the conditions on the campus." The process did not increase his political self-efficacy, for the "realistic assessment" of campus conditions fostered by PB made him "realize how little self-efficacy I had. That, as an individual, you know, pretty much everyone, except for . . . the very elite, are pretty much powerless to change anything according to their will." He described the Auraria Campus as an "extraction machine" that took money, time, and energy from students for the benefit of the institution rather than students.

However, Kyle made clear that this newfound knowledge about the conditions on campus, in his eyes, was not a negative development. On the contrary, his time working on PB had made him, in his words, "less naïve" about what was necessary to pursue activism for social justice. He no longer believed PB could be a useful process on the campus because of the recalcitrance of administrators. This realization left him disappointed, and the disappointment, he said, was "a tough pill to swallow, but a good one, nonetheless." After his experiences working on PB, Kyle concluded that democracy without popular power was meaningless. He said, "It [PB] made me more of a Leninist. . . . Without the means of coercion, you can't do anything, and you're just subject to the whims of others." Kyle believed that reformist policies, such as PB, would be ineffectual without a mass movement of organized people exercising their collective power through direct confrontation with those in power.

Overall, a minority of interviewees (n = 5; 36%) reported significant changes to their public participation and political self-efficacy after the conclusion of PB. Three of the five interviewees from Auraria PB reported significant changes in their public participation and political self-efficacy, whereas only two of the nine interviewees from Cole Has a Soul reported similar changes. Nevertheless, for those few interviewees who experienced changes in their public participation and political self-efficacy, the changes were drastic, oftentimes incorporating transformations to their approaches to public participation that reflected an activist orientation to pursuing social justice.

THE DURABILITY OF RELATIONSHIPS AND COMMUNITY CONNECTION

Both during Auraria PB and, especially, Cole Has a Soul, participants frequently commented upon the importance of forming relationships with one another and strengthening their sense of connection to their communities. As the COVID-19 pandemic had fractured so many social networks, I wondered about the durability of the relationships and community connections that the former PB participants had formed.

Most interviewees (n = 10; 71%) were no longer in contact with other former PB participants, with the remainder (n = 4; 29%) reporting that they maintained regular contact with former PB participants. Notably, none of the former Auraria PB participants were still in contact with other PB participants, and all four interviewees who were still in contact with former PB participants had participated in Cole Has a Soul.

Reasons for Unstable Participatory Budgeting Relationships

None of the Auraria PB interviewees were still in regular contact with former PB participants two years after the conclusion of the process, mostly because they reported that maintaining contact was unnecessary. Stephanie said that she viewed Auraria PB as being similar to a group project in a college course, working closely with people to complete the project for a semester, but once the project was completed, there was no reason to stay in touch. In her words, "I just didn't feel like I needed to stay in touch with them, and we didn't grow very close to begin with." Emma suggested that if the PB process had continued on Auraria, the relationships she formed might have continued. Kyle said that because he did not join Auraria PB to form friendships, he did not see his lack of ongoing contact with former PB participants as a failure of the process.

Nevertheless, all interviewees believed that Auraria PB was valuable for meeting people on campus, even if they were no longer in contact with them. Stephanie said that, before Auraria PB, she did not "hang out" with people who did not attend her university, and that "being able to get together with people of different perspectives and in different universities was incredibly helpful for me."

Emma and Luke, both of whom were first-year students new to the campus when they participated in Auraria PB, explained that participating in the process enabled them to meet a lot of people and become more comfortable with students on campus. For Emma, the other budget delegates on her committee encouraged her to run for student government. As she explained, PB made her feel confident on campus:

> When I first started PB, it was my first year, and I was in a new city, in a new place, and didn't know anyone, so I was really timid and shy, and kind of just getting used to it still. . . . PB definitely was a big part of [pushing past those feelings], as well as just getting to meet people and feeling more confident in, like, my place and my role on campus.

Luke echoed these sentiments, explaining that PB provided opportunities to communicate with a variety of campus students, administrators, and staff members, which helped him to "further some relationships, or make some relationships, at the very least." Hannah said that she benefitted from PB because "it definitely seemed like it was a great resource for community building."

From Cole Has a Soul, five of the nine interviewees reported not having regular contact with former PB participants; however, two of them were coordinators from Project Belay who did not live in the Cole neighborhood and, therefore, may not have been expected to maintain contact with former PB participants. These interviewees expressed views similar to some Auraria PB participants, who perceived the process as similar to a semester-long project. Cole interviewees explained their lack of ongoing interaction as part of the nature of the work: When PB ended, the need to stay in contact with participants also ended. Importantly, no interviewee from either PB process said that negative experiences in the process drove them to no longer interact with other former participants.

Susan, a steering committee member, explained that she only became close with one other steering committee member during the PB process, and that she was only occasionally in contact with her. However, Susan emphasized that she would always feel some connection to all former PB participants, saying: "I feel like I always have some kind of connection to those people.

When I do run into them, it's, like, you know, seeing an old friend kind of thing."

Maintaining Participatory Budgeting Relationships

The other four interviewees from Cole Has a Soul who were in regular contact with former PB participants tended to stay in touch with four to five of them, and much of the time, they knew those individuals before the PB process started. They reported that Cole Has a Soul deepened or evolved their friendships with these neighbors. For example, when I caught up with Amara, a steering committee member, she had been leading a process to redesign Russell Square Park in the Cole neighborhood, and she had contacted multiple PB participants to help with that work. She said that Tonya (a former steering committee member) was "an amazing partner" for the park redesign, and that Tonya had even been hired as a "community connector" for the project. In fact, as Amara reported, "I think quite a few members of Cole Has a Soul have at least been aware of the park project, [and] if [they have] not participated in all of the meetings, they've come to at least one." Finally, Amara said that she also had been working with Tamara in Tamara's new role as a community organizer supporting youth access to the outdoors.

In fact, Tamara appeared to serve as a central hub of connection for former PB participants because she reported regular interaction with many of them and discussed ways she had incorporated developments from Cole Has a Soul into other community projects. As she explained, "The connections have remained, but the things we're doin', they just keep evolving." Tamara also claimed that her professional network "is more robust as a result of bein' in this project [Cole Has a Soul], for sure." She was still in touch with Camila, the former project leader from Project VOYCE who was a Denver City Council member at the time of this interview, Connor from Warm Cookies of the Revolution, and other partners at Project VOYCE.

Tamara also offered narrative examples of how two of the projects from Cole Has a Soul (the inflatable movie screen and the community garden) had facilitated ongoing relationships among neighbors. Her team used the inflatable movie screen at an event in Russell Square Park to launch Amara's participatory design project, which Tamara represented as a moment when events came "full circle."

> Another thing that happened is one of our partners in the project, who is now our [Denver City] councilwoman, Camila, was able to join us [at the event] that night. . . . And Camila was able to come and kinda help in their launch. So it . . . almost felt like a full circle kinda thing, where we have a product of what we

> know people wanted [the inflatable movie screen], and we can use it as leverage to continue to raise engagement and activity and interest in our own community.

Tamara explained another moment from that park redesign launch event that illustrated how the inflatable movie screen continued to foster relationships among neighbors:

> The other thing that happened that first night we launched it—I feel super blessed to have had this experience. But there was a couple who were walking by, and . . . they asked, "Hey, who's in charge of this kinda thing?" I just happened to be walking by, [and] I'm thinkin' they're gonna have some comment that might not be as pleasant, but they were so excited [about the event]! They voted [in Cole Has a Soul], and they voted for the movie theater, so I was, like, "Oh, my gosh!" They didn't stop and stay; they were walkin' their dog, probably had other things to do, but they were involved, you know, with havin' that movie theater out there. So, it's just been, like, gifts that we could not have anticipated on the front end.

Another example of the ongoing gifts from Cole Has a Soul manifested in the community gardens that were implemented. Originally, the approved project was for a farmers' market in the Cole neighborhood, but after it was approved, organizers ran into logistical challenges that made a farmers' market impossible. Instead, they adapted the project to offer garden beds and gardening classes for Cole residents to learn to grow food. Although, initially, the garden beds were owned privately (they were installed in residents' private yards), many of the recipients opened their gardens to the community and established a network of neighborhood gardeners, making their garden plots communal. As Tamara explained:

> I don't know if you remember Miss Tonya [a steering committee member], but they're [Cole residents] in her backyard with a full garden, and she's happy because they're kind of helping manage her backyard. . . . She says, sometimes, she wakes up, looks in the backyard, and everything's been watered already. The other day, she was lookin' out her window sayin', "I need to go get these weeds," and the next day, before she woke up, it was done. So, there's still, like, this collectiveness that's happening around these [PB] projects.

Tamara elaborated that, because of the garden beds purchased through Cole Has a Soul, "people are developin' relationships, weeding for each other, waterin' grass, [and] talkin'." I interviewed Tamara in Summer 2020, during the COVID-19 pandemic, when Denver had implemented lockdown regulations limiting the number of people who could gather in one place. As Tamara explained, Cole residents were so engaged with their gardens that they risked violating public health guidelines:

> Miss Tonya says, the other day, it was so many people in her backyard, she was kinda scared they were over the limit because of COVID and all this, and I was, like, "What?!" It's, like, a party every Wednesday at her house, so it's crazy good. . . . It's, like, a buffet of all good things that you love, [with] all your favorites.

Thus, although not all interviewees reported being in regular contact with Cole Has a Soul participants, those who still were in contact reported that their friendships had deepened and evolved as a result of engaging in the PB process. Tamara and Amara even reported spillover effects: that the relationships forged through PB were supporting other community engagement initiatives and the PB projects, themselves, fostered ongoing connections among neighbors.

Connections to the Campus/Neighborhood

Luke was the only former Auraria PB participant who reported feeling more connected to the Auraria Campus after participating in the process. As Luke explained,

> Yeah, [PB] made it feel a little more like part of my community. . . . It made me feel more connected to it [the Auraria Campus], like, you know, I have a role on this campus and, like, this is my campus, in some sense.

Although not all of the Cole Has a Soul interviewees reported ongoing interpersonal connections after that PB process concluded, six of the nine reported feeling more connected to the neighborhood, which included feeling connected to both other residents and to the physical environment. For example, Jason, who had been highly involved in neighborhood activism prior to participating in the PB process, said that Cole Has a Soul increased his connection to the neighborhood because "I had more interactions with people in the neighborhood, in the community." He compared his PB participation to the time that he served on the Cole Neighborhood Association, saying: "You know, there may be 10 to 15 people, at most, at a good neighborhood meeting, whereas [through Cole Has a Soul] we reached 100 or a couple hundred. So, way more engagement."

Shirley also remained in regular contact with former PB participants. Although she did not live in the Cole neighborhood, she said that the PB process increased her sense of connection to that neighborhood: "It made me feel better about Cole to know that here are people willing to work to make their communities better, [and] not just whine about it."

Other interviewees who were not still in frequent contact with former PB participants also felt more connected to the Cole neighborhood. Susan said that the process "did increase that connection" for her, but "maybe not on a daily basis." Elise said that her feeling of connection to the neighborhood

> definitely increased . . . both with the steering committee people and . . . with, sort of, like, physically connected with the neighborhood, like, cuz I walked so many blocks of it just getting to know, like, really what the neighborhood looks like, and feels like.

Finally, although Taylor no longer stayed in frequent contact with Cole Has a Soul participants, she said that the PB process "made me feel more connected to the people that live in the neighborhood, rather than just being someone who lives in that area."

Rewarding Relationships

Four of the nine interviewees from Cole Has a Soul said that the friendships they forged were the most rewarding aspect of the PB process, demonstrating the long-term effects of getting to know others through PB. Notably, although some of those four interviewees were no longer in regular contact with former PB participants, they still identified the relationships that they formed as being the most rewarding aspect of the PB process. The other five interviewees reported that accomplishing the process and delivering tangible outcomes in the form of community projects were the most rewarding aspects of the process.

Elise and Susan were no longer in regular contact with former PB participants, but they both identified the relationships formed through PB as the most rewarding for them. For Susan, it was "building those relationships with the steering committee members and getting to know them and just feeling a greater sense of community connection." Elise said that it was rewarding "connecting with my neighbors . . . not just on the steering committee, even though they weren't, like, long-term relationships, but just getting out and talking to people . . . was pretty cool." Jason said that he "really enjoyed . . . the new relationships and the relationships I already had growing." When I asked him if there was anything about the PB process that disappointed him, he responded, "That I don't have as much interaction with some of the others [PB participants]." He regretted not seeing more participants more frequently, and he wished that he had "kept up" more with them. Thus, even though the friendships that Jason forged were the most rewarding aspect of the PB process, and he was in regular contact with some other participants, he still wished that he could have maintained those relationships with more PB participants.

Why Relationships Were Important

Interviewees also expressed why they believed that forming relationships was important for Cole Has a Soul, and why that process emphasized the dialogic aspects of public deliberation. Overall, participants reported that they viewed these friendships as a necessary first step for promoting social change. Additionally, getting to know their neighbors helped to establish trust and accountability, both within the PB process and with the broader community, which aided them when completing the arduous communicative work of PB. For example, Susan explained that Cole Has a Soul "was a lot of work," and that participants "needed to be able to, you know, count on each other," which was made easier when participants spent time getting to know one another. Elise also said that becoming friends with participants created a situation where "there were people who you were sort of accountable to, whether it was the committee members or the neighborhood." Jason explained that steering committee members and budget delegates "felt like family," which caused them to have a "vested interest in the outcome" of the process. Shirley extended that sense of accountability to the neighborhood writ large, offering that PB helped Cole residents to trust one another:

> When they [Cole residents] seen actual things happening, that made them have more trust in us, more belief in us, so that meant we could talk more freely and be more in their lives cuz they knew we weren't just blowin' smoke. We were actually doin' stuff that was gonna happen. And it did happen!

As she explained, the lack of follow-through from other parties had caused Cole residents to be distrustful of people purportedly working to improve the quality of life in the neighborhood. The dialogic encounters fostered through Cole Has a Soul humanized public participation such that Cole residents knew that their needs were being taken seriously by steering committee members and budget delegates.

Beyond accountability to one another and the neighborhood, some interviewees believed that forming relationships among PB participants was a necessary first step in developing allyship for promoting social justice. Tamara explained that the legacy of systemic oppression and exploitation experienced by Cole residents required that people needed to care about one another so that they would then be motivated to take public action on issues that affected the community:

> I don't think a whole bunch gets done without relationships, when you're talking about the kinds of changes we're trying to make. Because in our community, there are . . . complex social issues going on that aren't about one thing, like improving schools, or affordable housing, you know. It's layered. So, askin' people to come out to support [an] over-policing symposium or [an] access to healthy food summit, or something like that, it doesn't happen without relationships.

Nicole explained relationships as being both the "currency" and the "glue" through which feelings of community were built:

> That's the currency in which, like, community is built: through relationships and value-driven relationships, in particular. . . . I really believe that . . . a relationship in the context of, like, a community engagement effort is, like, a social arrangement that is meant to create some sort of positive social change in your community.

Thus, relationships formed through PB were meant to be political, aiding residents in exercising collective power to promote social justice.

As Nicole elaborated, these relationships were more than just friendships:

> It's beyond just a friendship. . . . It's a public relationship, right? And so it's just like a friend, but there's, like, an accountability there, there's a shared self-interest there, there's shared values, there's a goal. And that helps really build the glue to keep people in that relationship and in that network that can then be used for other purposes to create further change.

"Public relationships," according to community organizers, are unique from private interpersonal relationships because public relationships are not necessarily intimate or loving (although they can be); rather, public relationships emphasize civil encounters that establish trust over time through public work that advances a shared self-interest among parties (Christens 2010; Gecan 2002; Robinson and Hanna 1994). In other words, people in public relationships, over time, come to see each other as allies, comrades, or brothers and sisters in the fight for social justice.

Taylor, who, unlike Nicole, was not a trained community organizer, offered some evidence that PB participants came to see one another as entering into public relationships. When I asked why she thought that building relationships among participants was so important for Cole Has a Soul, Taylor—who was the only white budget delegate—revealed, "One thing that was valuable is me, as a white person, getting a, you know, Black perspective on things." Taylor had lived in the neighborhood for decades, but she had participated in few multiracial activist groups. The PB process offered an opportunity for her to learn firsthand from her neighbors about the effects of racial capitalism on their lives. As she interacted with other budget delegates, she came to see how they were connected in their struggle to live a good life, and she believed Cole Has a Soul fostered those realizations among other PB participants:

> I think whenever you have a situation like that, where there is sort of gentrification, it helps a lot to build relationships, so you don't have sort of, you know, these two other groups, you know, each perceiving the group as "other." To build a relationship creates a little bit more of a bridge between them, and hopefully an opportunity to kinda see both perspectives.

Thus, the public relationships, friendships, and alliances forged through Cole Has a Soul were intended to serve as a source of political power, a web of connections that could be leveraged collectively to improve the quality of life in the neighborhood. These relationships were just one aspect of PB's relationship to social justice, according to interviewees.

PERCEPTIONS OF PARTICIPATORY BUDGETING AND SOCIAL JUSTICE

The interviewees were split on the efficacy of PB in promoting social justice, whether it was the PB process in which they participated or PB processes in general, with eight of the 14 interviewees reporting that PB promoted social justice outcomes (two from Auraria PB and six from Cole Has a Soul), and the other six responding in the negative (three from Auraria PB and three from Cole Has a Soul).

Social Justice Shortcomings

Three of the five interviewees from Auraria PB did not believe that, in the end, Auraria PB was especially equitable or advanced social justice. Stephanie did not believe the process was equitable because the mere $30,000 that students allocated through Auraria PB was not enough to address large-scale inequities. Furthermore, despite my earlier finding in chapter 2 that concerns for equity were a significant theme during PB participants' deliberations, two years after the process concluded, Stephanie did not believe PB participants emphasized social justice in their outreach or their deliberations:

> It [Auraria PB] didn't advertise the social justice as much as I thought it would. . . . It's really important to get people involved in social justice, . . . but it [PB] didn't really motivate people to be active in social justice.

Hannah echoed this sentiment, saying that "The way it [PB] was presented on campus, it didn't really seem to be something for equity."

Kyle believed that Auraria PB was limited by structural issues in its ability to promote social justice:

> It feels like what students are really concerned with is their own financial insecurity, and I don't think PB could have addressed that. Where democracy is concerned, . . . our little three-month PB process isn't designed to sort of coordinate the kind of power that I think is necessary to effect a more democratic arrangement on campus.

Kyle said that if he were making a brochure for PB, he would put the terms "social justice" and "equity" on it; however, "I don't think it [Auraria PB] did that—or [that] it even could have. To me, those things are much bigger than what PB could achieve."

Even the small funding that PB offered may not have benefitted students as it had promised. Hannah offered the example of the Native American and Indigenous Student Retreat project, which Auraria PB voters approved and which was touted by organizers as an example of how Auraria PB could benefit historically oppressed student populations. However, according to Hannah, the university employee who was supposed to implement the project retired, and that position was still vacant when the COVID-19 pandemic struck, effectively shutting down much of the campus's operations for a time, including hiring a replacement for that staff position. The Indigenous student retreat appeared to be shelved with no anticipated date for implementation.

Three of the nine interviewees from Cole Has a Soul believed that the PB process failed to meet its objectives of promoting equity and advancing social justice. Susan said the process was not as inclusive and equitable as it could have been because of a lack of participation from Spanish-speaking residents, a comment supported by my quantitative analysis presented in chapter 1, which found that Cole Has a Soul underrepresented Spanish speakers and Latine residents through every phase of the process.

Nicole (one of the coordinators from Project Belay) expressed that Cole Has a Soul fell short in terms of promoting social justice because of the winning projects. Nicole thought that the inequalities in Cole were so deep and so structural that it was difficult to address residents' needs through a limited PB process:

> I think it [Cole Has a Soul] addressed some needs [in the neighborhood]. Like the need to bring people together . . . in a community that is going through some massive transitions, demographically and otherwise. . . . But the needs of the community are so deep and structural. The only way that PB can really get at them is to be ongoing processes that are sustainable year after year.

Thus, some of the interviewees believed Cole Has a Soul fell short of promoting social justice because it was not inclusive enough and because the approved projects were but a drop in the bucket for residents facing food insecurity, housing insecurity, environmental racism, and many other forms of oppression. Interestingly, however, for the other eight interviewees who believed PB promoted social justice outcomes, they compared the PB process to existing public governance systems, seeing PB as a potentially more equitable form of public decision-making than those existing systems.

Flaws in Other Governing Systems

Most interviewees understood PB as a meaningful and potentially powerful alternative to business-as-usual in existing democratic institutions. For example, Amara and Shirley compared PB to the broken promises of other institutions. During the PB process, participants often remarked about how government officials would collect surveys and conduct needs assessments in the neighborhood, but then no work would be completed. Shirley described these actions as, "You know, just messin' with people and surveyin' people endlessly, and there's nothin' comes of it. That's what . . . burns. And people are tired of that." Amara offered a more detailed explanation:

> I think that there's so much change happening in that [Cole] neighborhood. And I think that there's different pressures. . . . I mean, now, I think it's exacerbated by the [COVID-19] pandemic. But before, I think that there were some very clear pressures on the community from gentrification that was causing displacement, and, you know, the history of organizations or individuals coming into the neighborhood and wanting to do good, and doing these short-term projects that are supposed to be really great for the community, and then, you know, funding dries up, and they just disappear. And so I think this project [Cole Has a Soul] . . . met the needs differently for the community because it's so intentional about involving the community.

Interviewees also stated that local government forums were inaccessible. As Amara explained:

> I think a lot of folks don't think that they can attend city council meetings or have access to that level of government. And that's like, you know, starting at

> City Council, and then you're working up through government, it just feels like it's harder and harder to, as an individual citizen or resident, have a voice in that process.

Jason confirmed Amara's conjecture by explaining that participating in local government had been difficult for him:

> I've only been to a couple of city council meetings, and they're intimidating, and it kinda puts people off. . . . I felt more comfortable being involved with that board [the Cole Has a Soul steering committee] than some of the other interactions I've had in a public forum, be that city council, the [neighborhood association] board, or even voting, I guess, for that matter. I felt like I had more of a say and more of a choice [in Cole Has a Soul].

Jason reported that others felt similarly to him, saying, "People, I think, are kinda jaded with the democratic process now." He explained that elected officials "may not wanna cede power to people, whereas they'd much rather make the decisions for us than have us make decisions based on our needs and wants." Likewise, Tamara wanted to break down "old systems and old ways of thinkin' and knowing." She was interested in "tryin' to create somethin' beautiful together that's much more democratic and makes people feel sincerely alive."

Interviewees from Auraria PB also remarked that PB was more accessible than other government input processes. According to Emma, who had worked for a state legislator and learned what was necessary for people to provide input at the state Capitol, "I think it's [PB] just a lot less intimidating, a lot easier to access for more people, as opposed to, like, going to the Capitol and, like, dressing nice and sitting down and testifying for a bill or something." Luke also believed PB was more accessible for citizens than other forms of political decision-making because it did not require extensive wealth and civic knowledge:

> A lot of times, politicians get elected because they have the funds and the means to advertise and campaign. Whereas, a member of the community who might more closely represent the needs, or the wants, of its constituents is not elected because they don't have the financial capital to carry out a large-scale campaign.

Additionally, for Auraria PB interviewees, PB could advance social justice because it could provide increased accountability over other government institutions compared to the ways oppressed people can influence public spending in existing systems. For instance, Emma connected PB's significance for social justice to its ability to affect community members' material conditions: "To have a say in how money—that we contribute—is spent is really important, and kind of allows people to have more accountability over government, or universities, or whoever else, in general."

Luke offered an example regarding police accountability to illustrate how he believed PB could advance social justice. Luke explained that, in the midst of activist calls to defund or abolish the police, PB offered a more accountable path for allocating public dollars compared to existing budgeting processes:

> because, like, in a City Council meeting, especially we're seeing this now, like, there can be a popular demand where so many people support something [abolishing or defunding the police], but the elected officials can easily just ignore that, and basically face no repercussions.

In other words, city councilmembers lacked accountability for their spending decisions, and PB could offer a way to meet activists' demands.

Thus, PB processes were believed to hold the promise of promoting social justice because they provided an accessible form of public participation that was open to all people, especially those with low incomes who may not otherwise have the means to influence politicians. As I explain in the following sections, interviewees also believed PB offered an opportunity for people to, in Tamara's words, feel "sincerely alive" because marginalized people could exercise their collective power, the community could increase its resiliency, and the process facilitated a discursive shift to collective values.

Marginalized People Exercising Collective Power

Interviewees from Cole Has a Soul expressed that PB processes, in general, could advance social justice because PB promoted inclusion through horizontal power structures. For example, Jason thought Cole Has a Soul advanced social justice because the steering committee was comprised of people from historically marginalized backgrounds. In his words, they were people "that aren't usually included in those ideas," such as "older people, minorities, Hispanic, Black, women, and even kids." Taylor also appreciated the diversity in representation during Cole Has a Soul:

> I felt like people who, you know, have historically been denied access to the table—mainly, you know, Black folks—had, you know, . . . a voice, and they all had a place at the table. That was one of the things that I really valued about that process was it wasn't just, you know, white City Council people making decisions. . . . It was Black people making decisions for, you know, a neighborhood that's still largely Black and Latino.

Similarly, Amara thought the PB process "was an attempt to get closer to that equity goal [for public policy] because it's really trying to engage anyone and everyone, and decrease the barriers that might exist to participation, to resources, and to knowledge."

Other interviewees from Cole Has a Soul thought that PB went even further by not just including historically oppressed populations but also formalizing a way for them to exercise collective power. For Shirley, the PB process demonstrated that local residents did not need to wait on local government to address their problems:

> We can't wait for people way over there on [the] south end of town to come think they gonna take care of our people. They gon' take care of themselves. We need to know we can take care of our own. . . . If they [government officials] would trust us with some of those funds, and not just bureaucrats or whatever, then, you know what, they might get a lot more done than gets done now.

Shirley elaborated that, because of the COVID-19 pandemic, governments would need "communities to think about, 'Okay, how do we get back to some sort of normalcy?' And so, who should they go to . . . to learn that? Us, the communities." Amara offered that the PB process taught her about how to make social change because it showed that

> community actually has more power and more voice to make changes happen through different processes like PB. And that there are different things they can find and actually, you know, start those processes themselves rather than waiting on the city or government to implement something.

For Amara, PB offered "a new kind of support system" for the activism that was already occurring in Cole; it was "just one more way to support what community is already doing for themselves."

Tamara and Nicole (two of the coordinators from Project Belay) thought the PB process advanced social justice because it could transform power dynamics in a community. They agreed that Cole Has a Soul incorporated diverse residents, supported the activism that was already happening in the neighborhood, and helped residents realize they already had the power to make change in the neighborhood. Tamara and Nicole, though, believed the process could go beyond those benefits to offer a more permanent, equitable way of making collective decisions than other forms of social activism. Tamara had no desire to return to normal once the pandemic subsided:

> I am hoping that we do not return to the state we were in prior to this pandemic and social uprisings. . . . In times like these, we need tools and ways of

> rethinking, and re-engaging that actually give people agency. Sincerely, like, give them agency and guide them.

Nicole believed that PB offered a distinct form of activism that could change people's lives:

> Yes, it [PB] is an opportunity for folks to have direct democracy. But, like, there's also an opportunity for people to make a social change, or some other type of structural change, or impact their community in an important way beyond just building things, but like changing people's lives, and I want to see more of that in the conversation on PB.

Thus, interviewees believed PB promoted social justice because it legitimized the activism that was happening in the Cole neighborhood by providing a structure for public deliberations. It leveled power inequalities by incorporating diverse residents, and it provided opportunities for participants to exercise collective agency, perhaps changing lives.

Three of the five interviewees from Auraria PB also believed that the PB processes had the potential to advance social justice because the processes placed power over spending decisions into the hands of people who, too often, were not served by existing institutions—people who had been oppressed, excluded, or marginalized because of their income, race, physical ability, gender, and/or nationality, among many other factors. As Emma explained, PB, in general, had the potential to provide a significant power shift in the country: "I think it's a great process. And something that can definitely be . . . a really powerful tool in shifting our country, . . . like, the way we budget, and giving more power back to the people." Emma also mentioned PB's relevance for the Black Lives Matter (BLM) movement:

> We have no control over the millions and millions and billions of dollars that are allocated on our behalf. For instance, looking at the BLM movement, and the police funding and their budget, so many people want to see that reduced or spent in different ways. If we were asked, I think even people who don't realize it would support spending that money on other resources for communities.

Similar to some of the interviewees from Cole Has a Soul, interviewees from Auraria PB believed that the PB processes held the potential to alter significantly existing democratic power structures. Emma argued that PB "threatened" the current power system in society because "the people in power can make decisions that maybe aren't beneficial to the people and are beneficial to the government or to representatives or to interest groups or whoever else." PB, in her eyes, gave people a voice in public affairs, which was "a really powerful tool." Luke echoed Emma's sentiment that PB could shake up the status quo:

> PB is a really powerful process. And it puts power in the hands of masses of the community. So I think it would strongly change and disrupt, like, social order. And it has the opportunity to do that, especially when it's given the means—like, the community wealth on larger means.

Thus, PB held the promise to promote social justice and even transform power structures, especially if enough resources were dedicated to the process.

Increasing Community Resiliency

Despite the relatively small amount of money allocated through the two PB processes this study examined, many interviewees from Cole Has a Soul believed the process had already increased community resiliency, another important social justice outcome, given the history of oppression experienced by many of the residents in that neighborhood.

For example, Amara acknowledged that the portable movie screen project from Cole Has a Soul may seem superficial to some people, but it illustrated participants' value of "coming together" by providing some stability in a rapidly changing neighborhood:

> Buying an inflatable movie screen might seem kind of trivial. But I see it as the community saying, "We need to be able to come together in celebration. Come together to socialize, and be able to have those moments of the community building relationships," especially in a time where there's displacement of long-term residents, or a lot of the renters who had been there, you know, are being displaced because of the inflated housing market and things like that.

Shirley also explained how "coming together" through Cole Has a Soul would contribute to increased capacity for social change and trust among Cole residents:

> I mean, that [PB] just can make communities be so strong together because they're working together. And when you work together, [of] course you grow together, and you do things together, you live and flourish together. So yeah, a small little progress like that can really, I think, can really be a blessing to communities. And even if communities are startin' to gentrify, it's okay. Bring everybody in together and say, "Look, we still have to all work together." Even if you have a few more ideas, bring 'em to the table so that we all can live a balanced life. Or we all could have food on our tables, or we all can have a job. . . .

> So then let's just get together and all work together because [the] bottom line is, we are all human beings. We all are tryin' to live this life.

In this excerpt, Shirley described how "coming together" through PB could establish or increase residents' feelings of solidarity and their ability to perform activism for social justice.

In fact, Shirley had already seen some evidence of community resiliency derived from Cole Has a Soul. When Colorado went into lockdown because of the COVID-19 pandemic, Shirley saw Cole residents rely on the gardens that the PB process had funded:

> When they couldn't leave their houses and had to stay home, they could work out in their own little yard planting their own garden for some fresh vegetables. Which is what that neighborhood needed so much because it's a . . . food desert. You know, it's somethin' that can be ongoing, and people were able to learn—and 'specially when this COVID hit us, and right after—what was better than to have a little garden plot that you can garden from your home? 'Cuz you couldn't go nowhere else. Grow your own vegetables and stuff. And it's just, I mean, it's just like a blessin'.

Black and Brown communities were disproportionately impacted by the pandemic. Of course, Cole Has a Soul did not address many of those causes, such as environmental racism, healthcare inequalities, and the fact that people of color disproportionately work in frontline, essential occupations. However, Shirley believed the community gardens kept people healthy and fed at a time when visiting the grocery store was dangerous. Furthermore, access to homegrown vegetables could begin to address the underlying health conditions that disproportionately affect people of color and contribute to increased COVID-19 morbidity rates.

Discursive Shift to Collective Values

Finally, three of the interviewees from Cole Has a Soul expressed that PB could advance social justice because it provided a discursive shift away from values of self-interest and individualism to collective values of solidarity. Tamara believed that the COVID-19 pandemic had opened an opportunity to establish just and equitable social systems, and PB was one decision-making process that could help people reimagine democracy:

> We are a part of history where old systems are breaking down. We have to have something, some tools, that people can use to reestablish, reimagine, rethink their role in society and how we're gonna be together. We're not gonna be like we used to be [before the COVID-19 pandemic].

Elise believed PB advanced social justice because it was Other-oriented, reflecting the dialogic ethics essential to deliberative activism:

> I think putting other people before yourself, and sort of seeing how it can help somebody else as opposed to help yourself, I think that's one of the things that PB sort of is. You know, sort of promoting that social justice thing is about somebody else, not yourself, at least in my perspective. And so, I mean, that's just like a huge systemic thing to, you know, to sort of make people see the benefit of helping other people, as opposed to themselves.

Taylor also explained that Cole Has a Soul was a form of activism for social justice because it helped people exercise their power to reimagine their communities to benefit those who had been historically oppressed:

> I really feel like, as a nation, we're heading much more in that sort of direction of, you know, . . . direct citizen input and effect into government. Because I think people are sort of rising up, being like, "Wait, I wanna have some effect. Like, I wanna participate. I don't want to be pushed down anymore." And, you know, participatory budgeting is sort of one arm of that.

These comments reflect a similar finding from the PB process in Greensboro, NC, where the process facilitated a discursive shift from self-interest to the common good (Russell and Jovanovic 2020).

CONCLUSION

At the beginning of this chapter, I raised questions about PB's role as a "school for citizenship" or a "school for democracy" (Cohen, Schugurensky, and Wiek 2015, 10). To that end, findings from interviews with former PB participants provided additional insight into changes in public participation rates, feelings of political self-efficacy, feelings of connection to their communities, and perceptions of PB's relationship to social justice. Most of the interviewees ($n = 9$; 64%) reported no significant changes to their public participation rates and/or political self-efficacy, with those interviewees tending to have been highly engaged in community affairs prior to PB and reporting that their participation in the process reinforced their prior knowledge about and approach to public participation. However, for interviewees who did report changes in their public participation rates and/or political self-efficacy ($n = 5$; 36%), those changes were drastic. Some of those interviewees even reported that their experiences in PB contributed to their radicalization into activists for social justice, pursuing systemic change through grassroots social movements.

To assess feelings of connection to their community, interviewees were asked about the durability of the relationships they formed during the PB process, as well as to describe their feelings of connection to their geographic community (e.g., the Cole neighborhood). Most of the interviewees ($n = 10$; 71%) reported no longer being in regular contact with former PB participants, but those who maintained relationships with former PB participants ($n = 4$; 29%) reported that those relationships supported their ongoing activism for social justice. Six of the 14 interviewees (43%; all of whom were from Cole Has a Soul) reported feeling an increased connection to their geographic community after participating in PB, even though some of those interviewees were no longer in contact with former PB participants. Four of the 14 interviewees (29%; all of whom were from Cole Has a Soul) indicated that forming relationships with other PB participants was the most rewarding aspect of participating in PB, citing their importance both for making the PB process successful (promoting accountability and trust among PB participants when the process was occurring) and for encouraging allyship for social justice in general, with interviewees leaning on those relationships to support their ongoing activism after the conclusion of the PB process.

Finally, most of the interviewees ($n = 8$; 57%) believed that PB promoted social justice outcomes. The remainder of interviewees ($n = 6$; 43%) reported that PB did not contribute to social justice outcomes because the processes in which they participated were not inclusive enough or did not do enough to address macro-level systemic injustices (e.g., the limited amount of funds allocated through PB did little to address housing insecurity). Those who believed PB promoted social justice perceived PB as more accessible and inclusive than existing governing systems, believed it provided opportunities for people from oppressed communities to exert collective power, said it increased community resiliency, and thought it facilitated a discursive shift from values of self-interest in public decision-making to values of collective well-being and solidarity.

The past three chapters have offered a detailed look at the communication that occurred during these two PB processes, as well as the long-term effects of those processes on participants. In the remaining two chapters, I make sense of what these findings mean for PB scholarship, public deliberation theory, and the future of democracy.

NOTES

1. Notably, resident non-citizens were not eligible for the stimulus payments.
2. I interviewed 14 individuals, two of whom served in multiple roles in the PB processes. Kyle from Auraria PB worked as both a steering committee member and an organizer/facilitator. Jason from Cole Has a Soul worked as both a steering committee member and a budget delegate.

Chapter 5

Implementing Participatory Budgeting for Social Justice

If this machine had a soul, would it shoot missiles
  when the red button goes explode?
Would it drop bombs through drones?
Would it imprison children?
Would it bulldoze over family histories?
Would it kick mamas and abuelas out their homes?
Would it zone? Would it zone? Would it zone?

—Molina Speaks (Warm Cookies of the Revolution 2018b)

In his spoken-word performance produced by Warm Cookies of the Revolution, Molina Speaks asks a series of rhetorical questions that drive at the central purpose of the PB processes I have presented in this book: to put the "soul" into public participation processes, governance, and therefore, public policy. Speaks identifies the material effects of granting decision-making power to social elites: imperial military ventures abroad, the school-to-prison pipeline, and displacing vulnerable residents through neighborhood zoning that gentrifies neighborhoods and bulldozes their family histories and cultures into the dirt. With each revolution of the Earth around the Sun, the oppressive conditions of late-stage capitalism ratchet up to impart more and more suffering onto working-class residents. As people struggle simply to survive in neighborhoods across the United States, they oftentimes lack the energy, resources, and time to engage in democratic governance processes by providing input about proposed legislation or contacting their lawmakers.

Furthermore, as many of the PB participants articulated during this research project, even when residents do participate in existing governance systems, they are, at best, providing advisory input and, at worst, outright ignored. PB participants reported lacking meaningful decision-making power in shaping their communities, and they recognized that such disempowerment was by design. In other words, their experiences were not of a broken democratic system but rather a neoliberal democracy *working exactly as intended.* Thus, they sought PB as an alternative model for governance that could offer significant decision-making power to reshape their communities into ones self-governed by care and connection instead of extraction, profit-motive, and atomization.

The vision that Molina Speaks articulated in his poem is one rooted in social justice, and just as he steps back to ask "big" questions, so, too, do I, in this chapter, step back to assess the two PB processes from TMHS and their efficacy in promoting social justice. I mentioned at the beginning of this book that some scholars have raised concerns about PB's ability to promote social justice, especially when it is detached from grassroots support and implemented in the Global North, where material inequalities—while still significant—are less severe than in the Global South (Goldfrank 2012; Leighninger and Rinehart 2016). The two PB processes I studied arose from grassroots organizing, and they explicitly strove to promote social justice, so what can be learned from them to benefit other PB processes in the Global North?

In this chapter, I make what is a common analytical move for critical ethnographers who study more than one site by comparing the two PB processes to each other (see, e.g., Agar 2008; D. A. Carbaugh 1989; D. Carbaugh 2007; D. Carbaugh and Boromisza-Habashi 2015; Madison 2020; Scollo 2011). This comparison revealed two distinct approaches to implementing PB in Denver, CO—the instrumental approach in Auraria PB and the relational approach in Cole Has a Soul—that promoted social justice. Then, given the relative lack of research in the U.S. context of PB (Hagelskamp et al. 2016; Harvey 2009; Kinney 2012; Pincock 2012; Siu and Staniševski 2012), I combine both PB processes into a single dataset to identify insights that extend across both processes related to their effects on participants' civic engagement and their community's capacity for social change, and what those findings mean for PB processes, in general, that occur in the Global North. Finally, I end the chapter by offering practical recommendations to aid community organizers, implementers, facilitators, and other practitioners who employ PB to promote deliberative activism and strive to accomplish PB's social justice goals of including marginalized populations' participation in self-governance and achieving equitable outcomes.

TWO APPROACHES TO PARTICIPATORY BUDGETING AND THEIR COMMUNICATION CHARACTERISTICS

Scholarship about public deliberation has identified at least two approaches to implementing deliberation processes, such as PB: an instrumental approach and a relational approach. Although this distinction is somewhat artificial, as instrumental and relational communication pervade nearly every facet of public deliberation, which some public deliberation models reflect (see, e.g., Barge 2002; Black 2008; Burkhalter, Gastil, and Kelshaw 2002; Gastil 2008; Gutmann and Thompson 2004), constructing instrumentality and relationality as two poles on a spectrum of public deliberation approaches is useful for differentiating the implementation of Auraria PB and Cole Has a Soul.

Historically, the dominant, instrumental view endorsed by theorists (Bohman 1990; Farrell 1993; Myerson 1994; Nino 1996) is that participants engage in deliberation for the purpose of making legitimate and efficient political decisions (Kim and Kim 2008), and that they do so most effectively by advancing claims, offering supporting evidence, and considering counterfactual data (Ryfe 2002). In contrast, a relational approach to deliberation prioritizes participants engaging in dialogic encounters that acknowledge the Other's wholeness and humanity, providing the foundation for them to collaborate, reach agreement, and make decisions that promote social justice (Young 1997). That approach shifts the traditional emphasis that scholars and practitioners have placed on public deliberations' instrumental decision-making to standards of morality promoting participants' dialogic encounters (Christiano 1997). As detailed in the prior chapters, Auraria PB participants' deliberations while implementing the process skewed toward the instrumental pole, whereas Cole Has a Soul participants' deliberations skewed toward the relational pole.

Auraria Participatory Budgeting: An Instrumental Approach

Several findings illustrate the instrumental approach adopted by Auraria PB participants, as described in chapter 2. First, Auraria PB facilitators' high task orientation led them to be heavily involved in implementing the process, including, in the case of the steering committee, completing work that typically would be done by members, such as scheduling committee meetings, preparing meeting agendas, creating timelines for completing tasks, developing communication infrastructure for members to collaborate (e.g., Google Drive folders and group chats), creating promotional materials about the PB process, and participating in outreach activities. By taking on that work, the facilitators aimed to have steering committee members concentrate their work, primarily, on developing rules for the PB process. Although the number of budget delegate committees prevented the facilitators from fulfilling the same responsibilities that they did for the steering committee, they structured those budget delegate committees, established clear deadlines for completing committees' work, and offered committee members training sessions that included a manual explicating the project eligibility matrix procedure they needed to use to make decisions about projects appearing in the PB ballot. Not surprisingly, the facilitators' approach to PB influenced the steering committee members and budget delegates to adopt an instrumental, task-oriented approach to implementing Auraria PB themselves.

That approach stands in sharp contrast to the approach employed by Cole Has a Soul facilitators and PB participants described in chapter 3. For instance, with the exception of the voting event and the event to announce the winning projects, I never heard Cole Has a Soul participants discuss firm deadlines for completing PB tasks. Steering committee members also seemed to shift from the idea collection to the project proposal development phase when they thought that enough ideas had been collected, rather than because they were adhering to a predetermined timetable. Moreover, during the project proposal phase, whereas Auraria PB's budget delegates had multiple deadlines set to ensure timely and efficient completion of specific tasks, Cole Has a Soul budget delegates had no task-specific completion deadlines; they simply worked to have everything ready by the start of the voting phase. Additionally, whereas the Auraria PB budget delegates' training manual defined and explained how they should use "equity" to rate proposed project ideas, Cole Has a Soul budget delegates were given no manual. Instead, the budget delegates themselves defined equity and decided how to use that criterion to evaluate proposed project ideas.

The PB processes also differed in how they conducted outreach to recruit people's participation. Auraria PB participants' instrumental approach generated a coordinated focus on targeted outreach for the inclusion of people from oppressed populations. As explained in chapter 2, they developed a fairly robust plan for conducting targeted outreach about the PB process, with a detailed schedule for tabling and contacting interest groups on the Auraria Campus, especially those comprised of first-generation students and students of color. Importantly, participants engaged in that targeted outreach solely for the instrumental purpose of getting campus students to participate in the PB process, with, seemingly, no intent to get to know students with whom they interacted or to promote solidarity among the campus's students. Although Auraria PB steering committee members wanted students who participated in PB to form connections across institutions, as evidenced by steering committee members' rejection of labels that identified them with the college/university that they attended, they rarely engaged in dialogic encounters with one another or other PB participants to create and/or strengthen their interpersonal relationships. Instead, they seemed to assume that their shared experience of working on PB would increase their feeling of being connected with one another. Most importantly, the targeted outreach was conducted with the primary goal of ensuring that students who participated in the process demographically represented Auraria Campus's student populations, both to accord legitimacy to the process and to make decisions (e.g., projects funded) that met the needs of the student body.

Lastly, although those involved with Auraria PB wanted the process to promote students' "engagement" with the campus, which incorporated some dialogic elements of students getting to know others they did not know previously and increasing their feeling of being connected to the student community, the main focus was on the task-oriented work of the PB process, thereby increasing students' civic knowledge, capacity, and experience, rather than developing robust interpersonal connections that could be leveraged as resources for future social justice endeavors beyond PB. This instrumental approach to "engagement" and public participation was reflected in task group members' remarks that they viewed their PB involvement as being similar to their participation in a semester-long course assignment: They did the work required of them and then took individual lessons from that work into their future forays of activism for social justice, rather than relying on relationships formed/strengthened during PB as an ongoing source of collective solidarity.

Cole Has a Soul: A Relational Approach

In contrast to Auraria PB participants, as explicated in chapter 3, Cole Has a Soul participants privileged a more relational approach to implementing the PB process and, more generally, humanizing public participation. Specifically, those PB participants emphasized relationship building and the culturally significant communicative practice of "coming together" and its attendant cluster of values, including healing, cooperation, understanding, and justice, none of which were emphasized by Auraria PB participants. The differences between these two PB processes may have been due to one of two causes. First, Cole Has a Soul included a greater proportion of people from oppressed populations, who tend to be more responsive to relational deliberation practices (Polletta 2006), than did Auraria PB, which does not diminish Auraria PB's relative success, across all phases of the process, in recruiting participants who proportionately represented the campus's student demographics. Second, the Cole neighborhood was experiencing challenges that either were absent from or were less salient on the Auraria Campus, such as gentrification and community member displacement, racist police violence, food insecurity, environmental racism, and effects of the prison–industrial complex. Cole Has a Soul participants likely emphasized "coming together" as a way to overcome these and the other systemic forces of oppression they were experiencing.

Cole Has a Soul participants' relational approach to implementing the PB process also was reflected in the value that they placed on Cole residents listening to the unheard, which showed participants' desire for the process to promote dialogic encounters between and among neighbors. In contrast to Auraria PB participants' targeted outreach for the purpose of ensuring that students who participated in the process were demographically representative of Auraria Campus's student population, Cole Has a Soul participants were more concerned about the quality of their outreach interactions with Cole community members, wanting to spend time getting to know fellow residents and hearing their concerns about the neighborhood, even if that meant contacting fewer and less demographically representative residents.

Lastly, Cole Has a Soul participants saw the PB process as an empowerment opportunity for strengthening their social ties with other Cole residents, as expressed, for instance, in references to fellow participants as being "family." Moreover, as the second round of interviews revealed in the previous chapter, Cole Has a Soul participants viewed the relationships they formed as a resource to leverage for their future social justice activism, whereas Auraria PB participants focused on personal changes in democratic knowledge and skills that were relatively disconnected from other students and/or campaigns for social justice.

Effects on Participants

The effects of these differing approaches to implementing the PB processes were seen in changes to participants' civic engagement and the quantity and quality of their relationships with other students or neighbors after these processes ended. First, as explained in chapter 4, with regard to changes in participants' civic engagement, two of the five Auraria PB participants who were interviewed 21 months after Auraria PB concluded reported no changes in their civic engagement behaviors (one of whom was highly engaged in civic affairs prior to Auraria PB, and the other was not), but three interviewees said that participating in the process "radicalized" them, meaning they sought to address the root causes of injustice through their activism.

In contrast, seven of the nine Cole Has a Soul participants with whom I conducted a second round of interviews reported either no or minimal changes in their civic engagement, often because they had been (and still were) highly engaged in public affairs prior to the PB process. The other two interviewees indicated significant transformations in their quantity of and approaches to civic engagement, but neither would have described the process as "radicalizing" them. Thus, for interviewees who were not highly engaged in civic affairs prior to PB, Auraria PB appeared successful in developing the critical consciousness and civic capacities of individual participants.

Important conclusions can also be drawn from what the second round of interviews revealed about the effects of these two approaches to PB implementation on the quantity and quality of interpersonal relationships with other PB participants. As explained in chapter 4, none of the Auraria PB interviewees regularly contacted other PB participants, although that lack of contact may be due to the transitory experience of being college students, with many of them not living permanently on the campus of the university in which they were enrolled. Yet, given advances in communication technologies (e.g., social media), Auraria PB participants could easily be in contact with one another, but none even reported following former participants on social media.

In contrast, four of the nine Cole Has a Soul participants interviewed reported maintaining regular contact with others who participated in that PB process, and even those interviewees who did not maintain regular contact with former participants reported increased feelings of connection to the Cole neighborhood and residents. Thus, the instrumental approach that Auraria PB participants adopted does not appear to have promoted their ongoing interactions after the process ended, whereas for many Cole Has a Soul participants, their relational approach appears to have increased the number of social ties that they had in the neighborhood and the depth of those relationships.

The second round of interviews also revealed insights about these differing approaches with respect to PB's ability to promote social justice. Scholars have questioned whether using PB in the United States can promote social justice (Baiocchi and Ganuza 2017; Goldfrank 2012; Leighninger and Rinehart 2016). Three of the five Auraria PB interviewees believed that the process did not advance social justice because insufficient funding for PB projects prevented large-scale projects that could address systemic issues on campus, such as food insecurity. More generally, they were skeptical about PB's ability to meaningfully address the numerous crises of the twenty-first century, such as wealth inequality, racism, and climate change. The other two interviewees believed that Auraria PB advanced social justice because it had been accessible to people from oppressed groups, accountable to students, and gave power to students, granting them direct control over how money would be spent on the Auraria Campus.

In contrast, six of the nine follow-up interviewees from Cole Has a Soul believed that the PB process did advance social justice because it was accessible to residents from oppressed groups, gave power to community members to decide how to spend money to benefit the neighborhood, and facilitated a discursive shift among residents away from individual self-interest toward collective well-being. Only three of the nine Cole Has a Soul interviewees believed that the process fell short of achieving its goal of promoting social equity, primarily because of the small scale of the process and the lack of inclusion throughout the process of people who spoke Spanish.

Summary of the Two Approaches to Implementing Participatory Budgeting

Based on these findings, I can sketch the general parameters and effects of the two approaches to implementing PB (see table 5.1). First, there is the instrumental approach. The primary goal of this approach is to garner "engagement" from the community. Such engagement is focused on completing the work of the process: getting as many people as possible to submit project ideas, develop project proposals, and vote in the process. For steering committee members and budget delegates, the main goal of this "engagement" in the process is to develop one's individual capacities for public participation. The internal communication practices associated with this approach include facilitators completing work for the steering committee, providing a training manual to budget delegates, organizing and implementing outreach events, and providing multiple deadlines for the completion of participants' work.

The instrumental approach included targeted outreach to recruit people from oppressed populations to participate in PB. Such outreach recruited a greater number of participants, who were more representative of their community, than the relational approach in the Cole neighborhood. This outreach promoted relatively light "engagement" with the process, with most participants spending only a few minutes to submit a project idea or vote for projects they wanted to be funded (instead of extended periods of dialogue and/or deliberation that were present in the relational approach of Cole Has a Soul).

The instrumental approach distinctly affected participants' public participation and relationships with community members. As for public participation, most interviewees reported being "radicalized," demonstrating transformations in the quality of their civic engagement and dramatic increases in the quantity of public participation practices. However, no interviewees maintained regular contact with former PB participants. Lastly, the instrumental approach does not have a robust association with social justice. Most interviewees perceived the process as failing to promote social justice because of the limitations on what could be funded through PB.

In contrast, the primary goal of the relational approach is "coming together." In this approach, participants emphasize healing, cooperation, understanding, and justice. The desired outcome for all participants is to leave the process with increased social ties to their neighbors and the community, either in the quantity and/or quality of those relationships. Those

Table 5.1. Two Approaches to PB Implementation

Characteristic	*Instrumental Approach*	*Relational Approach*
Primary goals	Engagement, task completion, developing individuals' civic capacities.	Coming together, listening to the unheard, strengthening relationships among participants to be leveraged for future collective action.
Communication practices		
Internal communication	Facilitators complete work for the steering committee, provide a training manual to budget delegates, organize outreach events, and provide deadlines for task completion.	Participants reflect on what PB means for them and the community. They rarely discuss deadlines, instead transitioning to project development when "saturation" is reached. Budget delegates decide for themselves how to rank project proposals.
External communication	Targeted outreach to recruit people from oppressed populations. Garners more participants than the relational approach, but the participation is shallow.	Widespread canvassing. Focus on dialogic encounters among participants. Garners fewer participants than the instrumental approach, but the participation is deep.
Effects on participants		
Public participation	Most interviewees reported being radicalized for social justice activism, increased public participation rates, and increased critical consciousness.	Most interviewees reported little to no change in their public participation quantity and quality.
Feelings of connection to neighbors/community	Most interviewees reported no change in feelings of connection to their neighbors/community, and no interviewees maintained contact with former PB participants.	All interviewees increased feelings of connection to their neighbors/community, and increased quantity and quality of relationships with neighbors. Many interviewees maintained contact with former PB participants.
Ability to promote social justice	Most interviewees believed the PB process did not promote social justice due to limited funding and constrained project eligibility.	Most interviewees believed the PB process promoted social justice because it was accessible to people from oppressed populations, provided an opportunity to exercise collective power, and facilitated a discursive shift toward the common good.

relationships are perceived as a resource that can then be leveraged for future social justice activism.

The relational approach manifests through several communication practices. First, facilitators prompt participants to reflect on what PB means for them and the community, which was a frequent practice at meetings throughout the PB process. Participants minimally discuss deadlines. They also transition to the project development phase after believing that they have reached saturation in project ideas (to borrow a term from qualitative research methods) instead of according to a predetermined deadline. The facilitators guide steering committee members and budget delegates in making decisions, but the budget delegates and steering committee members are then responsible for doing most of the work that results from those decisions. For instance, the steering committee members and budget delegates are responsible for developing meeting agendas, organizing outreach events, conducting outreach, and developing criteria for evaluating project proposals.

The relational approach also affected outreach to community members. Instead of targeted outreach, these PB participants canvassed the neighborhood, with only one organized outreach event. Their outreach to neighbors focused more on the quality of interactions rather than the quantity. PB participants were supposed to engage in dialogic encounters with their neighbors and practice listening to the unheard. This type of outreach garnered fewer PB participants than the instrumental approach, but those who did participate were more deeply engaged in the process, often spending 15–60 minutes deliberating to identify problems in the neighborhood, the causes of those problems, and potential solutions to the problems.

The relational approach also had distinct effects on the PB participants' public participation and relationships with neighbors. As for public participation, most interviewees reported no or minimal changes to their civic engagement practices. As for their relationships with their neighbors, all the interviewees reported feeling an increased sense of connection to their neighborhood, and 44% maintained contact with former PB participants. The relational approach thus increased the quantity and quality of social ties that participants had with others in their community.

Finally, the relational approach affected participants' perceptions of PB's ability to promote social justice. Most interviewees believed the PB process promoted social justice because it was accessible to people from oppressed populations, provided opportunities for local residents to exercise collective power over their community, and facilitated a discursive shift away from neoliberal individualism and toward the common good.

My purpose, thus far, has been to compare and contrast the two approaches to PB implementation against each other, including their attendant goals, communication practices, effects on participants, and participants' perceptions of

PB's ability to promote social justice. Next, I shift my analysis to regard the two PB processes overall. That is, I treat the two cases as a single unit of analysis to understand what insights can be gained that extend across both processes. Specifically, I address lessons learned about the two PB processes' effects on the public participation of people from oppressed populations and their communities' capacity for social change.

EFFECTS OF PARTICIPATORY BUDGETING ON PUBLIC PARTICIPATION AND COMMUNITY CAPACITY FOR SOCIAL CHANGE

Prior research on PB has shown that the process tends to promote participation from historically oppressed populations and provide material benefits to those communities through the allocation of funds (Bhatnagar et al. 2003; Gonçalves 2014; McNulty 2011; Pateman 2012; Schneider and Goldfrank 2002; Shah 2007; Sintomer, Herzberg, and Röcke 2008; Su 2012; Touchton and Wampler 2014; Wampler 2012; The World Bank 2008). However, few studies have explored the effects of PB on participants, especially those from oppressed communities, including the quality of deliberations, whether and how members from oppressed populations engage in deliberation processes, and effects of PB participation on those population members' civic skills, attitudes, and behaviors (Hagelskamp et al. 2016). Beyond PB, public deliberation research, in general, has had relatively few ethnographic studies of public deliberation, with minimal exploration into how diversity affects deliberation, how deliberation affects participants' dispositions toward public participation, and how it builds community capacity for social change (Harvey 2009; Kinney 2012; Pincock 2012; Siu and Staniševski 2012).

Effects of Participatory Budgeting on Oppressed Participants' Public Participation

Overall, my research did not identify substantial changes to participants' civic engagement after the conclusion of the PB processes. Instead, study participants mostly reported small, relatively subtle shifts in their approach to and quantity of public participation. In interviews with Auraria PB participants approximately two years after the process's completion, only two of the interviewees were people of color. One of them, a Black man, reported that Auraria PB radicalized him, and he became a passionate community organizer in a local chapter of a socialist organization. However, the other interviewee, who was an Asian woman, indicated that PB did not have significant effects on her civic engagement. One white woman reported that Auraria PB radicalized her, even causing her to run for and win a student government position, but another white woman reported that PB had no effect on her civic engagement. She also ran for and won a position in student government after Auraria PB, but she stated that she already had plans to join student government before she participated in PB.

In Cole Has a Soul, most interviewees reported minor changes in their civic engagement after the PB process concluded. This group was already highly involved in civic affairs prior to the start of the PB process, so it was unlikely that Cole Has a Soul would increase their participation even higher. Instead, they reported that the deliberative activism they performed in Cole Has a Soul offered them an alternative approach to pursuing social change, and it motivated them to continue their community work, with several interviewees saying that Cole Has a Soul restored their faith in democracy and/or gave them hope about the possibility that democratic systems could respond to the needs of oppressed residents. Two of the follow-up interviewees (one Black woman and one white woman) experienced transformations in their approaches to and quantity of civic engagement.

Several conclusions can be drawn from these findings. First, the changes in civic engagement, for most interviewees, were relatively small, but that also may be because the PB processes themselves were relatively circumspect. They operated on a compressed timeline with limited funds and a relatively small pool of participants. However, this is not to discount the transformative changes experienced by four of the 14 second-round interviewees (29%), which ought to be considered a substantial result for a deliberation process that lasted only 4–5 months. Most importantly, three of the four participants who reported substantial changes in their civic engagement had minimal experience in civic affairs, activism, or public deliberation prior to PB. This finding suggests that in future studies, rather than focusing on demographic identity markers (e.g., race, household income, education level, gender, and so forth), a more insightful analytic lens may be participants' prior experience with public participation.

Certainly, one's identity offers an outsized role in their social location and perspective (e.g., Collins 2000; Meyer 2007; Shrikant 2014, 2015; Vakil et al. 2016; Young 2002), and I do not suggest minimizing that fact. As will be shown below, I argue that identity is an important aspect of PB's relationship to social justice. However, for the purposes of assessing changes in civic engagement from PB, this study suggests that an individual's race, gender, or class may not be as important for analytical purposes as their prior experience in civic affairs. After all, a cursory glance at history reveals that people of color, working-class people, women, and people with other stigmatized identities have been at the forefront of activist campaigns for social justice (Chafe 1981; Robinson 2019; Zinn 1980). Therefore, this study suggests that scholars cannot assume that a participant's socioeconomic status always relates to their prior civic involvement, and future studies could group participants according to their public participation rates before and after the PB process. My findings suggest that those who had the least experience with public participation received the most benefit from PB, because it radically altered their perceptions of social change and increased the quantity and quality of their public participation beyond PB.

Community Capacity for Social Change

When it comes to how PB affects a community's capacity for social change, the findings from Cole Has a Soul are most illustrative. This study has shown that the interpersonal relationships (what one interviewee termed "public relationships") formed through the PB process became resources for social activism after PB's conclusion. Interviewees reported that they relied on other former PB participants to promote social change, and the friendships they formed provided trust and a sense of accountability to each other. Cole Has a Soul launched a virtuous feedback loop for many of the participants: As they worked for social change in PB, they developed trust and accountability with one another to engage in social activism beyond the process. The work of community organizing did not stop after the conclusion of Cole Has a Soul, for, as one interviewee explained, the activist work simply evolved into other areas of community concern.

In Auraria PB, interviewees reported that the individual knowledge and experience they gained from PB contributed to community capacity for social change. Two interviewees assumed positions in student government and worked to make the schools more responsive to students' needs, translating what they learned in PB to governing. One interviewee who joined a socialist community organization credited the skills he developed in PB as invaluable for his community organizing to address homelessness in Denver.

These findings suggest two possible ways that deliberation can increase community capacity for social change, depending on the implementation approach that is adopted. In Cole Has a Soul, where relational communication was emphasized, participants developed and then relied on social ties to promote collective social change. In Auraria PB, where instrumental communication was emphasized, participants honed individual skills and knowledge for civic engagement, later devoting those skills to the public work of governing and community organizing. These conclusions lead me to the last section of this chapter: practical recommendations for implementing socially just participatory budgeting.

LESSONS LEARNED: PRACTICAL RECOMMENDATIONS FOR IMPLEMENTING SOCIALLY JUST PARTICIPATORY BUDGETING

Two justifications are warranted before providing my recommendations. First, I offer recommendations that can be applied across the two cases to PB processes in general; I do not provide detailed recommendations for Cole Has a Soul and Auraria PB as separate entities. Although I provided such recommendations to my community partners (Gardner and Russell 2020; Russell and Gardner 2019), I realize that the reader is likely more interested in ways to implement PB for social justice in general, not only in Denver, Colorado.

Second, the reader may notice that some of these recommendations are not, at first glance, related to communicative processes and practices in PB, so they may perceive my suggestions as emanating from someone with a lack of expertise in such affairs. In response to this criticism, I argue that rather than a deficit, these recommendations reflect the benefit of a critical, ethnographic, communicative approach to studying PB. That is, these recommendations address concerns expressed by many of the PB participants and are derived from studying how numerous factors impacted the quality of deliberation in the PB processes, both internal and external to the process. Therefore, I offer a recommendation such as allocating more money through PB for the purpose of improving the deliberation in PB processes, although the effects of implementing such a recommendation may have other important effects that would be of interest to researchers beyond the communication discipline.

My recommendations are derived both from the successes of TMHS, as well as the shortcomings. The recommendations for implementing socially just PB include allocating a significant amount of money through PB, scheduling an appropriate timeline for the process, incorporating structured idea collection events, conducting well-organized targeted outreach, and tailoring the process to residents' goals.

First, the case of TMHS demonstrates the importance of allocating a sufficient amount of money through PB. Auraria PB and Cole Has a Soul each allocated $30,000 to benefit their communities. Participants dedicate considerable time to the work of PB, especially steering committee members and budget delegates, and they need to believe that allocating their free time in such a manner is worthwhile. Although this study did not explore in-depth the material effects of PB (i.e., how the approved projects affected the communities in which they were implemented), the ability to have an impact on one's community is a significant motivator both in the recruitment and retention of PB participants. Participants of TMHS often remarked that they enjoyed PB because it granted them meaningful decision-making power and because they knew their work generated material impacts on their communities. With that being said, $30,000 is a relatively paltry sum for public works, especially given the decades of divestment in schools and infrastructure, with low-income areas and areas with large populations of people of color disproportionately affected. Indeed, the limited funds allocated through PB were a reason that some TMHS participants became disenchanted with the process, believing it was inadequate for addressing people's pressing material needs and thereby promoting social justice.

I cannot offer an exact amount of money to allocate through PB or what proportion of a public budget is best. In fact, other PB processes have ranged widely in how much they allocate through the process. In 2014–2015, North American PB processes allocated between $61,000 and $3.4 million, with the average being $1 million (Hagelskamp et al. 2016). When it came to dollars spent per resident, the amount allocated through PB ranged from $1.18 per resident to $69.85 per resident, with an average of $9.85 per resident (Hagelskamp et al. 2016). In 1999, residents of Porto Alegre, Brazil, allocated 21% of the city's budget through PB (Bhatnagar et al. 2003).

What is clear from the findings of this study is that practitioners must not only consider the amount of money when deciding how much material impact they want to make through PB. The size of the funds allocated has significant effects on participant recruitment and retention, and potential PB participants need to believe the time they spend on the process will be worthwhile for them, including the ability to promote social equity by addressing the effects of systemic discrimination on oppressed communities. For people from oppressed populations (whose time and energy are often stretched thin), the potential benefits of PB need to be substantial enough to justify them spending their free time deliberating in the process. In other words, residents need to perceive the amount of money allocated through PB as sufficient for making an impact on social inequality. Given the scale of inequality in the United States, and the shabby state of infrastructure around the country,[1] practitioners and policymakers should be ambitious in the amount of money they allocate through PB if they want the process to promote social justice. Similarly, activists should demand that the money allocated through PB be adequate to address their community's needs.

Second, TMHS demonstrated the importance of providing PB with an adequate timeline for completing the process. Although Cole Has a Soul launched in May 2018, a period of inactivity meant that the process effectively ran from August to December 2018. Similarly, Auraria PB participants began meeting in July 2018 and completed their process in December of that year. Thus, the processes ran only for 4–5 months. TMHS participants frequently remarked that the limited timeline was a hindrance to their deliberations. They wanted more time to conduct outreach and develop project proposals. In Cole Has a Soul, they wanted more time for outreach to ensure that residents felt they were being heard and to reach as many residents as possible, which could have, in turn, increased the number of people who volunteered to serve as budget delegates or vote in the process. In Auraria PB, budget delegates wanted more time to consider the numerous project ideas that people submitted. The compressed timeline of Auraria PB exacerbated conflicts between students and campus staff because campus staff were unable to offer the information that budget delegates required as quickly as the budget delegates needed it.

The limited timeframe for project proposal development affected project implementation in the Cole neighborhood and on the Auraria Campus. Cole Has a Soul was unable to implement the farmers market because they could not find a reliable community partner, a problem that could have been solved before the PB vote if they had more time. On Auraria, students approved the installation of more microwaves in the Tivoli, but that project ended up costing significantly more than anticipated because of required wiring renovations to support the microwaves—another development that could have been avoided if more time had been dedicated to project proposal development.

Providing more than 4–5 months for PB also would contribute to increased civic knowledge and skills for participants. Because of the experiential learning that occurs through PB, participants need an adequate amount of time to get the practice and exposure required to develop their civic capacities. Additional time working on PB could be especially useful for participants with limited prior public participation experience, as they may need more time than experienced activists to learn the skills necessary to engage in PB and beyond. TMHS would have benefitted from implementing the PB processes over 8 months, which is the national average for PB processes (Hagelskamp et al. 2016). The 4–5 months at TMHS clearly provided some benefits to the PB participants, but the extent of those benefits was hampered by the circumscribed timeline.

Third, PB implementers ought to implement structured idea collection events, sometimes called "neighborhood assemblies" by other PB practitioners. Cole Has a Soul only held one such event, which was their kickoff event in May 2018. Auraria PB held no structured idea collection events. Typically, at these neighborhood assemblies, which often last more than an hour, residents hear a brief presentation about PB and the specifics of its implementation in that geographic area (e.g., the rules, timeline, and how much money will be allocated). Then, attendees form small groups to identify problems in the community and propose project ideas that could address those problems.

These events extend the benefits of deliberation to residents by offering a chance for people to attend a single event, meet their neighbors, learn about challenges in the area, and deliberate about possible solutions for those challenges without committing to serve on the steering committee or as budget delegates. Incorporating these structured idea collection events into TMHS could have aided participant recruitment, generated better quality ideas, and spread the benefits of deliberation beyond the steering committee and budget delegates. Additionally, Cole Has a Soul participants often remarked that transparency in the process was limited because residents submitted ideas and then heard nothing from the organizers until months later when it was time to vote on projects. Providing structured neighborhood assemblies can increase transparency by getting budget delegates and steering committee members into the community to answer residents' questions and share updates about the process.

Fourth, PB implementers ought to develop a detailed plan for targeted outreach. Auraria PB was more successful than Cole Has a Soul in achieving proportional representation of the local community in its PB process. This was due in large part because the Auraria PB coordinators and steering committee dedicated much of their time to identifying marginalized constituencies on campus and developing plans to contact them for recruitment in the process. Interviewees from Cole Has a Soul often remarked that, although they enjoyed door-to-door canvassing, they wished they had developed a robust plan for sustained outreach to the community. These findings demonstrate that a direct, personalized invitation to community members is highly beneficial in securing their engagement, especially among people from oppressed communities. Those outreach strategies should be culturally appropriate for the targeted community, which may require creative strategies. For example, Michelle's suggestion to use a paletería to promote Cole Has a Soul may have aided in the recruitment of Latine residents in the neighborhood.

Finally, the findings from this study demonstrate the importance of tailoring PB processes to meet residents' goals. I have presented two models for implementing PB, which can be useful typologies for other PB implementers. Organizers can implement an instrumental approach to PB if residents hope to promote individual development in civic capacity and political education (e.g., the radicalized students from Auraria PB). However, implementers can emphasize a relational approach to PB to be culturally responsive to people of color and develop interpersonal ties among participants that can later be leveraged for community engagement, thereby promoting collective (rather than individual) development (e.g., "coming together" in Cole Has a Soul). In the previous chapters, I identified several significant communication practices and values that differ from traditional public participation processes by incorporating fun, humor, storytelling, and celebrations. These practices reflect the cultural preferences of the participants, and PB implementers ought to be sensitive to such dispositions (especially among participants from oppressed populations), which can promote participant recruitment, participant retention, high-quality deliberations, and projects that promote social justice.

NOTE

1. In 2021, the American Society of Civil Engineers estimated it would cost $2.6 trillion over 10 years to repair and expand infrastructure to meet the nation's needs (Stark 2021).

Conclusion

Reimagining Democracy: The Prefigurative Politics of Participatory Budgeting

As I dust off the bones of your dreams
In attempts to resurrect
In hopes of finding you again
Somewhere patiently waiting
Beneath the rubble of pillaged justice
My patience painfully fading
Over how they so easily spill our blood
And choke the life out of promise
In attempt to prune us
To train the tree not to grow these branches
But we are the roots and the riverbed
The seeds that they buried
Our blood nourishing the ground
Our hearts broken, heavy

—Kerrie Joy (Warm Cookies of the Revolution 2018a)

These PB processes helped many participants dust off the bones of their dreams—dreams about the kind of community in which they wanted to live, about how they would treat each other in that community, about who belonged in that community, and about the role of citizens in democracy. PB enabled these participants to reimagine their communities and their relationships with one another, both symbolically and materially. For instance, during the Auraria PB voting outreach that opened this book, the pitch to potential voters was, "Will you help us spend $30,000?" In the end, both PB processes enabled residents to decide the physical shape of their communities (e.g., by voting on and implementing PB projects).

Yet, the communication that occurred in PB was also symbolic (e.g., affected cultural discourses). For instance, in chapter 2, I described the Auraria PB steering committee's intense deliberations about whether administrators and campus police could participate in the process. Those and other deliberations reflected fundamental questions about who has a right to be heard in a democracy: Children? People who are unhoused? Undocumented immigrants? People with criminal records? As the PB participants deliberated, they created a vision for an inclusive and just community and, simultaneously, reimagined the structure and purpose of democracy, in general. One interview, in particular, highlights such prefigurative politics—"experiments in living, laboring or provisioning that are alternatives to 'what is' and prefigure 'what could be'" (Lin et al. 2016, 302).

In the Black Freedom Summer of 2020, I interviewed Tamara, a 44-year-old Black mother and former facilitator of Cole Has a Soul. During the PB process, Tamara and I had become friends, bonding over our mutual appreciation of Southern U.S. culture (she had lived for many years in Georgia and Virginia; I grew up in North Carolina). Tamara, as I described in chapter 1, was the first organizer from the Cole neighborhood who helped me feel welcome in the process. My interview in 2020 with her was the first time we had spoken in about 18 months. What began as a relatively formal interview process quickly evolved into a conversation between friends as we reconnected with one another and commiserated about all the social upheaval occurring at the time.

Tamara perceived PB as an essential tool for navigating that social change. What was most important about PB, in her words, was that it enabled "people to move forward together." The process was about "speaking from that place of uncertainty and breaking down old systems and old ways of thinkin' and knowing and tryin' to create something beautiful together that's much more democratic and makes people feel sincerely alive." She elaborated on the importance of PB in "times like these":

> I am hoping that we do not return to the state we were in prior to this pandemic and social uprisings . . . . In times like these, we need tools and ways of rethinking and re-engaging that actually give people agency . . . . We are a part of history where old systems are breaking down. We have to have something—some tools—that people can use to re-establish, reimagine, rethink their role in society. And how we're gonna be together. We're not gonna be like we used to be.

It is the power of PB to function as a site of prefiguration that is most significant and most underappreciated. If, in the words of Kerrie Joy, we are the seeds the oppressors tried to bury, then PB (and similar processes) may be what helps us bloom into the society of Tamara's dreams: one where people feel sincerely alive.

This book opened with a discussion of numerous crises facing democracies in the Global North—especially the United States—including record-breaking income and wealth inequality, decreased trust in governing institutions, increased political apathy and support for authoritarianism, the climate crisis, corruption, militarism, and elite capture of governing systems. In this final chapter, I return to those issues to describe insights that PB (and its attendant communication practices and values) can offer about potential ways to respond to these crises. I argue that the deliberative activism performed by the PB participants functioned as prefiguration. PB's ability to foster the reimagining of both the meaning and practice of democracy is what holds the most potential for citizens and their communities. Participants imagined and created through their communication a vision for a just society, robust communities, and new models of citizenship. Much has been written about PB's effects on material inequalities, and I summarized many of those findings in the introduction of this book. Yet more has been written about PB's ability to serve as a school for democracy, which I summarized in chapter 4. What this study adds to that important body of scholarship is a focus on the discursive effects and implications of PB (i.e., the constitutive nature of communication during and surrounding PB processes): the opportunities to create and enact alternative democratic processes, as realized through participants' communication. The previous chapter focused on practical lessons learned from the two PB processes I studied. Here, I turn my attention to the theoretical (rather than the applied), discussing the insights these findings offer for public deliberation scholarship.

THE LIMITATIONS OF PARTICIPATORY BUDGETING

Before delving into those insights, it is worth noting that PB is no silver bullet for the multitude of challenges facing U.S. society. PB cannot increase the minimum wage; it cannot increase unionization rates; it cannot implement universal healthcare; it cannot undo racist gerrymandering of political districts; it cannot secure reproductive and abortion rights; it cannot enact rent control; it cannot guarantee paid parental leave; and it cannot tax the rich. To illustrate, one recent study of PB across the United States stated its major findings:

> Two major positive impacts of PB emerged from the interviews. The first is that it served to boost civic participation, strengthen community ties, and demystify

> city government, resulting in residents' increased sense of civic agency. Second, it helped identify community needs often overlooked in a city's conventional outreach process. (Roth 2022, para. 6)

Importantly, what is missing from those findings is that PB meaningfully addressed residents' overlooked needs.

Even in areas where PB can intervene, much of it—at least in the United States—remains unrealized potential. For instance, the Movement for Black Lives endorsed PB as a tool for promoting racial justice (Phelps 2016), in part because of its potential to take money away from carceral punishment and direct it toward community care. However, PB, as it has been implemented in the United States, is not especially able to defund the carceral state. In most cities, when a city council approves PB, it stipulates how much money to allocate and from which budgetary buckets the money will come. No PB process has yet taken money from the police department to be allocated for community improvement instead. In other words, local government already dictates the amount and sources of money allocated through PB before residents gather to allocate those funds, thereby limiting the process's potential impact.

Furthermore, the amounts of money allocated through PB in the United States are unable to fully address many community problems. The average North American PB process in the 2014–2015 cycle allocated $1,015,756 ($9.85 per resident) and ranged from $61,000 to $3,365,644 ($1.18 to $69.85 per resident; Hagelskamp, Rinehart, et al. 2016b). At just $1 million, the average PB process cannot build more affordable housing, expand transit service, renovate a low-income school, or fully repair a city's crumbling infrastructure. It can help—perhaps by providing more Section 8 vouchers, purchasing a municipal bus, replacing bathroom stalls in a low-income school, or repairing a portion of a sidewalk—but those are only drops in the ocean of need for many communities around the country. Surely, PB supporters can and should advocate for more money to be allocated through any single PB process, and they can try to expand the sources from which PB money is derived (e.g., so as to defund police departments). Until those efforts bear fruit, however, most PB processes in the United States will only tinker around the edges of injustice.

Some of the PB participants I interviewed in 2020 acknowledged these limitations of PB. Nicole, a 37-year-old Black woman who had recently given birth to her first child when I interviewed her, was a former facilitator of Cole Has a Soul, and she remained realistic about what that PB process accomplished:

> I still think our system is rigged. . . . My view of what is possible within democracy has widened. But, like, the systems that oppress and, like, keep things in the status quo are still there, and they're stronger than ever.

Kyle, a 29-year-old white male graduate student who had participated in Auraria PB, began as a steering committee member and eventually became a co-facilitator with Jeremiah to help implement the process. He had become disillusioned with PB's social justice potential:

> It feels like what students are really concerned with are their own financial insecurity. . . . And I don't think PB could have addressed that. And where, like, democracy is concerned, our little 3-month PB process isn't designed to sort of coordinate the kind of power that I think is necessary to effect a more democratic arrangement on campus.

A final illustration of this perception among some PB participants comes from Emma, a 20-year-old, white undergraduate student and former Auraria PB budget delegate, who had volunteered in the process as a first-year student. Emma recognized the limitations of PB but made efforts to explain that her recognition of those limitations was beneficial to her understanding of social change. To capture the nuance of her view, I quote her at length:

> I would say it [PB] definitely has shown me, like, how much power we don't have in our current system. Like, it really has highlighted to me, like, that [so much] is so far out of our hands at this point. But it also showed me what can happen if people are actually given more power in any form [in] our democracy. . . . It [PB] showed me, like, if these systems are implemented, you can have so much say in it. But also—not to be, like, a pessimist—but it showed me, like, how much people [in power] can fight against these changes being made. And so, like, it showed me, like, what people aren't able to do at this point—what restrictions we have on us currently. But I'm not taking it as from a pessimistic point of view. It definitely has inspired me to, like, fight for more of these changes, and it showed me what can be done, like what the possibilities are.

These sentiments expressed by Nicole, Kyle, and Emma, thus, are not meant to dismiss PB outright but instead to be clear-eyed about the areas in which the process succeeds and the areas in which the process falls short.

Emma's quote, most importantly, illustrates something that has been underexplored by PB scholars and returns me to the central thesis of this chapter and, indeed, this book. That is, PB's promise is not simply as a tool of "good governance" that can realize more efficient spending, more transparency about public budgets, increased trust in government, and social justice projects. Nor is PB's promise, simply, that it can function as a school for democracy, wherein participants learn civic skills for navigating existing, unjust government systems. Rather, based on my findings from this study, the most significant aspect of PB—especially in the Global North, where its effects on material inequalities have been less substantial—is that it enables participants to (re)imagine democracy and democratic practices, to resist hegemonic discourses of civic participation and citizenship. In other words, the communication that occurs during PB processes enables participants to widen their view of what is possible in democracy (to paraphrase Nicole's remark above), to illustrate how much power residents can have in creating equitable communities, and, in Emma's words, inspire and equip them to fight for that vision of a socially just world.

THE PREFIGURATIVE POLITICS OF PARTICIPATORY BUDGETING

The notion of prefigurative politics from which I draw inspiration includes three central components: "a sense of relationality borne of desire, bids for self-determination derived from lived-experience, and intersectional engagement in coalitions" (Lin et al. 2016, 303). Relationality stipulates that the relational dimensions of collective action—such as friendships, disagreements, and trust-building—are necessary components for imagining and realizing political possibilities. The component of self-determination focuses attention on the fact that restructuring power relations in society and in social movements requires that demands for change come from those most impacted by the issue. Finally, intersectional engagement in coalitions facilitates the recognition that no one is truly free from oppression until everyone is free from oppression.

All three of these components were present in the PB participants' deliberations I have described in this book. The importance of relationships was demonstrated in Cole Has a Soul through the communicative theme of "coming together" and in Auraria PB through the emphasis on fun and friendships. Self-determination was demonstrated through the ability of participants to stipulate the rules of the process and then decide which projects they wanted to fund in their communities, and it manifested in their communication through themes of promoting activism (Auraria PB) and exercising power to reimagine the community (Cole Has a Soul). Lastly, the PB participants engaged in intersectional coalitions as they struggled together to implement the processes, as demonstrated by the communication themes of inclusion and equity (Auraria PB and Cole Has a Soul) and listening to the unheard (Cole Has a Soul).

Such threads of prefiguration have been woven throughout this book, and here, I magnify them by drawing attention to participants' quotes that illustrate the prefigurative communication that occurred during the PB processes. Some of these quotes have appeared in previous chapters, but by collecting them here, I intend to emphasize the transformative potential of these PB processes.

First, some participants explicitly spoke about how, during PB, they both imagined and practiced new possibilities for interaction. Riley, a white woman and graduate student, was a former budget delegate in Auraria PB. She had taken a leading role in developing the food pantry project that evolved into a Campus Kitchen described in chapter 2. In addition to food insecurity, Riley was passionate about addressing climate change, and she expressed that decision-making models such as PB were necessary for humanity's survival in a rapidly warming climate:

> I do personally believe that if we don't get serious about practicing decision making with each other, there is no way that our generation is, like, going to have a chance to create the large-scale change that we need to, like, ensure—or even have a chance at—like, a livable future for a lot of people. Right now, the world is not livable for a lot of people, and so I think that, like, increasing access to this model [PB] is really a practice of survival. . . . I think that processes like these help us map, like, when and why we might be giving away our power.

In another example from Auraria PB, Michelle was a 30-year-old white woman who co-facilitated the process with Jeremiah, and she expressed the importance of PB in helping students imagine possibilities. "The students," she said, "thought big and had no limit to their ideas. There's something really inspiring about students tackling big ideas." Jason was a 48-year-old Black father who served both as a budget delegate and a steering committee member for Cole Has a Soul. In an interview, I asked Jason how he felt about Cole Has a Soul being implemented independent of Denver's city government. His response emphasized the self-determination enabled through PB:

> We were allowed to come up with our own plan and implement it without some biases they may have had to enact from a city level. We had a fresh slate to do it the way we saw fit. Maybe some of their [city government] resources for outreach could have helped. But all in all, I'm happy we did it [PB] without [city support].

Other PB participants remarked that the PB process restored their hope and faith in democracy. Elsewhere in my interview with Jason, he stated that participating in the process "restored my faith in democracy a little bit. It's kinda more like what a democratic process should look like, where we've gotten kind of away from that." Taylor was a 48-year-old white woman who served as a budget delegate in Cole Has a Soul. She remarked, simply, "It [PB] gave me a little bit more faith in it [democracy]." Lastly, Luke was a 20-year-old Black undergraduate who was a first-year student when he participated in Auraria PB as a budget delegate. He offered in his interview:

> It [PB] gave me more hope. . . . It exposed me to, like, a process that is, in my opinion, much more democratic than the systems that we have in place now . . . . And it made me reflect on our current institutions, and how their democracy, in my opinion, is a really weak democracy.

Significantly, all of these quotes came from the second round of interviews I conducted in the summer of 2020. Despite the COVID-19 pandemic and the nightly police riots happening across the country, these participants still derived from their experiences in PB a fragile hope for democracy.

As a final illustration of the prefiguration that occurred through PB participants' communication, some interviewees remarked on the opportunities that PB enabled to challenge the hegemonic, oppressive status quo. Luke explained, "PB is a really powerful process. And it puts power in the hands of masses of the community. I think it would strongly change and disrupt, like, social order." Nicole also talked about the opportunities PB provides for people to make structural changes:

> Yes, it [PB] is an opportunity for folks to have direct democracy. But like, there's also an opportunity for people to make a social change, or some other type of structural change, or impact their community in an important way beyond just building things—by, like, changing people's lives. And I want to see more of that in the conversation on PB.

It is that potential for PB to change people's lives (beyond just funding projects) that is the crux of my argument about the importance of communication in PB to prefigure social justice.

Earlier in this chapter, I explained how, despite its promise, PB's implementation in the United States has not yet meaningfully addressed material inequalities. Instead, what is most significant about the process is that it creates discursive possibilities to imagine and create just relationships. As PB participants deliberate, they reimagine the social structure of their communities, how to relate to one another, how to engage in shared governance, and the role of citizens in their communities. Simultaneously, PB offers a chance to enact those new visions of a beloved community (King, Jr. 1964) as participants modify their communication practices to realize those visions. Such discursive transformations were illustrated in chapter 4, where I described participants' changes in civic habits after participating in PB.

The potential of PB, however, is only as good as its implementation. The process can be co-opted by elites and fail to promote social justice. Readers, therefore, should revisit the prior chapter for practical suggestions about how to avoid these pitfalls and structure PB so that it succeeds in providing discursive opportunities for participants to prefigure social justice. Given the importance of communication in PB processes (and other directly deliberative democratic innovations) for navigating prefigurative politics, the insights I have offered provide important lessons about communication activism for social justice.

IMPLICATIONS FOR COMMUNICATION ACTIVISM

Deliberative activism—one type of communication activism—occurs when people engage in social activism to institutionalize public deliberation processes (Fung 2005). Deliberative activism is unique from other forms of activism because it emphasizes dialogic encounters through listening, reasoning, and a readiness to transform one's opinions on the part of activists, wherein they pursue ethical commitments of responsiveness and reflexivity in their activism (Jennstål and Öberg 2019). Thus, deliberative activists typically offer justifications for their views and actions, and they are willing to engage in dialogue with whom they disagree (Talisse 2005). Deliberative activists strive to achieve these commitments by incorporating deliberative methods into their in-group communication, and they act under the assumption that opponents are willing to engage in good-faith deliberation, until they prove otherwise (Fung 2005).

The organizers of TMHS sought to use the PB processes as deliberative activism, with the goal of launching a campaign to advocate for PB's institutionalization following the conclusion of TMHS. My findings offer a nuanced picture of that approach. First, the use of PB *as* deliberative activism (rather than a traditional grassroots advocacy campaign with deliberative elements) was not especially successful in achieving the organizers' policy goals. Some evidence showed that the programmatic spending provided through Cole Has a Soul—a relative rarity for PB processes in North America (Hagelskamp, Rinehart, et al. 2016)—promoted community resiliency (e.g., the garden beds as a resource for nutrition and community bonding during the COVID-19 pandemic). Cole Has a Soul interviewees indicated that the process increased social ties in the neighborhood, and several former PB participants remained involved in activist work after the process's conclusion. One interviewee even reported that the deliberative activism she experienced through PB transformed her approach to other forms of public participation, for she strived to make those other forums more deliberative and participatory than they were previously. The PB processes, thus, were relatively successful in achieving cultural and discursive changes.

However, the bulk of the evidence suggests that PB was not an especially effective tool for achieving *policy* change. Neither PB process established a robust and active political constituency that was dedicated to advocating for PB's adoption. Former participants of Auraria PB launched an advocacy campaign, but it was hamstrung by a lack of participation from former PB participants and other students, and it was ultimately unsuccessful in securing PB's institutionalization. No one with whom I spoke from Cole Has a Soul engaged in activism to convince Denver officials to adopt PB, and the city's eventual approval of the process appeared to have little correlation with any advocacy from Cole residents. Thus, the findings indicate that engaging in a public deliberation process as deliberative activism, instead of a typical activist community organizing campaign, may not be especially effective in achieving policy change. The resources required to conduct PB were substantial, and many participants from Auraria PB and Cole Has a Soul expressed feeling burned out or exhausted by the end of their respective processes. They were not prepared to engage in an advocacy campaign after the conclusion of the PB processes.

Instead of limiting the concept of deliberative activism to actions promoting policy change (i.e., institutionalizing public deliberation processes), this study suggests that deliberative activism can also serve as a form of prefigurative politics. TMHS demonstrated the ability of deliberative activism to intersect with prefigurative politics because of its emphasis on developing intersectional public relationships and self-determination rooted in the experiences of PB participants. Thus, deliberative activism may not be understood only as social activism meant to intervene in public policy but also as social activism meant to intervene discursively. The deliberative activism of TMHS, as a form of prefiguration, sought to imagine "what could be" for local governance systems and the relationships among residents. The success of TMHS in its prefiguration was demonstrated by participant comments about the processes' ability to restore their hope and faith in democracy, with some commenting that PB revealed how local governance *should* operate, as well as reports of increased solidarity with other local residents.

Therefore, deliberative activism may not only be a pro forma commitment to ethical ideals of deliberative communication to achieve policy change. Even when it falls short of desired policy goals, deliberative activism can still create spaces of possibility, where activists transform social and power relations through their in-group deliberative practices. In this way, just as a new prefigurative politics exists within the context of people's struggle for liberation rather than a utopian ideal (Lin et al. 2016), the prefiguration of deliberative activism occurs within the group's communication as they create relationships and determine collectively a common interest. These internal transformations may be at a smaller scale than the policy changes that other deliberative scholars have imagined as they theorized deliberative activism, but such transformations are still impactful for the individuals who experience them, especially those from oppressed populations who struggle for liberation, dignity, and justice, as these findings have shown.

Another implication of this study relates to the scholarship of PB when it is implemented as a grassroots form of deliberative activism. Much of the public deliberation field is driven by a relatively small cadre of elite experts, both in its application and its study (Button and Ryfe 2005; Lee 2011). In practice, PB, as one specific type of public deliberation process, does not differ from the broader public deliberation field, with few PB processes implemented because of grassroots demand. Instead, most PB processes in the United States are implemented in a top-down manner, with powerful elites deciding to grant some power to non-elite citizens (Hagelskamp, Schleifer, et al. 2016). This factor has contributed to concerns among PB scholars that a globalized version of PB is being implemented in the United States and around the world, a form of the process that has been divorced from its radical, socially just, participatory origins in Brazil's Workers' Party (Baiocchi and Ganuza 2017; Goldfrank 2012; Leighninger and Rinehart 2016).

TMHS offers a unique perspective in the U.S. context because of its grassroots nature. It was implemented with minimal support from local governing institutions, reflecting the desires of a coalition of nonprofits to explore the possibility of a socially just way of allocating public resources. Although the general model that TMHS organizers followed was similar to the globalized form of PB, its explicit commitments to equity—a rarity for North American PB processes (Leighninger & Rinehart, 2016)—and culturally responsive design were closer to the grassroots origins of Brazilian PB than the highly technocratic approach implemented by some municipalities. Therefore, TMHS provides insights into the possibility of adapting PB to local contexts in the United States and its ability to advance social justice.

At least two benefits were derived from the grassroots approach of TMHS. First, in Auraria PB, several students became radicalized because of administrators' resistance to the students' self-determination. These PB participants became active in social justice campaigns, joining with others in the collective pursuit of social change. This finding supports the possibility that the implementation of PB can spur broader movements for participatory democracy, as happened in the Global South and Spain (Baiocchi and Ganuza 2017). Second, in Cole Has a Soul, residents reported that they increased their political self-efficacy. They felt more confident in their ability to take care of their neighbors, whether that was through mutual aid or political activism. This development was especially significant because of the COVID-19 pandemic, and the fact that, according to interviewees, government actors only provided limited support to vulnerable populations in Cole to cope with the public health and economic fallout of the pandemic.

However, TMHS also offered several cautionary tales about the possibility of grassroots PB initiatives in the United States and their ability to advance social equity. Because the PB processes were independent of governing institutions, they were relatively small in scope. Without a major funding source, such as what is available through public funds, TMHS organizers lacked the ability to fund large projects and implement a robust process. They had minimal ability to conduct outreach, maintain engagement, and research the potential effects and costs of PB projects. These factors limited the equity goals of the processes, as organizers sometimes struggled to reach people from marginalized communities, and the approved projects only scratched the surface of the deep, structural inequalities those community members experience.

Lastly, because of the independence of TMHS, PB participants were not able to develop much knowledge about navigating government bureaucracy, especially in Cole Has a Soul. This facet hampered PB participants' development as participatory citizens (Westheimer 2015; Westheimer and Kahne 2004) because participants had few opportunities to learn what departments perform what roles in local government—or on their university campus, in the case of Auraria PB. If one purpose of PB is to be a "school of democracy," many TMHS participants finished the process with little new knowledge about which levers in governing systems they could pull to benefit their communities, which may also explain why TMHS failed to secure policy change to adopt PB permanently.

COMMUNICATING FOR SOCIAL JUSTICE IN PARTICIPATORY BUDGETING

Social justice communication is promoted when all people possess the maximum freedom to talk about who they are, what they do, and how to envision their future in an ongoing process (Swartz 2006). The findings in this study illustrate that TMHS mostly met these goals by incorporating diverse residents and granting them the power to make collective decisions rooted in principles of equity and the all-affected-parties principle.

External and Internal Exclusion

People can be excluded from public participation in two ways: internally or externally. External exclusion refers to people being left out (un)intentionally from public participation, such as via backdoor brokering and lobbying, the inaccessibility of forums, media influence, political influence through campaign donations, and economic intimidation (Young 2002). External exclusion disproportionately affects oppressed populations because they typically lack the means to participate and/or are stigmatized because of their social location and are therefore prevented from participating in political spaces.

Internal exclusion refers to people participating in a public engagement process being prevented from influencing other participants and/or outcomes of the process, such as through process rules that allow particular ways of communicating and prohibit others (Young 2002). Again, internal exclusion disproportionately affects historically oppressed populations because they may lack the cultural resources to communicate in the approved way and/or will experience stigma for speaking from their social standpoint. Internal and external exclusion are significant barriers to social justice because of their effects on oppressed populations. TMHS offered several findings related to overcoming these obstacles.

External Exclusion

Both PB processes employed targeted and network-based recruitment strategies, with modest success in terms of demographic representation among PB participants. Latine representation in Cole Has a Soul was low, reinforcing other research findings that show targeted outreach is less successful with that population than with other minorities (Esterling et al., 2015; Fung & Lee, 2008). However, Latine participation in Auraria PB was representative of the student body, perhaps because language barriers were not as severe on the Auraria Campus as they were in the Cole neighborhood; all students had to demonstrate an adequate level of English-language proficiency to attend school at Auraria. Other ways that TMHS participants addressed external exclusion were by offering interpreter services at public events, providing food at meetings, and allowing anyone to submit project ideas (regardless of age, citizenship, or criminal record). Voting in the PB processes was more inclusive than typical government voting processes, with non-citizens and people with criminal records allowed to vote. Both PB processes also allowed people under the age of 18 to vote, demonstrating to young people their importance for making informed public decisions.

Internal Exclusion

Public deliberation processes can incorporate several strategies for addressing internal exclusion. First, they can promote an ethos of deliberative reciprocity (Ryfe and Stalsburg 2012), which sets standards for practices of mutual respect, with participants who disagree with one another providing each other equal recognition of their justification processes (e.g., reason-giving, storytelling, bargaining, and/or compromising). In addition to deliberative reciprocity, public participation processes can incorporate mutual culture recognition and acceptance of cultural diversity to address issues of inequality (McBride 2005; Young 2002). These suggestions emphasize the importance of public acknowledgment and recognition of cultural difference, including requiring participants to demonstrate pluralist openness and willingness to listen to diverse viewpoints (Habermas 1994).

In Auraria PB, Jeremiah promoted an ethos of deliberative reciprocity through skillful facilitation. He often invited people to participate in meetings and frequently repeated that PB participants needed to exercise their autonomy for the process to be successful. However, at least among the steering committee, none of the students ever led or facilitated a meeting; instead, Jeremiah offered deliberative reciprocity by regularly checking in with individual members to see if they had any contributions during meetings. Steering committee members and budget delegates in Auraria PB also demonstrated a willingness to respond to cultural differences, such as when they debated whether to allow security personnel and administrators to participate in the PB process. Although some students saw no problems with the security personnel, a majority ultimately supported other students who, because of their race/ethnicity, experienced negative interactions with security personnel. Another example involved the budget delegates' project eligibility matrix, which encouraged the consideration of minority experiences on campus (e.g., illustrative examples of the appropriateness of a Muslim prayer room project and an ADA-compliant ramp to access campus buildings).

However, much of the actual talk in Auraria PB reflected a rational, calm consideration of ideas that adhered to a hegemonic, middle-class, white deliberative ideal. Few stories or culturally significant ways of speaking broke through this hegemonic ideal; yet, the moments of humor and fun I documented during deliberations were an important deviation from that norm and made PB distinct from other public participation forums (e.g., city council meetings, school board meetings, or government committee hearings).

In contrast, participants in Cole Has a Soul incorporated several culturally significant communicative practices, including "coming together" and listening to the unheard. Certainly, these values and their corresponding communication practices can be found in U.S. American discourse of civic engagement writ large. However, I argue for the importance of these terms because of PB participants' frequent repetition of them and because it was precisely these forms of speaking that appeared, to me (a white, middle-class, male researcher), although not unintelligible, at least of minimal importance for a PB process. These cultural communication values combatted internal exclusion by centering the concerns of Cole residents, who, disproportionately, were people of color, low income, and/or spoke a language other than English. The specific communication practices that manifested from these deliberative values included greetings, demonstrations of care for the Other, and celebrations.

The findings from both PB processes complement the equity-driven model of PB (Pape and Lerner 2016). The equity-driven model of PB identifies process and communication rules for PB that could advance social justice, but it does not identify specific communication practices that also support that goal. This study has identified multiple ways of addressing internal exclusion, thereby promoting social equity, through communication practices. Future studies could explore if the values of "coming together" and listening to the unheard—along with their attendant practices of greetings, demonstrations of care for the Other, and celebrations—are significant for promoting participation from historically oppressed populations in other locales. In addition to addressing internal and external exclusion, the communicative ways participants navigate tensions between the values of equity and equality impact PB's relationship to social justice.

Tensions between Equity and Equality

Many public deliberation processes experience tensions between the values of equality and equity, where equality means "an approach to deliberative fairness that emphasizes the need to treat all deliberators the same, regardless of their power (or lack thereof) outside of the deliberative forum" (Abdullah, Karpowitz, and Raphael 2016, 1), whereas equity means "taking into account the advantages and disadvantages that have shaped participants' experiences, which may require treating participants differently in order to create conditions that achieve fair deliberation and decisions" (Abdullah, Karpowitz, and Raphael 2016, 1). On its face, it appears that deliberative practitioners cannot achieve one without violating the other.

How deliberative participants navigate these tensions is important for assessing a process's ability to promote social justice. For example, "the historically marginalized are often drawn to politics more by a hunger for more equitable policies than for opportunities to deliberate" (Abdullah, Karpowitz, and Raphael 2016, 2). Participants from historically marginalized communities—people who often are overworked, underpaid, and struggle with the material impacts of racist, classist, and sexist social structures—may be less interested in taking time to deliberate with neighbors if there is not a definitive opportunity to improve their conditions.

TMHS's successes in encouraging participation from oppressed communities likely were because it constituted a form of communication activism for social justice. Participants perceived an opportunity to make a meaningful difference in their communities both through the funds that were allocated and because participation was supposed to promote policy change to institutionalize PB. Participants often remarked that the opportunity to make material differences in their communities was one of the most rewarding aspects of TMHS and motivated them to volunteer in the process. Additionally, the PB participants perceived the independence of TMHS from governing institutions—because it constituted deliberative activism—as a benefit. TMHS participants, especially those from oppressed communities, were more trusting of their fellow neighbors/students/activists than they were of local government and school administrators, which contributed to their participation in the PB processes.

Furthermore, Moscrop and Warren (2016) argued that the extent to which a deliberative process is democratic depends on levels of equality and equity in the process, with equality meaning equal opportunities for participation and equity provided in processes and outcomes. Significantly, Auraria PB did not provide equal opportunities for participation in its process, as only students could serve on the steering committee, as budget delegates, and vote in the PB process. The students concluded that to achieve their goal of equity, they needed to reduce the potential influence of powerful stakeholders on campus (e.g., administrators and staff) in certain parts of the PB process. Although Moscrop and Warren might contend that the Auraria PB steering committee's decision limited the democratic nature of the PB process, participants believed that limiting participation to students increased Auraria PB's legitimacy. Therefore, future studies can further explore the appropriateness of limiting participation in PB at various phases of the process and that limitation's relationship to social justice outcomes.

This development from Auraria PB demonstrates that the participants were aware that dominant, hegemonic discourses are coercive forces that infuse all social relations, and those forces are not miraculously eliminated by entering a deliberative space. Thus, deliberative practitioners seek to impose rules and structures in their deliberation events to counteract these pervasive forces (Curato et al. 2017). In Auraria PB, participants navigated this tension between equal opportunity to participate and equitable opportunities to participate by engaging in meta-deliberation about who would be involved in the process and why they ought to be included or excluded. However, they did not engage in much meta-deliberation about the rules for budget delegate deliberations regarding project proposals.

In contrast, Cole Has a Soul participants engaged in meta-deliberation about the budget delegates' rules for project eligibility, explicitly creating an operational definition of "equity" and determining how that concept would be relevant to their PB process, and both Auraria PB and Cole Has a Soul made "equity" one criterion for the development of project proposals. Lastly, experienced African American community organizers coordinated, implemented, and facilitated both processes. These facilitators were dedicated to advancing social justice and ensured that concerns over equity remained on the minds of PB participants. All of these strategies aided in the navigation of tensions between equity and equality.

In their discussion of the relationship between equality and equity in public deliberation processes, Moscrop and Warren (2016) contended that, ideally, equality in deliberation enables equity in outcomes, saying:

> Equal distribution of empowerments such as votes, rights, and opportunities for voice should enable citizens to press for equity, to place equity claims on the agenda, and to deliberate about what equity requires in many different kinds of locations that comprise collectives of interdependent equals. (2–3)

However, the findings of this study demonstrate the inverse of that logic: equity would contribute to equality. Some people were barred from participating in the PB processes because the organizers wanted to address the historic legacies of racism, divestment, and disempowerment that had been occurring in these communities. TMHS participants favored some parties over others *in* PB in an effort to place them on equal footing *outside of* PB. Thus, equity in the distribution of empowerment in the deliberative space of PB sought to promote equity in outcomes that would contribute to equality. TMHS participants from oppressed communities would experience personal development of their civic capacities and fund projects that would provide material benefits to disadvantaged groups, contributing to material equality of resources. This attitude of TMHS organizers and participants was closer to the equity-driven model of PB (Pape and Lerner 2016) than it was to Moscrop's and Warren's (2016) ideal deliberative scenario. These findings, therefore, offer important insight into the deliberative practices that place values of equity at the fore to contribute to greater social equality.

Lastly, deliberation practitioners often pursue an all-affected-interests principle for inclusion (Fung 2013; Moscrop and Warren 2016; Young 2002). This principle holds that "if one is affected or potentially affected by collectivities, including structural locations within them, one should have a claim to voice in crafting agendas and a say within deliberative processes" (Moscrop and Warren 2016, 5). The all-affected-interests principle requires that those designing and participating in deliberative systems must consistently ask questions such as "What affects me or us most?" "What is most important to me or us?" and "How do those effects compare to the effects felt by others?"

This study demonstrated that the all-affected-interests principle was employed most frequently during budget delegate deliberations, with delegates asking repeatedly who would benefit from project ideas and how the project ideas aligned with their goals of promoting equity and community development. However, the all-affected-interests principle was also occasionally present when steering committee members deliberated about the rules of the PB process, such as when Auraria PB steering committee members discussed rules about who could participate in each phase of the process.

Notably, this value did not appear to be significant during the idea collection or voting phases of either PB process. During idea collection, Auraria PB pursued targeted outreach, which involved some consideration about which parties were affected disproportionately by existing power structures, but there was little explicit discussion about whether and why those groups constituted marginalized stakeholders. In Cole Has a Soul, the steering committee simply tried to reach as many people in the neighborhood as they could. In my observations of people submitting project ideas and voting, participants rarely were prompted to consider all-affected-interests. By incorporating my earlier recommendation of adopting structured idea collection events, PB practitioners could expand explicit consideration of all-affected-interests into that phase of PB, because residents could collaborate to identify issues impacting the community and thoroughly consider how possible projects would affect different stakeholders in that community.

CONCLUSION

This book opened with examples illustrating the public participation crisis facing the United States, driven, in part, by decreased trust in government institutions, increased social inequalities, and oppressive rules that make participating in civic affairs difficult or impossible for people who, historically, have been marginalized, oppressed, or excluded from civic engagement. The poem that opened this chapter illustrated the spirit of hope, perseverance, and possibility that activists maintain, despite those oppressive conditions.

The PB processes detailed in this study may offer the reader a fragile hope that participatory and deliberative forms of government can inject the soul of the people into the machine of electoral politics. Perhaps the most significant finding of this study was the discursive, cultural shift to collective values among participants as they (re)imagined democracy, which can have long-lasting and widespread implications for how people live and perform the public work of civic engagement. PB can humanize the necessary decision-making of collective action, as deliberators come to see the Other as a whole being rather than simply a cog in the machine of unjust social structures.

However, PB is not a silver bullet to all of these challenges, as evidenced by the participants who believed TMHS failed to advance social justice. This study, therefore, has offered insights into the boundaries of PB: when it can be successful, and when it may be an inappropriate model for social change, such as deliberative activism to achieve policy change.

Formal paths to public participation in the United States have been under attack for decades, as evidenced by the various forms of (racist) voter suppression, including voter purges, voter identification laws, the Electoral

College, and gerrymandering, among other strategies. Many of these efforts have existed since the founding of the United States, and they have only continued, and, in some instances, expanded into the twenty-first century. Activists, however, have also sustained their grassroots calls for social transformation to oppose the elite capture of democratic institutions. In recent years, social movements promoting antiracism; climate justice; gun control; universal health care; Indigenous sovereignty; lesbian, gay, bisexual, transgender, and queer rights; anti-imperial policies of perpetual war-making; working-class solidarity; and many more have been doing the difficult, life-affirming work of (re)imagining democracy in the United States. The United States stands at the threshold of a revitalized democracy, and PB offers a form of public governance that, when implemented effectively, realizes participatory and deliberative democracy that ensures all people live a life of dignity.

References

"2018 Doomsday Clock Statement." 2018. Bulletin of the Atomic Scientists. https://thebulletin.org/sites/default/files/2018%20Doomsday%20Clock%20Statement.pdf.

Aaronson, Trevor. n.d. "Alphabet Boys." https://alphabetboys.xyz/.

Abdullah, Carolyne, Christopher F. Karpowitz, and Chad Raphael. 2016. "Equality and Equity in Deliberation: Introduction to the Special Issue." *Journal of Public Deliberation* 12 (2): Article 1. https://doi.org/10.16997/jdd.253.

Abramowitz, Alan. 2010. *The Disappearing Center: Engaged Citizens, Polarization, and American Democracy*. New Haven, CT: Yale University Press.

Adams, Char. 2021. "Cities Vowed in 2020 to Cut Police Funding — but Budgets Expanded in 2021." *NBC News*, December 28, 2021. https://www.nbcnews.com/news/nbcblk/cities-vowed-2020-cut-police-funding-budgets-expanded-2021-rcna9864.

Agar, Michael H. 2008. *The Professional Stranger: An Informal Introduction to Ethnography*. 2nd ed. Bingley, UK: Emerald Group Publishing Limited.

Ahmed, Sara. 2012. *On Being Included: Racism and Diversity in Institutional Life*. Durham, NC: Duke University Press.

Alim, H. Samy, and Geneva Smitherman. 2012. *Articulate While Black: Barack Obama, Language, and Race in the U.S.* New York, NY: Oxford University Press.

Almasan, Oana. 2017. "Participation as Experiential Factor in Democratic Emancipation: Case of Cluj Napoca, Romania." *Pedagogika Społeczna* 3 (65): 85–98.

Alves, Mariana Lopes, and Giovanni Allegretti. 2012. "(In)Stability, a Key Element to Understand Participatory Budgeting: Discussing Portuguese Cases." *Journal of Public Deliberation* 8 (2): Article 3. https://doi.org/10.16997/jdd.147.

Auraria Participatory Budgeting and Participatory Budgeting Project. n.d. "Auraria Participatory Budgeting Budget Delegate Guide."

Baiocchi, Gianpaolo, and Ernesto Ganuza. 2017. *Popular Democracy: The Paradox of Participation*. Stanford, CA: Stanford University Press.

Baiocchi, Gianpaolo, Patrick Heller, Shubham Chaudhuri, and Marcelo Kunrath Silva. 2006. “Evaluating Empowerment: Participatory Budgeting in Brazilian Municipalities.” In *Empowerment in Practice: From Analysis to Implementation*, edited by Ruth Alsop, Mette Frost Bertelsen, and Jeremy Holland, 95–124. World Bank. http://documents.worldbank.org/curated/en/286191468315851702/pdf/350320Empowerm1ctice01OFFICIAL0USE1.pdf.

Bakhtin, Mikhael M. 1984. *Problems of Dostoevsky's Poetics*. Edited and Translated by Caryl Emerson. Minneapolis: University of Minnesota Press.

———. 1986. *Speech Genres and Other Late Essays*. Translated by Vern W. McGee. Austin: University of Texas Press.

———. 1993. *Toward a Philosophy of the Act*. Edited by Vadim Liapunov and Michael Holquist. Translated by Vadim Liapunov. Austin: University of Texas Press.

Barge, J. Kevin. 2002. “Enlarging the Meaning of Group Deliberation: From Discussion to Dialogue.” In *New Directions in Group Communication*, edited by Lawrence R. Frey, 159–78. Thousand Oaks, CA: Sage.

Beaty, Kevin. 2018. “Cole Neighborhood Will Spend $30,000 on Exactly What Its Residents Want.” *Denverite*, December 3, 2018. https://denverite.com/2018/12/03/cole-warm-cookies-participatory-budgeting/.

Bhatnagar, Deepti, Animesh Rathore, Magüi Moreno Torres, and Parameets Kanungo. 2003. *Participatory Budgeting in Brazil*. World Bank. https://siteresources.worldbank.org/INTEMPOWERMENT/Resources/14657_Partic-Budg-Brazil-web.pdf.

Black, Laura W. 2008. “Deliberation, Storytelling, and Dialogic Moments.” *Communication Theory* 18 (1): 93–116. https://doi.org/10.1111/j.1468-2885.2007.00315.x.

Blackman, Amanda. 2019. “Participatory Budgeting Addressing Student Needs.” *The Sentry*, February 27. http://cu-sentry.com/2019/02/27/participatory-budgeting-addressing-student-needs/.

Bohman, James F. 1990. “Communication, Ideology, and Democratic Theory.” *American Political Science Review* 84 (1): 93–109. https://doi.org/10.2307/1963631.

Bourdieu, Pierre. 1990. *The Logic of Practice*. Translated by Richard Nice. Stanford, CA: Stanford University Press.

Brenan, Megan. 2021. “Americans' Trust in Government Remains Low.” *Gallup* (blog). September 30, 2021. https://news.gallup.com/poll/355124/americans-trust-government-remains-low.aspx.

Buchanan, Larry, Quoctrung Bui, and Jugal K. Patel. 2020. “Black Lives Matter May Be the Largest Movement in U.S. History.” *The New York Times*, July 3. https://www.nytimes.com/interactive/2020/07/03/us/george-floyd-protests-crowd-size.html.

Burkhalter, Stephanie, John Gastil, and Todd Kelshaw. 2002. “A Conceptual Definition and Theoretical Model of Public Deliberation in Small Face-to-Face Groups.” *Communication Theory* 12 (4): 398–422. https://doi.org/10.1111/j.1468-2885.2002.tb00276.x.

Button, Mark. 2005. “Arendt, Rawls, and Public Reason.” *Social Theory and Practice* 31 (2): 257–80. https://doi.org/10.5840/soctheorpract200531211.

Button, Mark, and David Michael Ryfe. 2005. "What Can We Learn from the Practice of Deliberative Democracy?" In *The Deliberative Democracy Handbook: Strategies for Effective Civic Engagement in the Twenty-First Century*, edited by John Gastil and Peter Levine, 20–33. San Francisco, CA: Jossey Bass.

Cabannes, Yves. 2004. "Participatory Budgeting: A Significant Contribution to Participatory Democracy." *Environment and Urbanization* 16 (1): 27–46. https://doi.org/10.1177/095624780401600104.

Carbaugh, Donal A. 1989. *Talking American: Cultural Discourses on Donahue*. Communication and Information Science. Norwood, NJ: Ablex.

———. 2007. "Ethnography of Communication." In *The Blackwell International Encyclopedia of Communication*, edited by Wolfgang Donsbach. New York, NY: Blackwell Reference Online.

Carbaugh, Donal A., and David Boromisza-Habashi. 2015. "Ethnography of Communication." In *The International Encyclopedia of Language and Social Interaction*, edited by Karen Tracy, 537–52. Malden, MA: Wiley-Blackwell.

Carlson, Jake. 2017. "Expanding the Imagination of Democracy: PB in Paris." *Participatory Budgeting Project* (blog), June 13. https://www.participatorybudgeting.org/pbparis/.

The Center for Urban Development Studies. 2005. *Assessment of Participatory Budgeting in Brazil*. Washington, DC: Inter-American Development Bank. https://publications.iadb.org/publications/english/document/Assessment-of-Participatory-Budgeting-in-Brazil.pdf.

Chafe, William Henry. 1981. *Civilities and Civil Rights: Greensboro, North Carolina, and the Black Struggle for Freedom*. New York, NY: Oxford University Press.

Christens, Brian D. 2010. "Public Relationship Building in Grassroots Community Organizing: Relational Intervention for Individual and Systems Change." *Journal of Community Psychology* 38 (7): 886–900. https://doi.org/10.1002/jcop.20403.

Christiano, Thomas. 1997. "The Significance of Public Deliberation." In *Deliberative Democracy: Essays on Reason and Politic*, edited by James Bohman and William Rehg, 243–78. Cambridge, MA: MIT Press.

Chung, Jean. 2021. "Voting Rights in the Era of Mass Incarceration: A Primer." The Sentencing Project. https://www.sentencingproject.org/publications/felony-disenfranchisement-a-primer/.

City of Boston. 2022. "Youth Lead the Change." Boston.Gov. June 7, 2022. https://www.boston.gov/departments/youth-engagement-and-employment/youth-lead-change.

Clark, Susan, and Woden Teachout. 2012. *Slow Democracy: Rediscovering Community, Bringing Decision Making Back Home*. White River Junction, VT: Chelsea Green.

Cohen, Matthew, Daniel Schugurensky, and Arnim Wiek. 2015. "Citizenship Education through Participatory Budgeting: The Case of Bioscience High School in Phoenix, Arizona." *Curriculum and Teaching* 30 (2): 5–26. https://doi.org/10.7459/ct/30.2.02.

Collins, Patricia Hill. 2000. *Black Feminist Thought: Knowledge, Consciousness, and the Politics of Empowerment*. 2nd ed. New York, NY: Routledge.

Conquergood, Dwight. 1985. "Performing as a Moral Act: Ethical Dimensions of the Ethnography of Performance." *Literature in Performance* 5 (2): 1–13. https://doi.org/10.1080/10462938509391578.

"The COVID Racial Data Tracker." n.d. The COVID Tracking Project. Accessed August 1, 2023. https://covidtracking.com/race.

Curato, Nicole, John S. Dryzek, Selen A. Ercan, Carolyn M. Hendriks, and Simon Niemeyer. 2017. "Twelve Key Findings in Deliberative Democracy Research." *Dædalus* 146 (3): 28–38. https://doi.org/10.1162/DAED_a_00444.

De Souza, Rebecca. 2023. "Communication, Carcerality, and Neoliberal Stigma: The Case of Hunger and Food Assistance in the United States." *Journal of Applied Communication Research* 51 (3): 225–42. https://doi.org/10.1080/00909882.2022.2079954.

DelReal, Jose A. 2014. "Voter Turnout in 2014 Was the Lowest since WWII." *Washington Post*, November 10. https://www.washingtonpost.com/news/post-politics/wp/2014/11/10/voter-turnout-in-2014-was-the-lowest-since-wwii/.

DeSilver, Drew. 2018. "U.S. Trails Most Developed Countries in Voter Turnout." *Pew Research Center* (blog), May 21. https://www.pewresearch.org/fact-tank/2018/05/21/u-s-voter-turnout-trails-most-developed-countries/.

Dilanian, Ken, and Laura Strickler. 2022. "Theft from the Covid Relief Plan Known as PPP Was Even Worse than We Thought." *NBC News*, March 28. https://www.nbcnews.com/politics/justice-department/biggest-fraud-generation-looting-covid-relief-program-known-ppp-n1279664.

DiNardi, Gaetano. 2022. "PPP Loan Fraud: The Scam That Ruined America's Economy." *Aura*, June 5. https://www.aura.com/learn/ppp-loan-fraud.

Druckman, James N., and Kjersten R. Nelson. 2003. "Framing and Deliberation: How Citizens' Conversations Limit Elite Influence." *American Journal of Political Science* 47 (4): 729–45. https://doi.org/10.1111/1540-5907.00051.

Dryzek, John S. 2010. *Foundations and Frontiers of Deliberative Governance*. New York, NY: Oxford University Press.

Esterling, Kevin M., Archon Fung, and Taeku Lee. 2015. "How Much Disagreement Is Good for Democratic Deliberation?" *Political Communication* 32 (4): 529–51. https://doi.org/10.1080/10584609.2014.969466.

Farrell, Thomas B. 1993. *Norms of Rhetorical Culture*. New Haven, CT: Yale University Press.

Fendt, Lindsay. 2019. "Thanks in Part to Some Weird Art, Denverites Will Get to Decide How to Spend Taxpayer Money." *Denverite*, October 9. https://denverite.com/2019/10/09/thanks-in-part-to-some-weird-art-denverites-will-get-to-decide-how-to-spend-taxpayer-money/.

Fiske, John. 1991. "Writing Ethnographies: Contribution to a Dialogue." *Quarterly Journal of Speech* 77 (3): 330–35. https://doi.org/10.1080/00335639109383964.

Foa, Roberto Stefan, and Yascha Mounk. 2016. "The Democratic Disconnect." *Journal of Democracy* 27 (3): 5–17. https://doi.org/10.1353/jod.2016.0049.

Forester, John F. 1999. *The Deliberative Practitioner: Encouraging Participatory Planning Processes*. Cambridge, MA: MIT Press.

Foss, Sonja K., and Cindy L. Griffin. 1995. "Beyond Persuasion: A Proposal for an Invitational Rhetoric." *Communication Monographs* 62 (1): 2–18. https://doi.org/10.1080/03637759509376345.

Foucault, Michel. 1972. *The Archaeology of Knowledge*. Translated by A. M. Sheridan Smith. 1st American ed. New York, NY: Pantheon Books.

Frazer, Elizabeth. 2006. "Iris Marion Young and Political Education." *Educational Philosophy & Theory* 38 (1): 39–55. https://doi.org/10.1111/j.1469-5812.2006.00173.x.

Frey, Lawrence R., and Kristen C. Blinne. 2017. "Activism and Social Justice." In *The SAGE Encyclopedia of Communication Research Methods*, edited by Mike Allen, 1:12–15. Thousand Oaks, CA: SAGE. https://doi.org/10.4135/9781483381411.n6.

Fung, Archon. 2005. "Deliberation Before the Revolution: Toward an Ethics of Deliberative Democracy in an Unjust World." *Political Theory* 33 (2): 397–419. https://doi.org/10.1177/0090591704271990.

———. 2013. "The Principle of Affected Interests." In *Representation: Elections and Beyond*, edited by Jack H. Nagel and Rogers M. Smith, 236–68. Philadelphia, PA: University of Pennsylvania Press.

Fung, Archon, and Taeku Lee. 2008. *The Difference Deliberation Makes: A Report on CaliforniaSpeaks Statewide Conversation on Healthcare Reform*. Washington, DC: AmericaSpeaks. https://static1.squarespace.com/static/5ce018c4d711f30001ff4dab/t/5ce0b250a5f36b0001096c23/1558229593230/CASpeaksReportFinalv3.pdf.

Fung, Archon, and Eric Olin Wright. 2003. "Thinking about Empowered Participatory Governance." In *Deepening Democracy: Institutional Innovations in Empowered Participatory Governance*, edited by Archon Fung and Eric Olin Wright, 3–42. New York, NY: Verso Books.

Gardner, Natasha. 2019. "Disrupters: 15 People Who Are Changing Denver." *5280*, January 2. https://www.5280.com/2019/01/disrupters-15-people-who-are-changing-denver/.

Gardner, Therese, and Vincent Russell. 2020. "Cole Has a Soul 2018: Participatory Budgeting Research and Evaluation Report." https://scalar.usc.edu/works/participatory-budgeting-2019/index.

Gastil, John. 2008. *Political Communication and Deliberation*. Thousand Oaks, CA: Sage.

Gecan, Michael. 2002. *Going Public: An Organizer's Guide to Citizen Action*. New York, NY: Anchor.

Gilens, Martin, and Benjamin I. Page. 2014. "Testing Theories of American Politics: Elites, Interest Groups, and Average Citizens." *Perspectives on Politics* 12 (3): 564–81. https://doi.org/10.1017/s1537592714001595.

Gilman, Hollie Russon. 2016. *Democracy Reinvented: Participatory Budgeting and Civic Innovation in America*. Washington, DC: Brookings Institution Press.

Golden, Sherita Hill. 2020. *Coronavirus in African Americans and Other People of Color*. Johns Hopkins Medicine. https://www.hopkinsmedicine.org/health/conditions-and-diseases/coronavirus/covid19-racial-disparities.

Goldfrank, Benjamin. 2007. "Lessons from Latin America's Experience with Participatory Budgeting." In *Participatory Budgeting*, edited by Anwar Shah, 91–126. Washington, DC: World Bank. https://documents.worldbank.org/en/publication/documents-reports/documentdetail/635011468330986995/participatory-budgeting.

———. 2011. *Deepening Local Democracy in Latin America: Participation, Decentralization, and the Left*. University Park, PA: Pennsylvania State University Press.

———. 2012. "The World Bank and the Globalization of Participatory Budgeting." *Journal of Public Deliberation* 8 (2): Article 7. https://doi.org/10.16997/jdd.143.

Gonçalves, Sónia. 2014. "The Effects of Participatory Budgeting on Municipal Expenditures and Infant Mortality in Brazil." *World Development* 53: 94–110. https://doi.org/10.1016/j.worlddev.2013.01.009.

The Gravel Institute, dir. 2022. *How America's Best State Fell Apart*. https://www.youtube.com/watch?v=8PqZVcUBzvU.

Gregorčič, Marta, and Sabina Jelenc Krašovec. 2016. "Social and Learning Practices in Participatory Democracy Process: The Case Study of Self-Organized Communities in Maribor, Slovenia, Contextualised through the e-Participatory Budgeting in Reykjavík, Iceland." *Journal of Contemporary Educational Studies* 67 (4): 168–82.

Grillos, Tara. 2014. "Youth Lead the Change: The City of Boston's Youth-Focused Participatory Budgeting Process Pilot Year Evaluation." https://scholar.harvard.edu/files/grillos/files/pb_boston_year_1_eval_0.pdf.

Gutmann, Amy, and Dennis Thompson. 2002. "Deliberative Democracy Beyond Process." *Journal of Political Philosophy* 10 (2): 153–74. https://doi.org/10.1111/1467-9760.00147.

———. 2004. *Why Deliberative Democracy?* Princeton, NJ: Princeton University Press.

Habermas, Jürgen. 1982. "A Reply to My Critics." In *Habermas: Critical Debates*, edited by John B. Thompson and David Held, 234–47. Cambridge, MA: MIT Press.

———. 1984. *The Theory of Communicative Action*. Translated by Thomas McCarthy. Vol. 1. Boston, MA: Beacon Press.

———. 1991. *The Structural Transformation of the Public Sphere: An Inquiry into a Category of Bourgeois Society*. Translated by Thomas Burger. Cambridge, MA: MIT Press.

———. 1994. "Struggles for Recognition in the Democratic Constitutional State." In *Multiculturalism: Examining the Politics of Recognition*, edited by Amy Gutmann, 107–49. Princeton, NJ: Princeton University Press.

Hagelskamp, Carolin, Chloe Rinehart, Rebecca Silliman, and David Schleifer. 2016a. "A Process of Growth: The Expansion of Participatory Budgeting in the United States and Canada in 2015–2016." Public Agenda. http://www.publicagenda.org/files/AProcessofGrowth_PublicAgenda_2016.pdf.

———. 2016b. "Public Spending, by the People: Participatory Budgeting in the United States and Canada in 2014–2015." Public Agenda. https://www.publicagenda.org/reports/public-spending-by-the-people-participatory-budgeting-in-the-united-states-and-canada-in-2014-15/.

Hagelskamp, Carolin, David Schleifer, Chloe Rinehart, and Rebecca Silliman. 2016. "Why Let the People Decide? Elected Officials on Participatory Budgeting." Public Agenda. https://www.publicagenda.org/pages/why-let-the-people-decide.

Hartnett, Stephen John, and Laura Ann Stengrim. 2006. *Globalization and Empire: The U.S. Invasion of Iraq, Free Markets, and the Twilight of Democracy*. Tuscaloosa, AL: University of Alabama Press.

Harvey, Matthew. 2009. "Drama, Talk, and Emotion: Omitted Aspects of Public Participation." *Science, Technology, & Human Values* 34 (2): 139–61. https://doi.org/10.1177/0162243907309632.

Jenkins, Henry. 2016. "Youth Voice, Media, and Political Engagement: Introducing the Core Concepts." In *By Any Media Necessary: The New Youth Activism*, edited by Henry Jenkins, Sangita Shresthova, Liana Gamber-Thompson, Neta Kligler-Vilenchik, and Arely M. Zimmerman, 1–60. New York, NY: New York University Press.

Jennstål, Julia, and Per-Ola Öberg. 2019. "The Ethics of Deliberative Activism: In Search of Reasonableness and Dialogic Responsiveness in Provocative Art Exhibitions." *Policy Studies* 40 (6): 648–61. https://doi.org/10.1080/01442872.2019.1599840.

Jones, Robert P., Daniel Cox, Rob Griffin, Maxine Najle, Molly Fisch-Friedman, and Alex Vandermaas-Peeler. 2018. *American Democracy in Crisis: Civic Engagement, Young Adult Activism, and the 2018 Midterm Elections*. Public Religion Research Institute. https://www.prri.org/wp-content/uploads/2018/10/Civic-Engagement-NovB.pdf.

Jovanovic, Spoma, and Vincent Russell. 2014. "Voices of Grassroots Activists: Dollars and Sense in the City." *Carolinas Communication Annual* 30: 19–33.

———. 2019. "Constructing Civic Competence through Storytelling: Local Knowledge and Public Consequences in Participatory Budgeting." *Carolinas Communication Annual* 35: 33–47.

Kasakove, Sophie. 2022. "Colorado Jury Awards $14 Million to Demonstrators Injured in George Floyd Protests." *The New York Times*, March 26. https://www.nytimes.com/2022/03/26/us/denver-george-floyd-protests-ruling.html.

Khurshid, Samar. 2020. "First Citywide Participatory Budgeting Program on Chopping Block Because of Coronavirus." *Gotham Gazette*, May 12. https://www.gothamgazette.com/city/9386-first-citywide-participatory-budgeting-program-scaled-back-coronavirus-new-york.

Kim, Joohan, and Eun Joo Kim. 2008. "Theorizing Dialogic Deliberation: Everyday Political Talk as Communicative Action and Dialogue: Theorizing Dialogic Deliberation." *Communication Theory* 18 (1): 51–70. https://doi.org/10.1111/j.1468-2885.2007.00313.x.

King, Jr., Martin Luther. 1964. *Why We Can't Wait*. Boston, MA: Beacon Press.

Kinney, Bo. 2012. "Deliberation's Contribution to Community Capacity Building." In *Democracy in Motion: Evaluating the Practice and Impact of Deliberative Civic Engagement*, edited by Tina Nabatchi, John Gastil, G. Michael Weiksner, and Matt Leighninger, 163–81. New York, NY: Oxford University Press.

Lee, Caroline W. 2011. "Five Assumptions Academics Make about Public Deliberation, and Why They Deserve Rethinking." *Journal of Public Deliberation* 7 (1): Article 7. https://doi.org/10.16997/jdd.118.

Leighninger, Matt. 2006. *The Next Form of Democracy: How Expert Rule Is Giving Way to Shared Governance-and Why Politics Will Never Be the Same*. 1st ed. Nashville, TN: Vanderbilt University Press.

Leighninger, Matt, and Chloe Rinehart. 2016. "Brazil Has Reduced Inequality, Incrementally—Can We Do the Same?" Public Agenda. http://www.publicagenda.org/files/BrazilHasReducedInequalityIncrementally_PublicAgenda_2016.pdf.

Lerner, Josh. 2010. "Learning Democracy through Participatory Budgeting: Who Learns What and so What?" In *Learning Citizenship by Practicing Democracy: International Initiatives and Perspectives*, edited by Elizabeth Pinnington and Daniel Schugurensky, 242–51. Newcastle upon Tyne: Cambridge Scholars Publishing.

———. 2011. "Participatory Budgeting: Building Community Agreement around Tough Budget Decisions." *National Civic Review* 100 (2): 30–35. https://doi.org/10.1002/ncr.20059.

———. 2014a. *Everyone Counts: Could "Participatory Budgeting" Change Democracy?* Ithaca, NY: Cornell University Press.

———. 2014b. *Making Democracy Fun: How Game Design Can Empower Citizens and Transform Politics*. Cambridge, MA: MIT Press.

———. 2018. "VICTORY! NYC Voters Approve Citywide PB." *Participatory Budgeting Project* (blog), November 7. https://www.participatorybudgeting.org/nyc-voters-approve-citywide-pb/.

Lerner, Josh, and Daniel Schugurensky. 2007. "Who Learns in Participatory Democracy? Participatory Budgeting in Rosario, Argentina." In *Democratic Practices as Learning Opportunities*, edited by Ruud van der Veen, Danny Wildemeersch, Janet Youngblood, and Victoria Marsick, 85–100. Rotterdam, The Netherlands: Sense.

Lerner, Josh, and Donata Secondo. 2012. "By the People, for the People: Participatory Budgeting from the Bottom up in North America." *Journal of Public Deliberation* 8 (2): Article 2. https://doi.org/10.16997/jdd.148.

Levin, Sam. 2020a. "White Supremacists and Militias Have Infiltrated Police Across US, Report Says." *The Guardian*, August 27. https://www.theguardian.com/us-news/2020/aug/27/white-supremacists-militias-infiltrate-us-police-report.

———. 2020b. "Activist Suspected in Portland Shooting Was Fired at 30 Times by Police, Official Says." *The Guardian*, October 14. https://www.theguardian.com/world/2020/oct/14/activist-portland-shooting-michael-reinoehl-police.

Levinas, Emmanuel. 1982. *Ethics and Infinity: Conversations with Philippe Nemo*. Translated by Richard A. Cohen. Pittsburgh, PA: Duquesne University Press.

Lin, Cynthia S., Alisa A. Pykett, Constance Flanagan, and Karma R. Chávez. 2016. "Engendering the Prefigurative: Feminist Praxes That Bridge a Politics of Prefigurement and Survival." *Journal of Social and Political Psychology* 4 (1): 302–17. https://doi.org/10.5964/jspp.v4i1.537.

Lindert, Peter H., and Jeffrey G. Williamson. 2017. *Unequal Gains: American Growth and Inequality Since 1700*. Princeton, NJ: Princeton University Press.

Lindorff, Dave. 2018. "Exclusive: The Pentagon's Massive Accounting Fraud Exposed." *The Nation*, November 27. https://www.thenation.com/article/archive/pentagon-audit-budget-fraud/.

Lipari, Lisbeth. 2004. "Listening for the Other: Ethical Implications of the Buber-Levinas Encounter." *Communication Theory* 14 (2): 122–41. https://doi.org/10.1111/j.1468-2885.2004.tb00308.x.

Lowndes, Vivien, Gerry Stoker, Lawrence Pratchett, David Wilson, Steve Leach, and Melvin Wingfield. 1998. *Enhancing Public Participation in Local Government*. London: United Kingdom Department of the Environment, Transport, and the Regions.

Lüchmann, Lígia Helena Hahn. 2009. "Participatory Democracy and Political Learning: Lessons from Brazilian Experience." In *Learning Democracy by Doing: Alternative Practices in Citizenship Learning and Participatory Democracy*, edited by Katherine Daly, Daniel Schugurensky, and Krista Lopes, 646–59. Ontario: Transformative Learning Centre, Ontario Institute for Studies in Education, University of Toronto.

Madison, D. Soyini. 2020. *Critical Ethnography: Method, Ethics, and Performance*. 3rd ed. Los Angeles, CA: Sage.

Marquetti, Adalmir, Carlos E. Schonerwald da Silva, and Al Campbell. 2012. "Participatory Economic Democracy in Action: Participatory Budgeting in Porto Alegre, 1989–2004." *Review of Radical Political Economics* 44 (1): 62–81. https://doi.org/10.1177/0486613411418055.

Martin, Michael. 2014. "A Witness of Whiteness: An Autoethnographic Examination of a White Teacher's Own Inherent Prejudice." *Education as Change* 18 (2): 237–54. https://doi.org/10.1080/16823206.2014.907192.

Mathieu, Edouard, Hannah Ritchie, Lucas Rodés-Guirao, Cameron Appel, Charlie Giattino, Joe Hassell, Bobbie Macdonald, et al. 2020. "Coronavirus Pandemic (COVID-19)." *Our World in Data* (blog). https://ourworldindata.org/coronavirus.

McBride, Cillian. 2005. "Deliberative Democracy and the Politics of Recognition." *Political Studies* 53 (3): 497–515. https://doi.org/10.1111/j.1467-9248.2005.00541.x.

McCarthy, Justin. 2022. "U.S. Approval of Labor Unions at Highest Point Since 1965." *Gallup*, August 30. https://news.gallup.com/poll/398303/approval-labor-unions-highest-point-1965.aspx.

McNulty, Stephanie. 2011. *Voice and Vote: Decentralization and Participation in Post-Fujimori Peru*. Stanford, CA: Stanford University Press.

Meyer, Elizabeth J. 2007. "I Am (Not) a Feminist: Unplugging from the Heterosexual Matrix." In *Rocking Your World: The Emotional Journey into Critical Discourses*, edited by Andrew H. Churchill, 35–44. The Netherlands: Sense Publishers.

Miller, Peggy J., Grace E. Cho, and Jeana R. Bracey. 2005. "Working-Class Children's Experience through the Prism of Personal Storytelling." *Human Development* 48 (3): 115–35. https://doi.org/10.1159/000085515.

Minieri, Joan, and Paul Getsos. 2007. *Tools for Radical Democracy: How to Organize for Power in Your Community*. San Francisco, CA: Jossey-Bass.

Minkler, Meredith. 2004. "Ethical Challenges for the 'Outside' Researcher in Community-Based Participatory Research." *Health Education & Behavior* 31 (6): 684–97. https://doi.org/10.1177/1090198104269566.

Moscrop, David R. H., and Mark E. Warren. 2016. "When Is Deliberation Democratic?" *Journal of Public Deliberation* 12 (2): Article 4. https://doi.org/10.16997/jdd.256.

Moskowitz, P. E. 2019. *The Case against Free Speech: The First Amendment, Fascism, and the Future of Dissent*. New York, NY: Bold Type Books.

Myerson, G. 1994. *Rhetoric, Reason, and Society: Rationality as Dialogue*. Thousand Oaks, CA: Sage.

Nabatchi, Tina, and Matt Leighninger. 2015. *Public Participation for 21st Century Democracy*. Hoboken, NJ: John Wiley & Sons.

Nabatchi, Tina, and Dragan Staniševski. 2008. *Social Inclusion: Building Political Efficacy with Deliberative Democracy*. Chicago, IL. https://citation.allacademic.com/meta/p_mla_apa_research_citation/2/6/6/5/6/pages266566/p266566-1.php.

Nakayama, Thomas K., and Robert L. Krizek. 1995. "Whiteness: A Strategic Rhetoric." *Quarterly Journal of Speech* 81 (3): 291–309. https://doi.org/10.1080/00335639509384117.

Newall, Mallory, Chris Jackson, and James Diamond. 2022. "Seven in Ten Americans Say the Country Is in Crisis, at Risk of Failing." Ipsos. https://www.ipsos.com/en-us/seven-ten-americans-say-country-crisis-risk-failing.

Nez, Héloïse. 2016. "Does Participation Mean Reciprocal Learning? The Relationships Between Diverse Stakeholders During Participatory Budgeting in Paris." *Journal of Civil Society* 12 (3): 266–81. https://doi.org/10.1080/17448689.2016.1215371.

Niemeyer, Simon. 2011. "The Emancipatory Effect of Deliberation: Empirical Lessons from Mini-Publics." *Politics & Society* 39 (1): 103–40. https://doi.org/10.1177/0032329210395000.

Nino, Carlos Santiago. 1996. *The Constitution of Deliberative Democracy*. New Haven, CT: Yale University Press.

Norander, Stephanie. 2017. "Critical Ethnography." In *The SAGE Encyclopedia of Communication Research Methods*, edited by Mike Allen, 296–99. Thousand Oaks, CA: Sage. https://doi.org/10.4135/9781483381411.

Owen, David. 2007. "Towards a Critical Theory of Whiteness." *Philosophy & Social Criticism* 33 (2): 203–22. https://doi.org/10.1177/0191453707074139.

Pape, Madeline, and Josh Lerner. 2016. "Budgeting for Equity: How Can Participatory Budgeting Advance Equity in the United States?" *Journal of Public Deliberation* 12 (2): Article 9. https://doi.org/10.16997/jdd.261.

Participatory Budgeting Project. n.d.-a. "Case Studies." Participatory Budgeting Project. Accessed January 18, 2021. https://www.participatorybudgeting.org/case-studies/.

———. n.d.-b. "Participatory Budgeting in Schools." Accessed June 7, 2023. https://www.participatorybudgeting.org/what-is-pb/pb-in-schools/.

Pateman, Carole. 2012. "Participatory Democracy Revisited." *Perspectives on Politics* 10 (1): 7–19. https://doi.org/10.1017/S1537592711004877.

PB Chicago. n.d. "Get Involved with PB Chicago!" http://www.pbchicago.org/get-involved.html.

Pew Research Center. 2010. *Distrust, Discontent, Anger and Partisan Rancor*. Washington, DC. http://www.people-press.org/2010/04/18/distrust-discontent-anger-and-partisan-rancor/.

Phelps, Paulina. 2016. "How to Make City Budgets Racially Just? Let Citizens Do the Numbers." *YES! Magazine*, October 25. https://www.yesmagazine.org/social-justice/2016/10/25/how-to-make-city-budgets-racially-just-let-citizens-do-the-numbers/.

Pincock, Heather. 2012. "Does Deliberation Make Better Citizens?" In *Democracy in Motion: Evaluating the Practice and Impact of Deliberative Civic Engagement*, edited by Tina Nabatchi, John Gastil, G. Michael Weiksner, and Matt Leighninger, 135–62. New York, NY: Oxford University Press.

Pinnington, Elizabeth, and Daniel Schugurensky, eds. 2010. *Learning Citizenship by Practicing Democracy: International Initiatives and Perspectives*. Newcastle upon Tyne: Cambridge Scholars Publishing.

The Piton Foundation's Shift Research Lab. 2017. "Cole." Community Facts. http://denvermetrodata.org/neighborhood/cole.

Pogrebinschi, Thamy, and David Samuels. 2014. "The Impact of Participatory Democracy: Evidence from Brazil's National Public Policy Conferences." *Comparative Politics* 46 (3): 313–32. https://doi.org/10.5129/001041514810943045.

Polletta, Francesca. 2006. *It Was like a Fever: Storytelling in Protest and Politics*. Chicago, IL: University of Chicago Press.

Rao, Vijayendra, and Paromita Sanyal. 2010. "Dignity through Discourse: Poverty and the Culture of Deliberation in Indian Village Democracies." *The Annals of the American Academy of Political and Social Science* 629 (1): 146–72.

Reynolds, Andrew. 2016. "North Carolina Is No Longer Classified as a Democracy." *The News & Observer*, December 22. http://www.newsobserver.com/opinion/op-ed/article122593759.html.

Richardson, Jason, Bruce Mitchell, and Jad Edlebi. 2020. "Gentrification and Disinvestment 2020: Do Opportunity Zones Benefit or Gentrify Low-Income Neighborhoods?" National Community Reinvestment Coalition. https://ncrc.org/gentrification20/.

Robinson, Buddy, and Mark G. Hanna. 1994. "Lessons for Academics for Grassroots Community Organizing: A Case Study—The Industrial Areas Foundation." *Journal of Community Practice* 1 (4): 63–94. https://doi.org/10.1300/J125v01n04_05.

Robinson, Cedric J. 2019. *On Racial Capitalism, Black Internationalism, and Cultures of Resistance*. Edited by H. L. T. Quan. Black Critique. London, UK: Pluto Press.

Roth, Zachary. 2022. *Making Participatory Budgeting Work: Experiences on the Front Lines*. Brennan Center for Justice. https://www.brennancenter.org/our-work/analysis-opinion/making-participatory-budgeting-work-experiences-front-lines.

Russell, Vincent. 2023. "Communicating about Social Justice in Participatory Budgeting in the United States: 'Coming Together' to Benefit Communities."

Journal of Applied Communication Research 51 (5): 519–38. https://doi.org/10.1080/00909882.2023.2178856.

Russell, Vincent, and Therese Gardner. 2019. "Auraria Participatory Budgeting 2018 Research and Evaluation Report." https://doi.org/10.13140/RG.2.2.18940.90249.

Russell, Vincent, and Spoma Jovanovic. 2020. "Public Deliberation and Social Justice Sensibilities in Greensboro Participatory Budgeting." *Communication and Critical/Cultural Studies* 17 (2): 111–28. https://doi.org/10.1080/14791420.2020.1746371.

Ryfe, David Michael. 2002. "The Practice of Deliberative Democracy: A Study of 16 Deliberative Organizations." *Political Communication* 19 (3): 359–77. https://doi.org/10.1080/01957470290055547.

Ryfe, David Michael, and Brittany Stalsburg. 2012. "The Participation and Recruitment Challenge." In *Democracy in Motion: Evaluating the Practice and Impact of Deliberative Civic Engagement*, edited by Tina Nabatchi, John Gastil, G. Michael Weiksner, and Matt Leighninger, 43–58. New York, NY: Oxford University Press.

Saad, Lydia. 2019. "Socialism as Popular as Capitalism Among Young Adults in U.S." *Gallup*, November 25. https://news.gallup.com/poll/268766/socialism-popular-capitalism-among-young-adults.aspx.

Sachs, David. 2020. "Denverites Are Getting a $1.7 Million Allowance." *Denverite*, December 1. https://denverite.com/2020/12/01/denverites-are-getting-a-1-7-million-allowance/.

Schaul, Kevin, Kate Rabinowitz, and Ted Mellnik. 2020. "2020 Turnout Is the Highest in Over a Century." *Washington Post*, November 5. https://www.washingtonpost.com/graphics/2020/elections/voter-turnout/.

Schleifer, David, and Antonio Diep. 2019. "Strengthening Democracy: What Do Americans Think?" Public Agenda. https://www.publicagenda.org/wp-content/uploads/2019/08/Strengthening_Democracy_WhatDoAmericansThinkFINAL.pdf.

Schlozman, Kay Lehman, Sidney Verba, and Henry Brady. 2012. *The Unheavenly Chorus: Unequal Political Voice and the Broken Promise of American Democracy*. Princeton, NJ: Princeton University Press.

Schneider, Aaron, and Ben Goldfrank. 2002. *Budgets and Ballots in Brazil: Participatory Budgeting from the City to the State*. IDS Working paper 149. Brighton, UK: Institute of Development Studies. https://opendocs.ids.ac.uk/opendocs/handle/20.500.12413/3918.

Schugurensky, Daniel. 2006. "This Is Our School of Citizenship: Informal Learning in Local Democracy." In *Learning in Places: The Informal Education Reader*, edited by Zvi Bekerman, Nicholas C. Burbules, and Diana Silberman-Keller, 163–82. New York, NY: Peter Lang.

———. 2017. "Social Pedagogy Meets Local Democracy: Examining the Possibilities and Limits of Participatory Budgeting." *Pedagogika Społeczna* 16 (3): 9–32.

Schugurensky, Daniel, and John P. Meyers. 2008. "Informal Civic Learning through Engagement in Local Democracy: The Case of the Seniors' Task Force of Healthy City Toronto." In *Learning through Community: Exploring Participatory Practices*, edited by Kathryn Church, Nina Bascia, and Eric Shragge, 73–95. New York, NY: Springer.

Schugurensky, Daniel, Karsten Mundel, and Fiona Duguid. 2006. "Learning from Each Other: Housing Cooperative Members' Acquisition of Skills, Knowledge, Attitudes, and Values." *Cooperative Housing Journal* 2005/2006: 2–15.

Scollo, Michelle. 2011. "Cultural Approaches to Discourse Analysis: A Theoretical and Methodological Conversation with Special Focus on Donal Carbaugh's Cultural Discourse Theory." *Journal of Multicultural Discourses* 6 (1): 1–32. https://doi.org/10.1080/17447143.2010.536550.

Shah, Anwar, ed. 2007. *Participatory Budgeting*. Public Sector Governance and Accountability Series. Washington, DC: World Bank. http://documents.worldbank.org/curated/en/635011468330986995/pdf/394980REVISED0101OFFICIAL0USE0ONLY1.pdf.

Shall, Adrienne. 2007. "Sub-Saharan Africa's Experience with Participatory Budgeting." In *Participatory Budgeting*, edited by Anwar Shah, 191–224. The World Bank. http://documents.worldbank.org/curated/en/635011468330986995/pdf/394980REVISED0101OFFICIAL0USE0ONLY1.pdf.

Shrikant, Natasha. 2014. "'It's Like, "I've Never Met a Lesbian before!"': Personal Narratives and the Construction of Diverse Female Identities in a Lesbian Counterpublic." *Pragmatics* 24 (4): 799–818.

———. 2015. "'Yo, It's IST Yo': The Discursive Construction of an Indian American Youth Identity in a South Asian Student Club." *Discourse & Society* 26 (4): 480–501. https://doi.org/10.1177/0957926515576634.

Sintomer, Yves, Carsten Herzberg, and Anja Röcke. 2008. "Participatory Budgeting in Europe: Potentials and Challenges." *International Journal of Urban and Regional Research* 32 (1): 164–78. https://doi.org/10.1111/j.1468-2427.2008.00777.x.

Siu, Alice, and Dragan Staniševski. 2012. "Deliberation in Multicultural Societies." In *Democracy in Motion: Evaluating the Practice and Impact of Deliberative Civic Engagement*, edited by Tina Nabatchi, John Gastil, G. Michael Weiksner, and Matt Leighninger, 83–102. New York, NY: Oxford University Press.

Souza Santos, Boaventura de. 1998. "Participatory Budgeting in Porto Alegre: Toward a Redistributive Democracy." *Politics & Society* 26: 461–510. https://doi.org/10.1177/0032329298026004003.

Stafford, Kat. 2021. "Movement for Black Lives: Feds Targeted BLM Protesters." *AP News*. August 18. https://apnews.com/article/joe-biden-death-of-george-floyd-health-race-and-ethnicity-racial-injustice-07a91fd5c210f8b809d019292c3ec0c0.

Stark, Liz. 2021. "US Infrastructure Gets Slightly Better Grade on Engineers' Report Card: C-." CNN. March 3, 2021. https://www.cnn.com/2021/03/03/politics/us-infrastructure-report-card/index.html.

Stewart, Emily. 2018. "2018's Record-Setting Voter Turnout, in One Chart." *Vox*, November 19. https://www.vox.com/policy-and-politics/2018/11/19/18103110/2018-midterm-elections-turnout.

Stoudt, Brett G., María Elena Torre, Paul Bartley, Evan Bissell, Fawn Bracy, Hillary Caldwell, Lauren Dewey, et al. 2019. "Researching at the Community-University

Borderlands: Using Public Science to Study Policing in the South Bronx." *Education Policy Analysis Archives* 27 (56): Article 56. https://doi.org/10.14507/epaa27.2623.

Strand, Kerry, Sam Marullo, Nick Cutforth, Randy Stoecker, and Patrick Donohue. 2003. *Community-Based Research and Higher Education: Principles and Practices*. San Francisco, CA: Jossey-Bass.

Su, Celina. 2012. "Whose Budget? Our Budget? Broadening Political Stakeholdership via Participatory Budgeting." *Journal of Public Deliberation* 8 (2): Article 1. https://doi.org/10.16997/jdd.149.

———. 2019. "Research, Action, Activism: Critical Solidarities & Multi-Scalar Powers." *Education Policy Analysis Archives* 27 (57): Article 57. https://doi.org/10.14507/epaa.27.4450.

Svaldi, Aldo. 2017. "Northeast Denver Neighborhood Is Nation's Most Polluted." *The Denver Post*, February 16. https://www.denverpost.com/2017/02/16/denver-most-polluted-zip-code/.

Swartz, Omar. 2006. "Introduction." In *Social Justice and Communication Scholarship*, edited by Omar Swartz, xv–xvii. Mahwah, NJ: Lawrence Erlbaum.

Talisse, Robert B. 2005. "Deliberativist Responses to Activist Challenges: A Continuation of Young's Dialectic." *Philosophy & Social Criticism* 31 (4): 423–44. https://doi.org/10.1177/0191453705052978.

Touchton, Michael, and Brian Wampler. 2014. "Improving Social Well-Being through New Democratic Institutions." *Comparative Political Studies* 47 (10): 1442–69. https://doi.org/10.1177/0010414013512601.

Tracy, Karen, and Jessica S. Robles. 2013. *Everyday Talk: Building and Reflecting Identities*. 2nd ed. New York, NY: Guilford Press.

Tuck, Eve, and Monique Guishard. 2013. "Uncollapsing Ethics: Racialized Sciencism, Settler Coloniality, and an Ethical Framework of Decolonial Participatory Action Research." In *Challenging Status Quo Retrenchment: New Directions in Critical Research*, edited by Tricia M. Kress, Curry Malott, and Brad Porfilio, 3–27. Critical Constructions: Studies on Education and Society. Charlotte, NC: Information Age Publishing.

Vakil, Sepehr, Maxine McKinney de Royston, Na'ilah Suad Nasir, and Ben Kirshner. 2016. "Rethinking Race and Power in Design-Based Research: Reflections from the Field." *Cognition and Instruction* 34 (3): 194–209. https://doi.org/10.1080/07370008.2016.1169817.

Varieties of Democracy Institute. 2023. *Democracy Report 2023: Defiance in the Face of Autocratization*. University of Gothenberg. https://v-dem.net/documents/30/V-dem_democracyreport2023_highres.pdf.

Vera, Amir, and Jenn Selva. 2021. "Colorado Attorney General Report Found Aurora Police Racially Biased and Fire Department Administered Ketamine Illegally." CNN. September 15, 2021. https://www.cnn.com/2021/09/15/us/aurora-colorado-police-fire-department-investigation/index.html.

Wampler, Brian. 2000. "A Guide to Participatory Budgeting." Partizipation & Nachhaltige Entwicklung in Europa. http://www.partizipation.at/fileadmin/media_data/Downloads/themen/A_guide_to_PB.pdf.

———. 2007. "A Guide to Participatory Budgeting." In *Participatory Budgeting*, edited by Anwar Shah, 21–54. The World Bank. http://documents.worldbank.org/curated/en/635011468330986995/pdf/394980REVISED0101OFFICIAL0USE0ONLY1.pdf.

———. 2012. "Participatory Budgeting: Core Principles and Key Impacts." *Journal of Public Deliberation* 8 (2): Article 12. https://doi.org/10.16997/jdd.138.

Wampler, Brian, and Leonardo Avritzer. 2005. "The Spread of Participatory Democracy in Brazil: From Radical Democracy to Participatory Good Government." *Journal of Latin American Urban Studies* 7 (7): 37–52.

Warm Cookies of the Revolution. 2013. "About Warm Cookies of the Revolution." Warm Cookies of the Revolution, March 22. http://www.warmcookiesoftherevolution.org/about-us/.

———, dir. 2017a. *The Past Machine (Participatory Budgeting Training)*. https://vimeo.com/236994128.

———, dir. 2017b. *The Future Machine*. https://vimeo.com/247262279.

———, dir. 2018a. *Art - Kerrie Joy Poem*. https://vimeo.com/287697245.

———, dir. 2018b. *Art - Molina Poem*. https://vimeo.com/287698783.

Warren, John T. 2001. "Absence for Whom? An Autoethnography of White Subjectivity." *Cultural Studies/Critical Methodologies* 1 (1): 36–49.

Weissman, Evan. 2020. "It Feels Good to See Residents Win! We Worked for Over Three Years with Resident Leaders in Cole and Swansea." [Image attached] [Status update]. Facebook. November 16, 2020. https://www.facebook.com/evan.weissman.37/posts/2047685468701301.

Westheimer, Joel. 2015. *What Kind of Citizen? Educating Our Children for the Common Good*. New York, NY: Teachers College Press.

Westheimer, Joel, and Joseph Kahne. 2004. "What Kind of Citizen? The Politics of Educating for Democracy." *American Educational Research Journal* 41 (2): 237–69. https://doi.org/10.3102/00028312041002237.

Wike, Richard, Laura Silver, Shannon Schumacher, and Aidan Connaughton. 2021. "Many in U.S., Western Europe Say Their Political System Needs Major Reform." *Pew Research Center* (blog), March 31, 2021. https://www.pewresearch.org/global/2021/03/31/many-in-us-western-europe-say-their-political-system-needs-major-reform/.

The World Bank. 2008. "Brazil: Toward a More Inclusive and Effective Participatory Budget in Porto Alegre." 40144-BR. http://hdl.handle.net/10986/6275.

Young, Iris Marion. 1996. "Communication and the Other: Beyond Deliberative Democracy." In *Democracy and Difference: Contesting the Boundaries of the Political*, edited by Seyla Benhabib, 120–35. Princeton, NJ: Princeton University Press.

———. 1997. *Intersecting Voices: Dilemmas of Gender, Political Philosophy, and Policy*. Princeton, NJ: Princeton University Press.

———. 2002. *Inclusion and Democracy*. New York, NY: Oxford University Press.

Zakaria, Fareed. 2007. *The Future of Freedom: Illiberal Democracy at Home and Abroad*. New York, NY: W.W. Norton.

Zinn, Howard. 1980. *A People's History of the United States: 1492–Present*. New York, NY: HarperCollins.

Index

About the Author

Vincent Russell is an assistant professor in the Communication Department at Western Carolina University. He earned his PhD in Communication with a concentration in Community and Social Interaction from the University of Colorado Boulder, and his MA and BA in Communication Studies from the University of North Carolina at Greensboro. A critical ethnographer who employs community-based research methods, he specializes in communication activism for social justice scholarship. His research has appeared in the *Journal of Applied Communication Research*, *Communication and Critical/Cultural Studies* and *Annals of the International Communication Association.* His scholarly commentary has appeared in *The Atlantic*, *The Brennan Center for Justice*, *Financial Times*, and other outlets. Prior to entering academia, he was a community organizer who led the first successful grassroots campaign in the United States to implement participatory budgeting.

www.ingramcontent.com/pod-product-compliance
Ingram Content Group UK Ltd.
Pitfield, Milton Keynes, MK11 3LW, UK
UKHW041836031026
15587UKWH00002B/810

9 781666 942538